AF600528

South of the Future

SUNY series, Praxis: Theory in Action

Nancy A. Naples, editor

South of the Future

Marketing Care and Speculating Life in South Asia and the Americas

Edited by

Anindita Banerjee and Debra A. Castillo

Cover image by William Kremer

Published by State University of New York Press, Albany

Printed in the United States of America

For information, contact State University of New York Press, Albany, NY
www.sunypress.edu

Library of Congress Cataloging-in-Publication Data

Names: Banerjee, Anindita, author. | Castillo, Debra A., author.
Title: South of the future : marketing care and speculating life in south Asia and the Americas / Anindita Banerjee and Debra A. Castillo.
Description: Albany : State University of New York Press, [2020] | Series: SUNY series, Praxis : Theory in Action | Includes bibliographical references and index.
Identifiers: ISBN 9781438481074 (hardcover : alk. paper) | ISBN 9781438481081 (ebook)
Further information is available at the Library of Congress.

10 9 8 7 6 5 4 3 2 1

Contents

Acknowledgments vii

Introduction: Life and Care from South of the Future 1
Anindita Banerjee and Debra A. Castillo

Chapter 1
From Intercountry Adoption in Guatemala to Commercial Global Surrogacy in Gujarat and Beyond: Lessons Learned from Research and Human Rights 17
Karen Smith Rotabi

Chapter 2
On Cruelty and Care: Motherhood and the Crisis of Futurity 43
Kumkum Sangari

Chapter 3
Promissory Futures: Medicine and Markets in Speculative Fiction 73
Sherryl Vint

Chapter 4
The Surrogacy Public Interest Litigation in the Indian Supreme Court: Marginalizing the Marginalized 93
Sital Kalantry

Chapter 5
Wet Nurses and Migrant Nanas in Mexico's Imaginary Landscape 115
Emily C. Vázquez Enríquez

Chapter 6
Structures of Affect in Transactions of Care: From Surrogacy Discourses of the Womb to Mahasweta Devi's "Breast-Giver" 137
Kavita Panjabi

Chapter 7
Artificial Bodies: The Politics of the Posthuman in Argentine Science Fiction Novels 165
Silvia G. Kurlat Ares

Chapter 8
Unbearable Futures: The Science/Fiction of Care Markets in the Global South 189
Anindita Banerjee and Debra A. Castillo

Contributors 213

Index 215

Acknowledgments

The germ of this book was nurtured in an international symposium, Gujarat/Guatemala: Marketing Care and Speculating Life, generously sponsored by a National Resource Center grant to the South Asian Studies Program at Cornell University, along with cosponsorship from the Department of Comparative Literature, the Latin American Studies, and the Latina/o Studies programs. We are grateful to all the participants in the event for their generative ideas, including many who are participating in this volume, as well as Gladys Tzul Tzul, Kaushik Sunder Rajan, Cecilia van Hollen, Suman Seth, Himika Bhattacharya, and Pedro DiPietro, whose comments and contributions greatly informed the project, but who were not able to contribute chapters to this book. Our thanks go to Julie Lind, who applied her awesome academic and editing skills to help us prepare various parts and stages of the manuscript. We are profoundly grateful to Rebecca Colesworthy at State University of New York Press, whose astute guidance and steadfast support took the project from start to finish.

Introduction

Life and Care from South of the Future

Anindita Banerjee and Debra A. Castillo

Semi-Life and Semi-Care

> The Semi-Living Worry Dolls were the first tissue engineered sculptures to be presented alive in a gallery. . . . Inspired by the Guatemalan worry dolls given to children to whisper their worries and concerns to, these worry dolls were handcrafted out of degradable polymers (PGA and P4HB) and surgical sutures. The dolls are then seeded with living cells [specifically, endothelial (skin), muscle, and osteoblast (bone) tissues: AB and DC] that, throughout the exhibition, will gradually replace the polymers within a micro-gravity bioreactor that acts as a surrogate body. The worry dolls become partially alive. These semi-living dolls represent the current stage of cultural limbo, characterized by childlike innocence and a mixture of wonder and fear of technology. This work invites you to whisper your worries to the worry dolls—will they take your concerns away?
>
> —Artists' Statement

Semi-Living Worry Dolls is a bio-artistic project conjured by two Australians, Oron Catts and Ionat Zurr, and annexed to a folk art tradition of tiny, mostly female gendered figurines from indigenous Guatemala. They were first presented in an Ars Electronica festival in Linz, Austria, in 2000 and toured for over a decade since then. In exhibition, each of Catts and Zurr's seven semi-living dolls represents a different worry: "the worry of biotechnology," "demagogy, and possibly destruction," "the fear of fear itself," "our fear of hope," and so on. These semi-living dolls speak to the continuities and collisions between three related discourses that constitute the central concerns of this book. They highlight how the generation of life and the work of caring are inextricably interwoven; how the Global South, historically and contemporaneously a vital resource for the sustenance of life and care, is emerging anew as the symbolic and embodied locus of our collective hopes and anxieties for the future; and how the relationship between giving and supporting life, dependent on both physical and affective flows of gendered labor from the south, is becoming increasingly mediated by speculative technologies in the twenty-first century.

On the face of it, "care" seems the polar opposite of technological mediation. The most intractably human of terms, "care," in fact, differentiates humanity from other forms of existence. It punctuates language as a noun, adjective, and verb: care workers care for others. They ameliorate their cares. They care, it seems, especially for those who cannot easily care for themselves—hence the repetition "children-childlike" in Catts and Zurr's artist statement. Typically associated with "traditional" southern societies of the globe where caring is imagined to be more intrinsic to communities, in the transnational exchanges with the Global North, southern laborers sell their services, their care work, precisely at the intersection of the economic and affective labor markets. Whether what they sell is the use of their bodies for gestational surrogacy (or sex work), the loving-kindness of their interactions with our children, or the use of their hands to clean the bodies of the elderly and infirm, their work is valued because "they care," while at the same time the reality of capital extracts affect from the economic calculations of their worth on the labor market. The United States, for instance, has a special category of B-1 visas for domestic workers accompanying diplomatic families. Like the worry dolls, such care work is cathected most frequently to female bodies, and the peculiarity of their labor resides in the fact that the very nature of their job description brings together affective and emotional labor along with physical exertion—this is the difference with other kinds of nongendered, or frequently male-gendered service work, like that of dishwashers or janitors. The care worker's job is to worry on others' behalf.

Guatemalan worry dolls are scraps of wood and cloth that already have a semi-living function, pointing to the slippage between people/objects that care for us / that we care about. They are popular tourist items and are sold semi-seriously for precisely the affective labor they perform. One tourist site tells us: "The indigenous people from the Highlands in Guatemala created Worry Dolls many generations ago as a remedy for worrying. According to the Mayan legend, when worrying keeps a person awake, he or she tells a worry to as many dolls as necessary. Then the worrier places the dolls under his or her pillow. The dolls take over the worrying for the person who then sleeps peacefully through the night. When morning breaks, the person awakens without the worries that the dolls took away during the night" (Shamans). What is suggested is that with the worry dolls, we nonindigenous northerners can imagine ourselves into a time of childlike innocence and wonder, into a time when, like now, placebos really worked. And, of course, the childlike quality evoked both in the Shamans Market and in Catts and Zurr's description of their project—both the innocence and the fear—are exactly why we need the affective soothing in the first place. Scientific studies agree. A report in *Harvard Health* 2012, for instance, documents the growing recognition that what we call the placebo effect may involve changes in brain chemistry—and that the placebo effect may in fact be an integral part of good medical care and an ally that should be embraced by doctors and patients alike. It is, this article notes, "an effect of care that's caring" ("Putting").

The labor of the Guatemalan doll, then, is imagined as a gift, though there is an exchange of a modest amount of cash to secure them. At the same time, they represent an investment in a certain kind of emotional/affective labor that is buffered by the ability to see people as objects and things as human. For the northern consumers of women's care work, the value added of southern labor is their imagined investment in a global care chain, distinct from the poor women of the Global North, who imaginarily don't show the proper care for their loved ones. Like other transnational migrants, the semi-living dolls move north to sell their labor, but the employer wants to buy their affect—while not putting an economic value on it, nor compensating the worker for their "care."

The Australian semi-living dolls also represent a kind of monstrous pregnancy within a bioreactor body. As one of the creators notes, "This emergence of [a] new class of object/being, which is positioned in the fault line of our psychological dichotomies in regard to the life continuum, might become more and more visible as our abilities to manipulate life increases. As these creations will contain different gradients of life and sentiency[,] new relationships will be formed with our objects, our environment and with the concept of life itself. Parts of our own bodies can be sustained apart from us as independent autonomous entities (currently only small fragments). What kind of relationships are we going to form with these entities? Will we care for them or abuse them?" (Catts). In exhibition, it seems that the semi-living dolls added to people's worries rather than alleviating them; many spectators were concerned by their uncanny aliveness and asked what would happen to the dolls after the show, prompting the artists to a statement that they treated the remains respectfully, even giving them funerals.

The semi-living dolls are more monstrous than ever because scientific advances are continually closing in on the possibility of their movement from object to full life: thus, for example, the 2017 successful in vitro gametogenesis, which resulted in living mice from mouse tail cells. Already there are many uncanny echoes with technological advances that bridge object, animal, and human. Chinese scientists have been developing what they call semi-living embryos to develop heritable modifications to the human genome that can eradicate disease—and, by the way, enhance beauty and intelligence. In a controversial article released in April 2015 they reported successfully using embryos sourced from a local fertility clinic to edit the genetic code and remove a gene responsible for a potentially fatal blood disorder. Readers were quick to note other uses for the versatile and easy to use gene-editing technology CRISPR, including—in a more recent iteration—the Brad Pitt clone scenario evoked by James Vincent. By 2018, this science-fiction scenario became a real-time controversy as the Chinese bioengineer He Jiankui announced the birth of the first child with genes edited to eliminate the human immunodeficiency virus (Bruenig).

One familiar definition of modernity is its drive to mythologize and celebrate prolepsis. The convergence of age-old care work and rapidly emerging biotechnologies in our unfolding present—hypostasized in the speculative project of the semi-living worry dolls—puts a new, cautionary spin on this drive. As Catts and Zurr noted at the turn of the millennium, when they first developed their "symbiotica" from an artifactual template based upon an explicitly gendered, racialized, and commodified embodiment of the Global South, fear and anxiety about the technologization and financialization of life itself seemed imminent over the horizon of the future. Nearly two decades later, what remained unacknowledged in the artists' choice of cultural object has become part and parcel of the north's imaginary of futurity. Semi-life has not only arrived at its shores in numbers too critical to ignore but is here to stay. What is more, the worry doll from south of the future has revealed itself to be a constantly transmogrifying repository of semi-care that is at once intimately familiar and terrifyingly alien.

South of the Future

Flickering in the asymptote of histories of the future, the miniaturized subject-object of the artistic imagination serves at once as donor and recipient of care, biotechnologically productive yet incapable of biological reproduction, hypothetically immortal but managed by the assignment of a limited shelf life. The longings and fears called forth by the worry doll are correspondingly Janus-faced. Appropriating an all-too-familiar plaything from a commodified version of the south recuperates nostalgic conceptions of care vested in a racialized, gendered body even as its technologically conjured "vibrant matter" (Bennett) serves as the staging ground for a brave new world in which affective and reproductive labor are simultaneously mechanized and generated to excess.

The seemingly timeless template of semi-life, consequently, is joined at the hip with modern vectors of migrant care work, epitomized by the nanny or eldercare worker providing succor across geopolitical and economic boundaries between north and south. As a traveling exhibit, additionally, the worry doll pits its own premodern and modern prototypes against the perpetually future-oriented plasticity of biomatter and bioinformation fueled by rapid advances in tissue engineering, in vitro fertilization, and synthetic biology over the last three decades. Consonant with the mutating components of the figurine, the holistic caregiver and caretaker from the south fragments and reconstitutes itself into donors, surrogates, and biomedical infrastructures that enable life to be traded as both commodities and futures across unimaginable distances around the globe.

The most incendiary potential of the tightly managed yet unpredictably proliferative worry doll from the turn of the millennium might lie in the in-built anticipation of its own uncanny returns in a future imperfect long after the exhibition's end. In the two years during which this book emerged from conception to completion, the worry doll has repeatedly come back to life as the quintessential migrant pair of mother and child, washing up on the shores of North America and Western Europe on the highest wave of demographic displacement since World War II. Their twinned bodies, though increasingly spectralized, are subjected to ever more futuristic methods of surveillance and violence. The paradoxical pairing of affect and technology, once condemned to perpetual uncertainty in the artistic imagination of the worry doll but now a real threat to the geopolitical imaginary of the Global North, stands at the center of the twilight zone in which semiologies of care, technologies of the body, and ontologies of the future coconstitute each other. Nowhere is their mutuality more vividly visible than at the borderlands of South Asia and the Americas, the two regions that this book brings into generative comparison.

On April 29, 2015, five days after Nepal was hit by a devastating earthquake, the Israeli newspaper *Haaretz* designated as its "picture of the week" a newborn baby, "wrapped in a woolen blanket and in a piece of blue and white cloth, snuggling in the strong arms of an Israeli Defense Forces soldier in a pressed uniform" (Narayanan). Although the soldier most certainly represented what his uniform and insignia stood for, the baby was not just any baby: it was the product of a commercial contract between an Israeli same-sex couple and a clinic located in Nepal that employed women who had come across the open border from India to serve as surrogates. The IDF's response to the earthquake inadvertently revealed not just a two-tier system of care, in which the state's future citizens were airlifted while their gestational vessels remained both invisible and left behind, but also a bizarre reversal of the traditional trajectories of gender, labor, and migration between the two South Asian countries of India and Nepal. As India's largely unregulated international surrogacy market, whose revenues grew to an annual two billion dollars since its inception in 2004, began to be increasingly restricted by the government, Nepal—a long-standing source of childcare workers for middle- and upper-class Indian households—became a lucrative destination for potential surrogates. This encounter between radically divergent scales of migrant biomatter and technologically mediated care, however, reveals a larger picture of the south as a simultaneous repository of anxiety and hope.

At a seemingly unimaginable distance from the Himalayan highlands, a similar paradox of semi-care and semi-life now dominates the public imagination of the divide between the United States and Latin America. As the US administration pursues an exponentially aggressive policy of separating children from caregivers at the southern border with Mexico as part of its zero-tolerance strategy to deter migration, the ethics of care has emerged as a primary battleground for the politics of life itself. Media dispatches from the border now look like scenes that could be lifted from Alfonso Cuarón's 2006 cinematic dystopia *The Children of Men*, featuring a brown-skinned prospective mother navigating a northern metropolis littered with cages full of migrants—with the additional twist that in real life, it is children rather than adult migrants who feature as the inmates of fenced enclosures and tent cities. Asked about the state's plans for the future of such minors, the White House chief of staff casually speculated that they would be sent to "foster care or whatever" (Burnett). Fox News commentator Laura Ingraham, following her much-reviled description of child detention centers as "summer camps" (Wootson), put forward an even more insidious proposal: the influx of young life from south of the border, she speculated, would solve the perpetual shortage in the domestic adoption market. Media critics pointed out the particular irony of the remarks given Ingraham's own history of adopting a girl from Guatemala (Timmons).

These contradictions, however, are hardly limited to the current moment; they have always been inherent to and symptomatic of the global business of marketing care and speculating life. Commercial surrogacy, and especially transnational commercial surrogacy involving northern intending parents seeking out low-cost options for family-making in the Global South, provides a compelling case in point. Despite the literally rosy images of altruism projected by commercial surrogacy providers, scandal has persistently shadowed the industry, both with accusations of human trafficking involving women forced by poverty to allow themselves to be exploited in baby factories as surrogates and by the trafficking of the babies themselves. The commercial side of this transaction has become notoriously evident in high-profile cases of parents dissatisfied with the outcome of their venture, who refuse to accept their biological children for a range of reasons including mental illness and physical challenges. As many scholars have noted, even in locations where the practice is legal, the patchwork of law and policy does little to adequately protect surrogates or the children themselves (Torres et al.; Pande; Rotabi and Kalantry in this volume).

Thus, transnational commercial surrogacy has become a rapidly changing enterprise, moving from place to place as local governments catch on to the stigma attached to it. Thailand (2015), Nepal (2016), Cambodia (2016), and Mexico—where commercial surrogacy was only legal in Tabasco, but banned in 2016, and is now treated as a form of human trafficking—and India (2018), all banned transnational commercial surrogacy in quick succession after booms, or the promise of major booms. Russia is considering a ban, though its commercial surrogacy companies mostly serve nationals, and Ukraine is reeling under a 2019 crisis as reports appear of parents abandoning "imperfect" babies (Hawley). April 2019 brought news that Nigeria, Kenya, and Ghana seem to be the next places this fast-moving industry is trying to land (Fenton-Glynn). Given the loose regulatory environment in these countries—there is neither explicit legislation nor an outright ban—reports of baby factories in Nigeria are popping up ("Nigeria Police"). As attention rapidly moves to the next great place for middle-class foreigners to commission a child, the countries are getting quicker and quicker to shut it down.

Regardless of location, however, the nexus of semi-care and semi-life continues to rely on an instantly recognizable paradox: while age-old tropes of dehumanization and demographic panic inform the denial of care, the south nevertheless remains an essential repository of surplus reproductive potential, a resource of vitality ripe for biopolitical and technopolitical extraction in the proleptic imagination of the north. This is the commonality that provides this book with its object of study and conceptual point of departure. *South of the Future* follows the intersecting and intertwined trajectories of semi-life and semi-care across two regions that have not only been historically entrenched in transnational flows of care work but also, more recently, become flashpoints of global traffic in speculative technologies of life. By examining them in juxtaposition, it comprises the first comparative and interdisciplinary investigation of care markets and biomarkets in the Global South.

Care and Life in Interdisciplinary Comparison

This volume seeks to add a new conceptual frame and a new methodological toolkit to the body of recent scholarly work that attends to the outsourcing of both biological risk and the burden of care (Hochschild; Hochschild and Ehrenreich). By examining traditional types of migrant care work such as milk-nursing and nannying in close engagement with speculative technologies of producing, managing, and financializing the building blocks of life itself, it aims to reveal the historical continuums and structural contiguities between older forms of affective and reproductive labor and the newest pathways through which migrant life is mediated by traveling technologies across the asymmetries of the north and south. While engaging deeply with recent theorizations of this transformation—articulated through concepts such as "biocapital" (Sunder Rajan), "clinical labor" (Cooper and Waldby), and "tactical biopolitics" (Da Costa and Philip)—the essays in this volume perform an altogether different kind of work than the macrostructural studies previously cited.

Our contributors approach the south not as an abstract space and a general category of inequality, but as a constellation of concrete sites and embodied subjectivities that are deeply imbricated in broader global movements and flows. This disaggregating impulse is evident in the diverse ways in which the chapters that follow address multipronged vectors of biotechnology and differential imaginations of care, accounting for cultural and political imaginaries that constantly cross the line between mimetic and speculative modes. Focusing on specific places, languages, histories, and texts while demonstrating the theoretical and methodological value of comparison, our contributors repopulate the umbrella term of the south with gendered, racialized bodies. Such an approach puts into generative comparison two regions not usually studied together at the conjunctures of geo-, bio-, and technopolitics despite their visible convergences. The rich body of scholarship on migrant care work in the Americas, for example, has never been put in dialogue with landmark recent studies of outsourcing life on the Indian subcontinent (Pande; Vora), and literary and cultural debates on the subjects rarely intersect with the deliberations of public policy and law. The chapters in this volume, separately and together, bridge precisely these gaps while also retaining each author's deep attention to local, regional, national, and transnational conditions.

Consonant with the objectives outlined earlier, contributions to this volume are organized to simultaneously illuminate and provoke interrogations of the intersections between histories of care and technologies of life in the two regions. To that end, the eight essays that follow may be read sequentially in cross-reference with each other, or contrapuntally in thematic and conceptually related pairs. The first essay, by Karen Smith Rotabi, lends a unique on-the-ground perspective to the comparative study of intercountry adoption in Guatemala and international surrogacy in the state of Gujarat in western India. For well over a decade, Rotabi had been involved in intercountry adoption (ICA) research, with an emphasis on identifying adoption fraud and reforming systems to meet international standards of ethical practice. With the ascension of commercial global surrogacy (CGS), she began a comparative study of the human rights issues that extended from the "old" economy of adoption to the emerging Wild West of commissioning babies beyond borders. Rotabi's chapter considers the lessons learned along the way as she interfaced with the dynamic marketplaces of ICA and CGS, emphasizing that one of the most important questions researchers can ask is how we can truly address and alleviate the underlying index of poverty that serves as their driving force. She argues that perhaps this is the only real question in the scheme of global realities, since desperate conditions push women into all sorts of exploitation—much of which puts lives in danger and not only traumatizes the people immediately affected but scars families and entire communities as economic inequality becomes ingrained.

Community also provides the fulcrum for Kumkum Sangari's comparative investigation of the poetics and politics of motherhood in contemporary

South Asia. Drawing upon a range of literary and cultural imaginaries of competing futures, she contends that uneven temporal relations between distant dystopias and existing polities, between realms of fiction and the realities of policy, can provide an entry into the dislocations, displacements, and de- or renationalizations of the figure of the mother across the Global North and South. In Hasan Manzar's "A Requiem for the Earth" and P. D. James's novel *The Children of Men*, the mother materializes as a guarantor of orderly social reproduction, species-sameness, and survival. These anxious and relatively denationalized fictive future imaginaries emerging from Pakistan and England resonate, retrospectively, with contemporary misogynist and sectarian social imaginaries centered on fertility and motherhood in India. Both modes, as her essay shows, revolve on common axes of total or partial extinction, de- or renationalization, social reproduction or care, local or global surveillance, enclavization, eco-destruction, and the production or repression of heterogeneity. She then proceeds to situate the anxieties of these futuristic fictions in the allied controversies around commercial surrogacy and cow slaughter in India. The recent policies to curb both practices converge in a divisive nationalism even as they seek to pull surrogate mothers and cows out of the transnational market economy and seem to go against the grain of neoliberal state policies. The altruistic surrogate as a "close relative" and cows revered as "collective mothers" become, ironically, neoliberal subjects who are also expected to continue the violent political work of enclavizing lower-caste citizens and religious minorities. Yet, the anthropomorphism of the cow as a mother binds the human with the nonhuman in a single servicing economy of care, a care that still depends on the servicing labor of excluded others. In opening up questions of human/nonhuman subsistence and unconditional care in a neoliberal era, this figure of the mother is caught in the crisis of futurity.

The third chapter, by Sherryl Vint, positions the bio-socio-technological imaginary of the future in a different kind of borderland, marked by the multiethnic traces of migration between the United States and a number of locations in the Global South. Through a powerful corpus of contemporary fiction and film by minority and diasporic authors, she posits the search for biological and affective citizenship in North America as a mode of inquiry in itself—an inquiry into the work of speculation in an age of radical reorganization and financialization of life. The border emerges in her work not as a geopolitical or ethnocultural abstraction but as a fraught space for negotiating the economics of bodies and health. Whether these are transnational borders relevant to transplant and surrogacy markets, the walls that separate the privileged from the dispossessed in accessing the conditions of well-being, or indeed the states of incarceration that inevitably attend traffic in racialized and gendered conditions of providing care and generating life, the speculative narrative in Vint's analysis is uniquely equipped to expose their entanglements. Through the trope of promissory futures, a rearrangement of time that colonizes the imagination by generating value in the notion of futurity itself, the essay pushes the boundaries between near-future scenarios and the unfolding present.

In contrast with the work of the imagination, Sital Kalantry's contribution deals with the intricacies of legal procedure and public policy in India's unregulated market of gestational care. She focuses on the turning point of 2015 when the government turned from favoring robust growth to a prohibitionist stance, denying surrogacy visas to foreigners and later proposing a bill to completely ban surrogacy. She documents the little-known but crucial role played by the Indian Supreme Court in this change, which, though never issuing a final opinion, effectively ordered the executive branch to crack down through numerous oral hearings. The Court held these hearings in a public interest litigation (PIL) brought by one woman who believes that surrogacy violates surrogates' fundamental rights under the constitution. While PIL is a special procedure created in the 1980s by the Court to give voice to marginalized communities, in this case surrogates were never consulted by the lawyer who brought the case. When they sought to intervene in the case to claim they had a right to sell gestational care, they were not given voice in the proceedings.

"Altruistic surrogacy," the Indian government's proposed alternative, is taken up again by Emily Vázquez Enríquez as a much older figure of life support in Mexico. The archetypal site of contestation she examines is the body of the wet nurse, which from colonial times all the way to the end of the twentieth century served as an epicenter of debates about the cultivation of the future. Enríquez identifies anti–wet nursing discourses with prejudicial structures against both minority and gendered identities, with anti–wet nursing advocates worrying that subordinate subjects could contaminate the biology or behavior of the infant and thus shape the character of the nation. The transformation of this earlier biologic is catalyzed by the confluence of modern technology and migrant care work, namely, through the appearance of formula and domestic workers called *nanas*, who were devoted to child care without the organic obligation of providing nutrition. It was not until after wet-nursing as a form of labor disappeared and wet nurses were replaced by nanas, Enríquez contends, that the maternal surrogates were not only accepted but also transformed into ideal subjects in the Mexican popular imagination.

The inherent contradictions of agency and voice that attend transnational economies of mother substitutes return as the subject of Kavita Panjabi's analysis of affective discursive structures of the Indian surrogacy debates. Tracing the modes by which motherhood is "both shaped and conscripted" for "a culture of biotechnological innovation to take root" (Sunder Rajan, 78), her essay takes up the aftermath of the PIL in which the Indian government proposed a system of "altruistic" surrogacy to replace its commercial incarnation. Panjabi contextualizes the concept of altruism in this context through the intersecting markets of care and biotechnology, pointing out the asymmetry of different positions of the surrogate mother and a neoliberal transnational industry, the lack of access to the standpoint of the surrogate mothers, and the unacknowledged "excess" appropriated in the creation of the "commodity" of new life. She locates the ruptures in the disciplining discourses of commercial surrogacy—the silences, the ambiguities, and the contradictions—showing how they constitute an ethical lens that reveals suppressed concerns. The concluding section of the essay returns, via the discursive privileging of sacrificial love, to other disturbing questions confronting the future prospect of official "altruistic" surrogacy by law.

The last two essays in the collection are oriented toward posthuman horizons of marketing care and speculating life, a dive into predictive storytelling in the Americas and South Asia that identifies the gendered, racialized work of care and reproduction with the feminization of labor on a global scale. Silvia Kurlat Ares examines the redefinition of the living to include artificial systems, along with the attendant concepts of autonomy and agency, in Argentine science fiction of the new millennium. She surveys these futuristic texts as a chronicle of transition from traditional party systems to neoliberal and populist agendas, engendering the displacement of blue-collar workers from their traditional forms of employment, and the emergence of new forms in consumer and visual cultures. Placed in dystopian worlds that clearly read as a future Argentina, novels like *El corazón de Doli* (2010, Doli's heart), by Gustavo Nielsen, and *Casa de Ottro* (2009, Ottro's house), by Marcelo Cohen, create new idioms of life through radically reconfigured forms of subjectivity—a speculative dynamics of reproduction mediated through transgenic clones and cyborgs. In this chapter, Kurlat Ares explores how these other-bodies, these other-biologies, allow for a meditation on the value of agency in the absence of community. The concluding essay by the editors extends the analysis of millennial science fiction across South Asia and the Americas toward a necropolitics of "unbearable" futures—futures in which the trade in tissues, organs, fetal matter, and bioinformation has divided the world into a supranational north of bioconsumers and a south of *abhumans* suspended in zones of etiolated care.

Drawing from fields as diverse as anthropology, law, literary studies, public policy, and social work, each contribution to this collection draws upon the most diverse of genres, discourses, texts, and contexts. Through the loci of South Asia and the Americas—separately, in juxtaposition, and inevitably from south of the future—they offer multifocal approaches to the ongoing afterlives and possible incarnations of the figure that once coalesced in the artistic imagination as the semi-living worry doll. Together, the essays simultaneously amplify and offer a rich tapestry of responses to the question that Elizabeth Povinelli posed in *Economies of Abandonment*: "To care is to embody an argument about what a good life is and how such a good life comes into being. . . . [W]hat do we believe care to consist of, such that when we experience a form of relating to one another socially, we experience that form of relating as a form of caring for others?" (160).

Works Cited

Bennett, Jane. *Vibrant Matter: A Political Ecology of Things*. Duke UP, 2010.

Bruenig, Elizabeth. "Technology Will Soon Be Able to Tinker with Who We Are. Are We Ready?" *Washington Post*, 3 Dec. 2018, www.washingtonpost.com/opinions/technology-will-soon-be-able-to-tinker-with-who-we-are-are-we-ready/2018/12/03/6f61632c-f4d4-11e8-bc79-68604ed88993_story.html?noredirect=on&utm_term=.0c812f7143f3. Accessed 12 Nov. 2019.

Burnett, John. "Transcript: Interview with White House Chief of Staff John Kelly." *National Public Radio*, 11 May 2018, www.npr.org/2018/05/11/610116389/transcript-white-house-chief-of-staff-john-kellys-interview-with-npr. Accessed 12 Nov. 2019.

Catts, Oron. "Fragments of a Designed Life: The Wet Palette of Tissue Engineering." *Biomediale*, 2004, biomediale.ncca-kaliningrad.ru/?blang=eng&author=catts. Accessed 10. Nov. 2019.

Catts, Oron, and Ionat Zurr. "Semi Living Worry Dolls." lab.anhb.uwa.edu.au/tca/semi-living-worry-dolls/. Accessed 10 Nov. 2019.

Cooper, Melinda, and Katherine Waldby. *Clinical Labor: Tissue Donors and Research Subjects in the Global Bioeconomy*. Duke UP, 2014.

Cyranoski, David, and Sara Reardon. "Chinese Scientists Genetically Modify Human Embryos." *Nature*, 22 Apr. 2015, www.nature.com/news/chinese-scientists-genetically-modify-human-embryos-1.17378. Accessed 12 Nov. 2019.

Da Costa, Beatriz, and Kavita Philip. *Tactical Biopolitics: Art, Activism, and Technoscience*. MIT P, 2010.

Fenton-Glynn, Claire. "Surrogacy: Why the World Needs Rules for 'Selling' Babies.' " *BBC News*. 26 Apr. 2019, www.bbc.com/news/health-47826356. Accessed 12 Nov. 2019.

Hawley, Samantha. "Damaged Babies and Broken Hearts: Ukraine's Commercial Surrogacy Industry Leaves a Trail of Disasters." *ABC News*, 9 Apr. 2019, www.abc.net.au/news/2019-08-20/ukraines-commercial-surrogacy-industry-leaves-disaster/11417388. Accessed 10 Nov. 2019.

Hochschild, Arlie. *The Outsourced Self: What Happens When We Pay Others to Live Our Lives for Us*. Picador, 2013.

Hochschild, Arlie, and Barbara Ehrenreich. *Global Woman: Nannies, Maids, and Sex Workers in the New Economy*. Holt, 2004.

Lewin, Tamar. "Babies from Skin Cells? Prospect Is Unsettling to Some Experts." *New York Times*, 16 May 2017, www.nytimes.com/2017/05/16/health/ivg-reproductive-technology.html?_r=0. Accessed 10 Nov. 2019.

Narayanan, Nayantara. "Why the Nepal Earthquake Has Got India and Israel Talking about Cross-Border Surrogacy." *Scroll.in*, 1 May 2015, www.scroll.in. Accessed 12 Nov. 2019.

"Nigeria Police Raid Lagos 'Baby Factory." *BBC News*, 30 Sept. 2019, www.bbc.com/news/world-africa-49877287. Accessed 30 Oct. 2019.

Pande, Amrita. *Wombs in Labor: Transnational Commercial Surrogacy in India*. Columbia UP, 2014.

Povinelli, Elizabeth A. *Economies of Abandonment: Social Belonging and Endurance in Late Liberalism*. Duke UP, 2011.

"Putting the Placebo Effect to Work." *Harvard Health Publications*, Apr. 2012, www.health.harvard.edu/mind-and-mood/putting-the-placebo-effect-to-work. Accessed 12 Nov. 2019.

Rathi, Akshat. "For the First Time Ever, Scientists Have Edited the Genetic Makeup of Viable Human Embryos." *Quartz Media*, 10 Mar. 2017, qz.com/929773/crispr-has-been-used-to-genetically-modify-viable-human-embryos-for-the-first-time/. Accessed 10 Nov. 2019.

Shamans Market. "The Legend of the Worry Dolls." blog.shamansmarket.com/the-legend-of-the-worry-dolls/. Accessed 12 Nov. 2019.

Sunder Rajan, Kaushik. *Biocapital: The Constitution of Postgenomic Life*. Duke UP, 2006.

Timmons, Heather. "Laura Ingraham's Latest Racist Rant Is Aimed at Legal Immigrants—Like Her Own Daughter." *Quartz Media*, 9 Aug. 2018, qz.com/1352412/laura-ingrahams-fox-news-anti-immigrant-rant-overlooks-her-adopted-daughter/. Accessed 12 Nov. 2019.

Torres, Gloria, et al. "A Review of Surrogate Motherhood Regulation in South American Countries: Pointing to a Need for an International Legal Framework." *BMC Pregnancy and Childbirth*, vol. 19, no. 46 (2019): bmcpregnancychildbirth.biomedcentral.com/articles/10.1186/s12884-019-2182-1. Accessed 10 Nov. 2019.

Vincent, James. "Scientists in China Edit Human Genome in Embryos for the First Time." *The Verge*, 23 Apr. 2015, www.theverge.com/2015/4/23/8477491/human-genome-editing-embryo-china-crispr. Accessed 10 Nov. 2019.

Vora, Kalindi. *Life Support: Biocapital and the New History of Outsourced Labor*. U of Minnesota P, 2015.

Wootson, Cleve R. "Fox News's Laura Ingraham Says Immigrant Child Detention Centers Are Essentially 'Summer Camps.'" *Washington Post*, 19 June 2018, www.washingtonpost.com/news/arts-and-entertainment/wp/2018/06/19/fox-news-laura-ingraham-says-immigrant-child-detention-centers-are-essentially-summer-camps/?utm_term=.601b2c49958f. Accessed 12 Nov. 2019.

1

From Intercountry Adoption in Guatemala to Commercial Global Surrogacy in Gujarat and Beyond

Lessons Learned from Research and Human Rights

Karen Smith Rotabi

For well over a decade I have been involved in intercountry adoption (ICA) research with an emphasis on identifying adoption fraud and reforming systems to meet international standards of ethical practice and ultimately preserve the practice. That area of inquiry is rooted in human rights; the rights of women and children within their family and community life anchor my research questions. Then, as there was a shift to commercial global surrogacy (CGS), I also began to inquire into this different yet parallel area with multiple human rights concerns. As I reflect on my research, to better understand the phenomena of ICA and CGS and inform social policy and systems of care, I will consider the lessons learned along the way as I interfaced with the dynamic marketplace of ICA and CGS (Goodwin 5).

I began my ICA research in Guatemala dating back to the turn of the millennium. At that time, I was working for the Peace Corps as a technical trainer in child health education in rural Guatemalan schools. While it was not entirely clear what was occurring in rural communities, I soon observed that there was a significant exodus of very young children and infants as adoptees, mainly bound for the United States. When I was in Guatemala City, I observed many infants and toddlers leaving in the arms of mainly college-educated white Americans. When boarding the plane with multiple children departing as adoptees, the flight crews often delighted in seeing the children who were, in their view, escaping the extreme poverty of Guatemala for a far more prosperous life. More than once I had a flight attendant tell me of the joy found onboard the "baby flight," and I began to realize that the departure was one of the first steps in shedding Guatemala for the individuals and couples (adoptive parents) who were shocked by the devastating poverty on the ground (Rotabi and Bromfield 65).

For anyone paying attention, the nexus point of power and privilege was undeniable as the brown children were conveniently called "orphans" and their white adoptive parents were viewed as saviors. The biological families were silenced as if they hardly ever existed. I have known of this phenomenon of silencing the social history of adoptees, an erasure of the past, but I began to think about the "disappeared" of the Civil War, and it became clear to me that some of these very young children and infants were the "living disappeared" in post-conflict Guatemala (Rotabi, "Child Adoption" 169). The children were disappearing into families in the United States, and in time, as I began to explore the human rights issues, I came to realize that the right of a child to remain in his or her community and biological and kinship system was clearly spelled out in the United Nations Convention on the Rights of the Child (CRC) along with other critical ideas like identity. Furthermore, as per the CRC, countries like Guatemala were expected to provide oversight of adoptions with competent authorities to verify the unparented status of the child, among other concerns (Roby and Maskew 57).

The Concept of Orphan

The common narrative in ICA—one in which the helpless and poor child is rescued from the orphanage—is all too often a myth (Joyce 1). As with many complicated ideas, things are not always what they seem. In the case of Guatemala there were far too many cases of child sales under the guise of ethical ICA (Comisión Internacional Contra la Impunidad 10; "Report on Players" 3). In fact, we now know that many children were not truly orphans—that is, both parents being deceased or social orphans who were unparented and truly abandoned in institutions without the incentive of the ICA industry. Rather, an unknown but significant number of children were *manufactured* to meet the demands of the business of ICA (Rivera). Of course the process necessary in the making of an orphan includes an erasure of social history and identity; the human rights dimensions are profound.

My story of research in this area actually starts with the moment when I began to suspect something was terribly wrong with ICA in Guatemala, with the idea of the *orphan* being a central concept. Today, more than a decade later, my research has now emerged on a global scale as I have investigated many countries (e.g., Ethiopia, Cambodia, India, and Russia). More recently, my research agenda has also included CGS in India, and the mix of knowledge in the area of ICA and the history of the practice has been quite informative when considering global surrogacy contracts (Rotabi and Bromfield 3).

Historical Background on Intercountry Adoption

ICA largely dates back to the end of World War II and at least one million children have been adopted around the world since then, half of those joining US families (Selman 12). Many other children joined families in Western Europe, Canada, Australia, and elsewhere; most frequently these children left impoverished environments/families and immigrated to be adopted by comparatively wealthy families. What began as a legitimate humanitarian intervention, with South Korean children being the first major migration of "war orphans," eventually became a practice in which thousands of children were joining families throughout the world annually (Herman 11). Global inequalities and privilege versus poverty played out with each country having its unique social context and underlying dynamics, with war being one of the most obvious catalysts in the early days (Rotabi and Bromfield 5). As the intervention of ICA shifted from a humanitarian solution to a marketplace, one where a child was found for a paying individual or couple (rather than a family found for a child), a corrupted model of practice emerged in countries where children were available due to nothing more or less than the conditions of poverty (Cheney 69).

In the sixty-plus years since World War II, the impact of ICA has been profound; the research on gains in child development and health improvement alone make a strong case for the practice of ICA (Bakermans-Kranenburg et al. 279; Juffer and van Ijzendoorn 175). In addition, that story of developmental gains and health improvement has often been told in the media with compelling case examples of the idyllic "love conquers all" happy ending of family life. However, more recently another story is also being told—that of illicit adoption practices, which violate children's rights to their family and community life (San Román and Rotabi 3). This other side of the story is now heard more and more frequently in the media. For example, the *Economist* ran a 2010 story entitled "Saviours or Kidnappers? International Adoption." This is just one press story that continues to be told as the dramatic decreases in the practice continues to generate discourse about the *whys* and *hows* of the changes in ICA. Part of that story is how one ICA-country of origin closes as another country starts to boom. Eventually that next boom country runs into problems as the adoption entrepreneurs become aggressive and cross ethical lines in order to meet marketplace demands. In time, one country after another closes in what is called an ICA "moratorium." These closures and related corruption activities are the culprits of a massive global decrease in ICA.

There has been an over 70 percent decrease since ICA reached a peak in 2004 with approximately forty-five thousand children being adopted internationally on a global scale, of which 22,884 children were sent to the United States (Selman 11). To make this point, the following graphic of adoptions to the United States, from 1990 to 2017, indicates the stark reality at hand. The graph indicates the shift in adoption practices in the most frequent countries of origin, in recent history, specifically in these countries' sending patterns to the United States. Each of these countries has its own problematic ICA history.

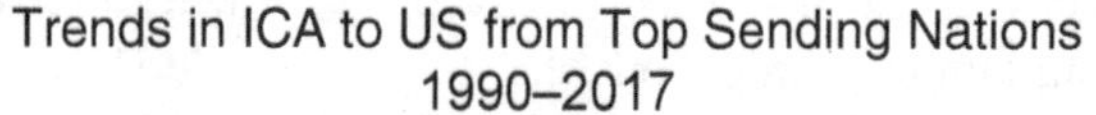

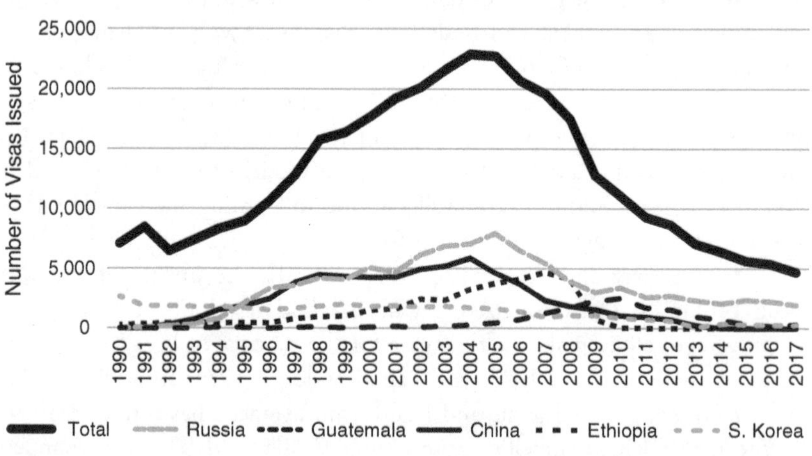

Total Adoptions to the United States from Russia, Guatemala, China, Ethiopia, and South Korea (1990–2017).

Russia's downturn is related to bilateral problems stemming from child deaths; at least twenty adoptees have died at the hands of their adoptive parents (Rotabi, "Child Adoption" 13), many of them dying as a result of head injuries (Hegar et al. 182). Ethiopia recently entered into an adoption moratorium in 2017 as a result of wide-scale fraud in the country, to include child sales into adoption; this fraud has been a known problem for the past decade (Bunkers et al. 132). China has its own dynamics for downturns in the practice, some of which have been driven by fraud and after years of a relatively fast processing of cases (many of which were healthy girls), and today China has a long process of five to six years or more. Most children departing the country have special needs (Johnson 109). And, then there is the moratorium in Guatemala (Bunkers and Groza 119).

Before I proceed with further details of Guatemala, I will look at Cambodia first as a case study of *how* fraud is carried out. This small, post-conflict country with a history of genocide was home to gross abuses of human rights related to adoption fraud (Roby and Maskew 55; Maskew 619); United States law enforcement investigation provides us with a detailed account of the various steps in *creating* the orphan for child sales into adoption (Cross 1; Smolin, "Child Laundering" 115). The case is quite instructive for setting the framework for how illicit adoptions are constructed and the steps of fraud.

Cambodia: The Ugly Truth and How Illicit Adoptions Were Orchestrated

Cambodia provides a case study because it was one of the first countries with rigorous investigation and prosecution of a US adoption agency director and facilitator. A relatively detailed account of wide-scale fraud was documented by US federal marshals who investigated the case on the ground where multiple crimes took place in the making of orphans (Cross 1). Lauryn Galindo and her sister Lynn Devin pled guilty in federal courts of Washington state in 2004, and the story that emerged was a stunning web of deceit within a multimillion-dollar scheme (3).

Galindo was working in Cambodia as an "adoption facilitator," employed by Seattle Adoptions International. Galindo orchestrated a child sales into adoption scheme through the systematic manner in which she pulled together nexus points necessary for fraud / illicit adoptions in this deeply impoverished country with little to no formal systems of social care at that time. The country was ripe for the fraud that emerged, and the investigating US federal marshal reported the illegal activities consistent with organized crime, including bribery, falsified paperwork, wire fraud for money laundering and related tax fraud, and immigration/visa fraud (Cross 4).

When individuals and couples would travel to Cambodia to pick up their child, after spending thousands of dollars on adoption fees, they would be told to carry in at least $3,000 in crisp $100 bills for an "orphanage donation" (Cross 10). It was later determined that Galindo would deposit this cash into offshore bank accounts hidden from the US federal government to avoid taxes. Tax evasion was one charge that was the ultimate demise of the sisters, in the end. At the time of the fraud, there were simply inadequate human trafficking laws to prosecute for the crime of child sales.

Inadequate legal systems for regulation and prosecution were the norm at this juncture in history, especially for adoptions to the United States. The human rights abuses that took place were compelling and occurred at multiple nexus points necessary to construct the orphan. The story goes as follows.

Galindo would buy children from residential care institutions as well as hire "child finders" who would move across the small country, seeking impoverished families willing to hand over their children for a better life. These finders worked on contingency; they were paid based on the number of children secured for adoption. Galindo's practice of only paying a finder based upon success of securing a child was obviously flawed—quite simply ethical adoptions *are never* based on an operation of *finding* a vulnerable child in this manner with financial incentives.

We now know that in many cases, the finders promised families that their child would return to visit but enjoy a good life with an excellent education under the sponsorship of another relatively rich family in a second country (Cross 4). Many Cambodians saw the opportunity to send their children away to school as being not unlike a boarding school scheme; they simply did not understand the paperwork that they were required to sign, severing their legal ties to their child. These adoption relinquishment papers were often written in a language that the impoverished people of Cambodia did not understand due to both illiteracy and a lack of appreciation for the severance of parental rights. As they signed the papers, acting upon the trust of the finder/facilitator, they were often given a mere $50 in US dollars or perhaps a bag of rice (3).

One may ask how a family could be duped in this way, and the answer is poverty combined with hope and ultimately exploitation. Extreme poverty is an experience that those of us with access to resources such as education often fail to fully appreciate. Mothers and fathers who desperately try to feed their children on a daily basis (often falling short in calories), with little hope for a better future including decent educational opportunities, are susceptible to a dream presented by the child finders. In the end, a smooth sell of hope ultimately uses a number of techniques of force, fraud, and coercion, the three internationally agreed-upon elements of human trafficking (Rotabi and Bromfield 74).

While some argue against the term "child trafficking" when considering adoption fraud—especially since the end point is *not* exploitation for the child in question (Brown and Roby 63), the means and mechanisms used to buy and sell children in Galindo and Devin's scheme had all the hallmarks of organized crime necessary for illicit adoptions (Smolin, "Child Laundering" 115). The process included falsified identity documents in which the child was presented to United States (and other) embassy officials as *orphans* for the travel visas/paperwork necessary to depart Cambodia. Most of the children were anything but orphans as they had Cambodian families, and the idea of both parents being deceased or legitimately lost was simply false in most instances. In the case of Galindo, she presented the children as "orphans," and the "orphanage" was a theater she constructed so that prospective adoptive parents could see the horrifying conditions of institutionalized children in Cambodia.

When Galindo was prosecuted, it was due to Galindo's depositing this cash into offshore bank accounts hidden from the US federal government to avoid taxes. In the end, tax evasion was one charge that was the ultimate demise of the sisters. That was just one crime of many when one factors in both countries.

As a result of the detailed investigations into Galindo and Devin's enterprise, the racket of child abduction into adoption was identified, and the term "child laundering" began to be used in earnest as a result of David Smolin's determined push to explore the legal and social protections needed for ICAs. Smolin explains "child laundering" used to legitimize ICAs as follows: "The term 'child laundering' expresses the claim that the current intercountry adoption system frequently takes children illegally from birth parents, and then uses the official processes of the adoption and legal systems to 'launder' them as 'legally' adopted children. Thus, the adoption system treats children in a manner analogous to a criminal organization engaged in money laundering, which obtains funds illegally but then 'launders' them through a legitimate business" ("Child Laundering" 115). In this definition, Smolin captures what appears to be the clean side of Devin and Galindo's activity; a nice little adoption agency headed up by Devin in Seattle served as the conduit for fees for service before the families ever arrived in Cambodia. Devin operated the agency with little more than a website, a spare room in her home, photographs of "waiting" children in Cambodia, and formal procedures of child adoption, which all seemed quite legitimate to the families paying for the service of an adoption provider. Fundamentally, Devin, a licensed professional counselor at that time, appeared to be operating a respectable adoption agency, and the federal marshal who investigated the case admitted that Devin herself was largely unaware of the dark side of Galindo's activity on the ground. For this reason, Devin eventually offered testimony against Galindo (her sister), resulting in lesser charges and avoidance of jail time. Galindo was stripped of her wealth, including a beachside home, luxury car, and other trappings of wealth she maintained in Hawaii. In the end, Galindo served a relatively brief sentence in a US federal prison.

Eventually Cambodia, like other countries, entered into an adoption moratorium. The fraud was profound as there were others operating just as Galindo had. Highly placed Cambodians were also implicated, misusing their status and positions in humanitarian organizations to push along illicit adoptions. Indeed, many Cambodian bureaucrats participated in the process of fraud by issuing false paperwork, and Galindo admitted to bribery of these individuals (e.g., public record clerks issuing identity documents) calling the payments "tips." When Galindo was interviewed by the press about her activity in Cambodia, she clearly saw herself as being persecuted and continued to identify herself as a child saver rather than trafficker (Cross 7). For example, she justified the "tips" as being related to the fact that Cambodian government employees were paid so poorly. While that may be true, the magnitude of the distortions of reality were such that you cannot look at Cambodia without concluding that wide-scale illicit adoptions occurred and lives were forever changed.

Guatemala: A Human Rights Catastrophe

When one talks of the problems related to ICA, the use of emotive words can come easily and I try to moderate my choice of words. This is essential for me as a researcher as objectivity is critical in how I frame research questions and discuss results of analysis. After years of work in this field, I have settled on the term "child abduction into adoption" when talking about such cases in Guatemala. I have also settled on the word "catastrophe" as the correct concept for that which occurred in Guatemala. Part of this decision to use the dramatic word catastrophe links back to Guatemala's roots of war and genocide that, not unlike Cambodia, ultimately set off the adoption boom. This baby and young child boom began to build in the 1990s before the 1996 Peace Accords (Bunkers and Groza 119; Dubinsky 3).

The truth and reconciliation process in Guatemala captured testimony from military leaders and others who were personally involved in the removal of young indigenous children from their communities and resocialization with ladino (Spanish origin) families in Guatemala (Recuperación de la Memoria Histórica 35). This is not only an act of war but also an internationally identified form of genocide dating back to the 1948 Genocide Convention that was drafted as a result of World War II. For example, in the case of Guatemala, an excerpt of truth and reconciliation testimony is very telling: "In 1984, the mayor of Rabinal ordered the auxiliary mayors to take children between the ages of five and ten from the Pacux settlement to the Children's Home of the Church of the Nazarene in San Miguel Chicaj. They took twenty boys and girls against their parents' wishes. . . . Later, in 1988, the families complained to the parish priest that their children had been turned into evangelical Christians; they wanted their children returned to them. They were returned that same year" (Recuperación de la Memoria Histórica 38). In this case, the children were returned home. However, an unknown number of children disappeared into adoption during the war years; some remained in Guatemala and often they were raised by military families, reared by the oppressor with the child unaware of their social history (Rotabi, "Child Adoption" 172). Other children departed the country as international adoptees; the precise numbers of either group are unknown as would be expected in clandestine operations. Today, there have been some attempts above and beyond the truth and reconciliation testimonies to unearth the identities of those lost in adoption. For one's identity is a human right that cannot be underestimated.

Most recently, an adoptee in Belgium has lodged a case in Guatemalan courts, seeking the truth about her case (Cruz). The case is ongoing and without resolution at this juncture. However, the implications can be quite significant because in the case of child abduction into adoption, it may well work out that this is one crime that can continue to be prosecuted today. This was found to be true in the case of Argentina, when adoptees there sought truth as war crime prosecutions took place, including the trial and imprisonment of one of their top generals (Caistor 1). In the case of child abduction into adoption during war, the statute of limitations was found (in some cases) to extend to the child's age of majority and thus the crime is prosecutable for many years after the fact (Briggs and Marre 9).

The Millennium Adoption Surge in Guatemala

Globally, there was what I call the "Millennium Adoption Surge." This was certainly the case in Guatemala, and in the year 2000, the BBC ran a story entitled "Guatemala's Baby Business" (Goldsmith 1); that year saw approximately 1,500 children depart for the United States alone. Also in 2000, the United Nations released a report by a special rapporteur who documented gross human rights abuses including pregnant sex workers being forcibly housed with midwives, women coming out of labor and delivery and being told a falsehood by a doctor or nurse that their child died in childbirth, pregnant housemaids being forcibly separated from their infants by their employers, and other means not unlike the Cambodia fraud and child finders searching across the countryside. As the numbers of children departing continued to rise, reaching a peak in Guatemalan press accounts included "robo de ninos" (theft of children) as stories emerged about illicit adoptions in the years following the year 2000 reports (Dubinsky 30; Mónico 15). By 2007, 4,726 children departed as adoptees to the United States after a steady increase since the year 2000. Negative press reports seemed to have little effect on the system that saw a consistent flow of prospective parents. Publications such as the *New York Times* were consistently running negative stories by the year 2002–2003, culminating in very descriptive examples of fraud. Nonetheless Guatemalan adoption lawyers continued to capitalized on lax adoption processes by representing the paying family / prospective parents as well as the birth mother (in a dual relationship allowable by Guatemalan law at the time). The lawyers became wildly enriched; many became adoption millionaires, buying lavish homes in Miami and elsewhere, not unlike Galindo's Hawaiian getaway. On the adoption agency side of the equation, in the United States where most of the agencies were physically located, those organizations started to spring up overnight. Those starting small agencies did so with very little influence or oversight by seasoned child welfare professionals who understood the complexities of adoption ethics and the imperative of viewing a vulnerable child as a member of a biological family, a kinship group, and a community with rights (Roby 48; Roby and Maskew 56).

Simultaneously, violence against women was gaining attention just after the turn of the millennium and the crimes were so grotesque that I began to also consider the disturbing social climate and context of ICA ("Guatemala" 1). An exchange with a US embassy official working in Guatemala City on security-related issues is one that I will never forget. I met this individual socially and had the opportunity to very privately ask if the rumors of violence against women and adoption fraud were true. Specifically, I asked if it was true that women's bodies were being found at homicide scenes in which they had experienced a cesarean section for labor and delivery prior to their murder. He confirmed that there were cases of pregnant women being killed and that US embassy officials were well aware of the suspicions that these killings were related to the dark side of Guatemalan adoptions. Later, these killings were confirmed to me by human rights defenders, including Norma Cruz, who is internationally recognized for her tireless advocacy for women who have experienced societal and family violence in Guatemala (Cruz et al., "Violence" 1).

It became clear that the scenario was not just one of illicit adoptions, but the context was impunity and violence against women ("Guatemala" 1) combining in an insatiable adoption marketplace mainly in the United States. On the side of the Americans seeking to adopt were powerful politicians who put extraordinary pressure on embassy officials to keep adoption from Guatemala open. It was a compelling political scenario in which politicians saw their constituents as well-meaning people and hopeful parents. The highly charged political nature of adoption became very clear as politicians went to Guatemala on fact-finding missions to persuade officials to keep the system open. On the Guatemalan side of the equation, human rights defenders were hard at work to cease the abuses and ultimately close the system (see Casa Alianza et al. 1).

The turning point in building momentum for change eventually came as those committed to prevention of violence against women stepped in as advocates. As my colleague Norma Cruz tells the story, she decided to involve herself when she realized that stealing a woman's child is the worst form of violence as it inflicts eternal suffering upon a mother (Cruz et al., "Violence" 2). As a result, Cruz threw herself full force into supporting the mothers searching for their children; among other things, Cruz and a small group of brave women collectively went on a hunger protest to demand a means to bring their cases before the courts (Rotabi, "Guatemala City" 1).

In time, Cruz and her team of her lawyers at Survivor's Foundation were successful in helping to bring Loyda Rodriguez's case to court, and ultimately the nullification of the adoption of the child in question (including nullifying her passport, which had been constructed with a false identity).

Sadly, even with a court order to return the child to Guatemala, Loyda still has not seen her child in the eight-plus years since that court order. The adoptive family, in the United States, refuses to adhere to the order. Specifically, the US Department of Justice has also refused to involve itself in enforcement of the Guatemalan court ruling (Cruz et al., "Stolen 5).

The United States' unwillingness to enforce the court ruling was particularly disappointing as Loyda experienced classic child abduction. Loyda briefly turned her back on her child as she unlocked a gate and the young girl was snatched on the roadside. Loyda dedicated herself to bringing her cherished daughter home, searching and begging for help from law enforcement and other authorities. After quite a struggle to have the case heard, a verdict to return the child resulted in Loyda finally speaking with sympathetic international press about the case. She demonstrated her sincere intent as a dedicated mother: "All I want to tell them [the adoptive parents] is to return my girl. I don't have anything against them because perhaps they took my daughter without knowing that she had been stolen from me. That's why I want to ask them to return her to me," said Rodriguez (Romo 1). The case remains unresolved today as the adoptive family has made a public statement that they do not view returning *their* daughter to be in her best interests. Even with Loyda's grace in her pursuit of reunification, the family appeared on a news show, viewed by millions in the United States, to make their position known. Their statement is clear and, in the long run, this young girl will be confronted with some difficult social history as she becomes an adolescent, then adult, likely to eventually learn of her past and about the decisions others made on her behalf. Her position is a difficult one and I fear for her long-term sense of self and emotional life as she finds her way in the world. Her human rights have been violated and she will have much to reconcile as she considers the meaning of family.

Even without resolution in this case, the documentation of Loyda and other women's cases is not to be underestimated in the process of unearthing the truth. As Guatemalan-born adoptees themselves begin homeland tours and asking questions, the truth continues to emerge. These journeys are taking place within the context of the knowledge gained from a wide range of documentation of fraud, ranging from the United Nations' documentation to high-quality investigative reporting that has documented other cases of child abduction into adoption (Siegal 1). Today, it is recognized that an unknown but significant number of Guatemalan adoptions were illicit as the system was deeply corrupt ("Report on Players" 2; Rotabi, "Force" 1). There are so many cases that those adoptions that were legitimate—and there were ethical adoptions during the boom years—are overshadowed with dark questions at this point in history.

Commercial Global Surrogacy Takes Off as Intercountry Adoption Declines

One thing is certain, the global "baby market" (Goodwin 1) continues on and some individuals and couples simply want a healthy infant. In that desire, the marketplace began a shift into CGS in India, which eventually became a significant player in the billion-dollar surrogacy business. While surrogacy arrangements have been taking place for decades, especially in the United States, India provided the opportunity to secure an infant for $20,000 in US dollars or less dating back to the year 2002. This was an attractive price tag as one considers the fact that ICAs were estimated to cost on average $25,000 or more for American citizens in 2006 (United States Government Accountability Office 10). In truth, the cost of adoption was surging well beyond that sum in the peak years of ICA in the United States (some adoptions costing $50,000 or more). In the meantime, surrogacy arrangements in the United States are known to range upward to $75,000 and more.

Before turning to the case of Gujarat, India, and that which we learned there, it is important to note that CGS in India is now in its own moratorium. While surrogacy is still taking place in India (on a domestic level), CGS has been blocked as the practice was suspended in 2015 while the Indian Supreme Court deliberated on international contract pregnancies / CGS. There remains no resolution today, in terms of a ruling by that court, and the global business of surrogacy has now ceased in India for the time being. It is speculated that the business will not resume, as the practice was simply an embarrassment to a country dedicated to promoting an ethical medical tourism model (orthopedics, cardiac care, cancer care, etc.) worth billions of dollars (Rotabi and Bromfield 151).

Commercial Global Surrogacy: The Case of Gujarat, India

Historically, the epicenter of the surrogacy boom in India is in Gujarat. It is in this state, known for a fierce entrepreneurial spirit, that surrogacy clinics began to spring up. The practice of CGS and the techniques of advanced reproductive technologies interfacing with impoverished women (often called gestational surrogates) is a compelling story that captured international media attention (Carney 69). As one may expect, there was outrage as the world learned that many women were housed in dormitories during gestation, separated from their own children and husbands while they carried out the work of pregnancy and labor for a paying customer. It was a compelling story that raised an alarm on many fronts, most obviously discourse about right and wrong and inherent human rights, most especially the rights of women contracted as gestational surrogates (Carney 69; Pande 3). It should be noted that these CGS contracts were based on embryo transfer and the child was not the genetic offspring of the surrogate mother. This was a particularly attractive aspect of the Indian surrogacy industry, and the practice of gestational surrogacy (rather than traditional surrogacy) is the most common today on a global scale.

In my own work, I've considered *exploitation* and I've learned that the concept is incredibly complicated depending on one's position in view of the problems in question. In some cases, those who are exploited can find themselves participants in their own exploitation as they are navigating the terrain of extreme poverty with few choices. This is one of the many themes in research on prostitution / sex work in which women bear the physical burdens in a marketplace.

Amrita Pande has carried out the most important and seminal research on surrogate mothers in Gujarat, India, and she explores the notion of "dirty work" as well as sex work, along with the various dimensions of exploitation (1). The intermingling of CGS with sex work as a concept is one that has required a deeper look as one of the concerns for the well-being of the surrogate mothers in India and the shame and stigma that comes with work in the sex industry. Pande has found that the women she studied are very clear that they were *not* involved in sex work (30). Rather, some of the women speak of the virtue of the work of helping build a family. By and large, the surrogates of India view the endeavor of CGS as work in which their blood and health as a mother is necessary to help and serve those paying for her service as a surrogate.

Upon reviewing Pande's ethnographic work, I wanted to know more as I began to interrogate the idea of *what* is acceptable to sell in the globalized marketplace in which neoliberal policy has resulted in some gains and many losses for the people living in poverty. In thinking out loud about these ideas, I started asking others about their opinion of the practice of CGS. Many Indians that I spoke to were unaware of the activity. Others were aware, but they did not seem interested in meaningful discussion of CGS (and, of course, there were exceptions such as Indian scholars and human rights defenders). As I probed more deeply, I never really came to understand why there might be a disinterest except for my own theory of poverty fatigue and the outrageous stories of exploitation in India with its population of well over a billion people, many of whom live in extreme poverty, and the reality of the wide array of human rights abuses that emerge in such a context.

Then, we decided to simply ask the women their view of the contract pregnancy as ultimately their voices are critical in any discourse about the practice of CGS. Now, I turn to our results focusing on (1) the cost-benefit analysis that the women undertake in deciding to become a surrogate, (2) the emotional burden of being a surrogate mother for pay, (3) the benefit that came to the women and their families as a result of their participation in a CGS contract, and (4) perceptions of exploitation. These four areas of results of our research in Gujarat, and an expanded discussion of these interviews with twenty-five surrogate mothers, can be found in (Rotabi and Bromfield 145).

1. Cost-Benefit Analysis Made by Surrogate Mothers

Poverty was a clear thread throughout the interviews and some of the stories were unforgettable. One mother talked of trying to feed her own children and spoke of her cupboards being empty. Another woman spoke of selling her blood for cash. This is not unlike the study by Karandikar and colleagues that identified one woman and her husband who considered the idea of selling a kidney (236). Once she considered her options, she chose surrogacy as the better option for earning money.

We also found that women were often comparing surrogacy to other far less attractive work options. These are jobs that will never enable the woman to save or get ahead. This reality is combined with long work hours that take her away from daily family life, and other issues such as workplace safety in factories and other undesirable locations of labor available to women.

It should also be mentioned that our study did not probe into problems in the surrogate's personal life that may factor into motivation. However, Deomampo found surrogates in Mumbai who reported making the decision to participate with a history of divorce and marital separations; serious problems like physical abuse and partner substance abuse were reported by some of the women she interviewed (516).

All of this considered, there is clearly a cost-benefit analysis equation operating in which perceived threat and perceived benefit are factored into the decision-making process. A decision-making model was clearly operating for women who were weighing a broad array of unattractive options to earn a living, and CGS offered a way to get ahead. The social exchanges are complex with the constant of poverty as a hard-pressing social context.

2. The Emotional Burden of the Surrogate Mothers

The surrogate mothers that we interviewed, by and large, reported a sense of loss and the associated pain is the emotional burden of CGS. However, in our study, the surrogates were known to have contracted through a respected fertility clinic in which the doctor who is in charge takes her international reputation seriously, including appearances in international media such as the *Oprah Winfrey* show, where she spoke of CGS as a win-win practice. Here, a surrogate mother speaks of her emotional burden and the interface with the medical doctor, whom she refers to as "madam": "I didn't feel good because I kept them in my belly for nine months. When they took them away, I cried a lot. I felt like I was giving away my own children and I regretted it a lot. I went back home and couldn't eat anything, I was crying a lot. Then my husband explained that those were their babies and of course they will take them away. Madam also told me that they were not my kids. So like that slowly I forgot about it."

3. The Benefit That Came to the Women and Their Own Families as a Result of the Surrogacy

Of the twenty-five surrogates mothers interviewed, we found that nearly all of them mentioned educating their own children (paying school fees and buying uniforms and books) as well as the construction of a home. Some spoke of also giving happiness in the process of CGS: "I needed to get my daughter married, educate my sons, fix the house. In nine months, forget that. Even if I worked for five years, I wouldn't have been able to make this amount of money. And it is a good job. Money is good but then to give happiness to someone is a big thing." The preceding quote is particularly telling as the surrogate mother mentions dowry first, that is, the need to marry her daughter with a dowry. This is another unfortunate gendered reality in India that is an extreme burden on families living in poverty. This surrogate mother is quite practical in her explanation, just as another woman explained similarly, who mentions her husband's role in the decision to contract a pregnancy: "I didn't have a house before. To build a house I told my husband that I wanted to be a surrogate. Our salaries were less so couldn't have built a house with that. My husband didn't agree with this, but I told him that I will definitely go for it. I said only if I become a surrogate will the house be built, otherwise it wouldn't. And if anything is remaining I will keep some for my child for his education. That is how I decided. Later my husband and I were on the same page."

4. Surrogate Mother: Perceptions of Exploitation

This research began with questions about exploitation and it was startling when the women were simply asked about being "used or taken advantage of." All twenty-five women said they did not feel exploited. The responses shed light on not only the cost-benefit analysis mentioned earlier but the practical view that the woman took of the practice: "Why will (the paying couple) take advantage? They haven't asked me to become a surrogate. It was my situation which pushed me into becoming a surrogate. I went there (to the fertility clinic) myself. I thought if someone else benefits only then will I benefit. They have no advantage here. It's a good work as someone got a child and our poverty also got erased." Another woman simply said, "No. The benefit was mine. They didn't come to my house to ask me to come for it. I was the one in need and so I came. So benefit was mine."

Several women responded by explaining the informed consent process with this particular fertility clinic when responding to this question of feeling taken advantage of. One said, "No. Nothing like that. They give us counseling, make us sign an agreement so it's all taken care of." Another woman spoke of the benefit in the following quote, "No never felt like that (taken advantage of). I like this life. I will keep this experience close to me my whole life. From here on life will be good."

Concluding Thoughts on Lessons and What Is Next in My Research Agenda

In our CGS research in India, it was clear to me that you simply cannot generalize from our findings. As mentioned previously, the fertility clinic related to these women's CGS contracts has an international reputation and arguably it is one of the best clinics in India (Rotabi and Bromfield 150). I have no doubt that there are many poorly managed clinics in this country with a population of well over a billion people. Our research did not reach any women who reported poor or unethical care and practices. Research with women who can identify the problems of poor and unethical practices as well as illicit activities is important, especially since domestic surrogacy is still a major marketplace, albeit far less profitable for the women of India. The reality is that foreign couples were seen to be more desirable than domestic/Indian couples because the outsiders (from high-resource countries) were willing to compensate the women more handsomely (Pande 60).

Thinking more broadly about which are the important lessons, a few thoughts are not necessarily new but these ideas were reinforced as a result of the experience. For example, whenever possible, *do not* speak for others as they express their opinions and views, especially when you yourself do not share in their experience of poverty, problems, and complicated decision-making processes. Always look for a way for vulnerable people to express themselves so that we may better understand their circumstances and *how* we may protect them with effective social policy.

In the case of *exploitation*, recognize that in many cases there are multiple variables that come together in complicated social contexts, especially when poverty is a driving force. In CGS, there are children who must also be considered. In the case of India and other low-resource settings, the children born as a result of CGS have yet to tell their stories and their views on the best interests of the child. I suspect that there will be as many unhappy individuals born as a result of CGS as there will be happy and grateful individuals. Perhaps not—I am open to the idea that many of those conceived by CGS will ultimately see the arrangement as essential in their own existence (rather than exploitive) and thus view the contract and process pragmatically. Only time will tell and there will invariably be differences between those individuals born to US surrogates versus those gestated by women in poverty in countries like India.

In ICA research, adoptees are vocal, with those who view ICA as an overreach, a neocolonial act, speaking loudly and clearly in their work against the expansion of ICA. Of course, there are also ICA adoptees that see the practice positively. There are clearly different camps within ICA discourse (Gibbons and Rotabi 3). For CGS, research on the views of those born of such contracts in impoverished countries shall emerge. This is an area for others to explore; I am more interested in other topics for future research.

In the process of research, have I come to some conclusions in terms of a moral position? Yes, some things should not be *bought* and *sold* as the human cost and price are too high. When it comes to ICA, the answer is clear as a child should *never* be sold under the guise of adoption. Do I similarly include CGS in the "never" category? The answer depends on *how* the transaction/contract is organized and managed. In this answer, I am leaning on the side of recognizing surrogacy as a "service" that can be contracted, even though I have discomfort in the idea when it comes to the relatively rich individual/couple contracting with a women living in poverty with few options for work that is paid at a fair wage. Ultimately, I think that low resource countries, like India, with the context of deep poverty and limited opportunities for women, are fraught with opportunities for exploitation. In my view, it is impossible to set up an assembly line, on a mass scale as had been built in India, without serious human rights abuses emerging in an insatiable marketplace. This is particularly true in a country known for violence against women and limited access to justice for those living in poverty. Finally, just like ICA, we do not know the actual scale of abuse in CGS in India and other impoverished countries, but anyone who argues against the abuse occurring in an unknown number of cases is either willfully blind *or* being enriched by the industry! I certainly have learned that lesson from interfacing with those who work in ICA and refuse to have a meaningful conversation about the problems in the process and opportunities to strengthen and ultimately build a more ethical system.

I cannot conclude without considering the surrogate mothers in the United States. In this particular country, surrogates have a great deal of autonomy over the process. Many of the surrogates invest significant time and energy in reviewing and choosing the couples/individuals with whom they contract as many see the process to be a relationship (Rotabi and Bromfield 138). The evidence is that surrogates in the United States see themselves as exercising self-determination and many view the process as a gifting of family life (a gift child) to an individual or couple. Some see the act as one of social justice for gay men (Rotabi and Bromfield 136). While the activity in the United States and India uses the same technology and some of the women in India also mentioned the idea of giving the gift of a child, the two countries are quite different in social realities and the risks of CGS, including a context necessary to truly exercise self-determination. Therein lies a serious distinction as it may be argued that women in India do not have a fair playing field in this aspect of ethical engagement and informed consent.

It is obvious that CGS must be regulated as the marketplace will inevitably shift to other low-resource countries with limited infrastructure in terms of legal protections. Briefly, after India and Thailand closed, Cambodia appeared to be an emerging location. However, that Southeast Asian country was ultimately not a friendly location and the government has closed the door to the opportunity of CGS there (an Australian nurse is being prosecuted on charges related to human trafficking in the summer of 2017). Now, it appears that the marketplace may be shifting to neighboring Laos. The shifts are predictable if one looks at the history of ICA. The regulation of CGS with internationally agreed-upon policy and procedures for cross-border surrogacy is essential. Today, there is international private law that regulates many of the ICA transactions in the world (Bunkers and Groza 120). We shall see if such a regulatory structure can be developed for CGS. I do fear the wide-ranging consequences *if* there is no international regulation.

As for my future research agenda, I am looking more at the deinstitutionalization of children in low-resource settings via means other than ICA. That is, supporting and preserving family life with preventive measures that preclude the need to abandon a child to such a setting. This research into family preservation interventions and the need for trained social workers is an area that I feel I can look to in order to satisfy my need to make a difference. Also, domestic adoptions in low-resource countries is another area in which I see the potential for expanding my research agenda because ethical domestic adoption as a social intervention is so very important. When domestic adoption systems are fully functioning, *then* the ICA system can ethically coexist as a child is only released to an international adoption once domestic options are fully explored and exhausted. On the subject of ICA systems, I remain committed to seeking ethical pathways for the practice to remain a viable solution for truly appropriate children.

Finally, I want to close with the following. As we consider the concerns about women in poverty being exploited in surrogacy contracts or unethical adoptions, I submit to the reader that one of the most important questions is *how* we can truly attack and alleviate the poverty. Desperate conditions of poverty pushes women into all sorts of exploitation—much of which puts lives in danger and not only traumatizes the people affected but scars families and entire communities as economic inequality becomes ingrained. Without social development with true poverty-reduction interventions, we will continue to see gross human rights abuses. That is a simple truth that cannot be denied, and oppression of the poor, including reaching across borders in globalized marketplaces, is a poison for humankind with far-reaching consequences.

~

I would like to express my sincere appreciation to Lopamudra Goswami, research assistant for the Gujarat project. Lopa took an interest in CGS and became a partner in field research. I am proud to mentor Lopa along in her next stages of research training as she has much to give.

Works Cited

Bakermans-Kranenburg, Marian J., et al. "Earlier Is Better: A Meta-Analysis of 70 Years of Intervention Improving Cognitive Development in Institutionalized Children." *Monographs of the Society for Research in Child Development*, vol. 73, no. 3, 2008, pp. 279–93.

Briggs, Laura, and Diana Marre. *International Adoption: Global Inequalities and the Circulation of Children*. New York UP, 2009.

Brown, Taylor W., and Jini L. Roby. "Exploitation of Intercountry Adoption: Toward Common Understanding and Action." *Adoption Quarterly*, vol. 19, no. 2, 2016, pp. 63–80.

Bunkers, Kelley. M., and Victor Groza. "Intercountry Adoption and Child Welfare in Guatemala: Lessons Learned Pre and Post Ratification of the 1993 Hague Convention on the Protection of Children and Cooperation in Respect of Intercountry Adoption." *Intercountry Adoption: Policies, Practices, and Outcomes*, edited by Judith L. Gibbons and Karen S. Rotabi. Ashgate Press, 2012, pp. 119–31.

Bunkers, Kelley M., et al. "Ethiopia: Intercountry Adoption Risks and Considerations for Informal Care." *Intercountry Adoption: Policies, Practices, and Outcomes*, edited by Judith L. Gibbons and Karen S. Rotabi. Ashgate Press, 2012, pp. 131–42.

Caistor, Nicholas. "Obituary: General Jorge Rafael Videla: Dictator Who Brought Terror to Argentina during the 'Dirty War.' " *The Independent*, 17 May 2013, www.independent.co.uk/news/obituaries/general-jorge-rafael-videla-dictator-who-brought-terror-to-argentina-in-the-dirty-war-8621806.html. Accessed 15 May 2016.

Carney, Scott. "Cash on Delivery: Gestational Dormitories, Routine C-sections, Quintuple Embryo Implants. Brave New World? Nope, Surrogacy Tourism." *Mother Jones*, Mar./Apr. 2010, pp. 69–73.

Cheney, Kristen E. "Giving Children a 'Better Life'? Reconsidering Social Reproduction and Humanitarianism in Intercountry Adoption." *European Journal of Development Research*, vol. 26, 2014, pp. 247–63.

Cross, Richard. "Operation Broken Hearts: Transcript of Richard Cross Video." 15 Apr. 2005, Samford University, cumberland.samford.edu/files/rushton/Richard_Cross_transcript.pdf. Accessed 10 June 2006. Lecture.

Cruz, Norma. Personal correspondence. 15 Aug. 2014.

Cruz, Norma, et al. "Violence against Women in Guatemala: Global Connections and Action in the US University of Central Florida." *YouTube*, uploaded by University of Central Florida, 29 Mar. 2010, www.youtube.com/watch?v=xPtJadrhZzk.

Cruz, Norma, et al. "Stolen Children: Illegal Practices in Intercountry Adoption and the Need for Reform." Human Rights Impact Litigation Clinic of American University, April 2010, Washington College of Law, Washington, DC. Presentation.

Deomampo, Daisy. "Gendered Geographies of Reproductive Tourism." *Gender & Society*, vol. 27, no. 4, 2013, pp. 514–47.

Dubinsky, Karen. *Babies without Borders: Adoption and Migration Across the Americas.* U of Toronto P, 2010.

"Fact Sheet: Femicide and Feminicide." Guatemala Human Rights Commission/USA, 2009, www.GHRC-USA.org/Publications/FemicideFactSheet2009.pdf. Accessed 8 Aug. 2009.

Fundación Myrna Mack. "Adoptions in Guatemala: Protection or Business?" *Informe adopciones fundación Myrna Mack*, Brandeis University, 2007, www.brandeis.edu/investigate/gender/adoption/docs/InformedeAdopcionesFundacionMyrnaMack.pdf.

Gibbons, Judith L., and Karen S. Rotabi, eds. *Intercountry Adoption: Policies, Practices, and Outcomes*. Ashgate Press, 2012,

Goldsmith, Rosie. "Guatemala's Baby Business." *BBC Crossing Continents*, British Broadcasting Corporation, 1 Sept. 2000, news.bbc.co.uk/1/hi/programmes/crossing_continents/879859.stm. Accessed 5 July 2004.

Goodwin, Michele B. *Baby Markets: Money and the New Politics of Creating Families.* Cambridge UP, 2010.

Gresham, Katie, et al. "Intercountry Adoption from Guatemala and the United States: A Comparative Policy Analysis." *Journal of Immigrant & Refugee Studies*, vol. 1, no. 3/4, 2004, doi:10.1300/J191v01n03_01, pp. 1–20.

Goicoechea, Ignacio. "Report of a Fact-Finding Mission to Guatemala in Relation to Intercountry Adoption." Hague Conference on Private International Law [HCCH], 26 Feb.–9 Mar. 2007, www.hcch.net/upload/wop/mission_gt33e.pdf. Accessed 5 June 2009.

"Guatemala: No Protection, No Justice: Killings of Women in Guatemala." Stop Violence Against Women Campaign, Amnesty International, 2006, lib.ohchr.org/HRBodies/UPR/Documents/Session2/GT/AI_GTM_UPR_S2_2008anx_KillingsofwomeninGuatemala.pdf. Accessed 17 June 2017.

Honeyman, Derek. "Lynch Mobs and Child Theft Rumors in the Guatemalan Highlands." University of Alberta, 1999. Diss.

Hegar, Rebecca, et al. "Child Fatality in Intercountry Adoption: What Media Reports Suggest about Deaths of Russian Children in the US." *Children and Youth Services Review*, vol. 55, 2015, pp. 182–92.

Herman, Ellen. *Kinship by Design: A History of Adoption in the Modern United States*. U of Chicago P, 2008.

Human Rights Office, Archdiocese of Guatemala. *Guatemala Never Again!* Recovery of Historical Memory Project: The Official Report of the Human Rights Office, Maryknoll, 1999.

Johnson, Kay. "Challenging the Discourse of Intercountry Adoption Perspectives from Rural China." *Intercountry Adoption: Policies, Practices, and Outcomes*, edited by Judith L. Gibbons and Karen S. Rotabi. Ashgate Press, 2012, pp. 103–18.

Joyce, Kathryn. *The Child Catchers: Rescue, Trafficking, and the New Gospel of Adoption*. Public Affairs, 2013.

Juffer, Femmie, and Marinus van Ijzendoorn. "Review of Meta-Analytical Studies on the Physical, Emotional, and Cognitive Outcomes of Intercountry Adoptees." *Intercountry Adoption: Policies, Practices, and Outcomes*, edited by Judith L. Gibbons and Karen S. Rotabi. Ashgate Press, 2012, pp. 175–86.

Karandikar, Sharvari, et al. "Economic Necessity or a Noble Cause? Exploring Motivations for Gestational Surrogacy in Gujarat, India." *Affilia: Journal of Women and Social Work*, vol. 29, no. 2, 2014, pp. 224–36.

Maskew, Trish. "Child Trafficking and Intercountry Adoption: The Cambodian Experience." *Cumberland Law Review*, vol. 35, 2004, pp. 619–38.

Mónico, Carmen. "Implications of Child Abduction for Human Rights and Child Welfare Systems: A Constructivist Inquiry of the Lived Experience of Guatemalan Mothers Publicly Reporting Child Abduction for Intercountry Adoption." VCU Digital Archives, Electronic Theses and Dissertations, 2013, hdl.handle.net/10156/4373. Diss.

Pande, Amrita. *Wombs in Labour: Transnational Commercial Surrogacy in India*. Columbia UP, 2014.

Portenier, Giselle. "Killer's Paradise." British Broadcasting Corporation, 4 May 2006, news.bbc.co.uk/2/hi/programmes/this_world/4965786.stm. Accessed 8 Aug. 2009.

Recuperación de la Memoria Histórica (REMHI, Recovery of the historical memory). Guatemala Never Again! Orbis, 1999.

"Report on Players Involved in the Illegal Adoption Process in Guatemala Since the Entry into Force of the Adoption Law (Decree 77-2007)." Comisión Internacional Contra la Impunidad, 1 Dec. 2010, cicig.org/uploads/documents/informes/INFOR-TEMA_DOC05_20101201_EN.pdf. Accessed 25 June 2011.

Rivera, Claudia. Personal communication. 9 Apr. 2009.

Roby, Jini L. "From Rhetoric to Best Practice: Children's Rights in Intercountry Adoption." *Children's Legal Rights Journal*, vol. 27, no. 3, 2007, pp. 48–71.

Roby, Jini L., and Trish Maskew. "Human Rights Considerations in Intercountry Adoption: The Children and Families of Cambodia and Marshall Islands." *Intercountry Adoption: Policies, Practices, and Outcomes*, edited by Judith L. Gibbons and Karen S. Rotabi. Ashgate Press, 2012, pp. 55–66.

Romo, Rafael. "Guatemalan Mother Says Daughter Kidnapped, Adopted in U.S." CNN, 17 Aug. 2011, edition.cnn.com/2011/WORLD/americas/08/15/guatemala.kidnapping.adoption/index.html. Accessed 17 June 2017.

Rotabi, Karen S. "Child Adoption and War: 'Living Disappeared' Children and the Social Worker's Post-Conflict Role in El Salvador and Argentina." *International Social Work*, vol. 57, no. 2, 2012, pp. 169–80, 10.1177/0020872812454314.

———. "Force, Fraud, and Coercion: Bridging from Knowledge of Intercountry Adoption to Global Surrogacy." *ISS Working Paper Series / General Series*, vol. 600, edited by Kristen E. Cheney, International Institute of Social Studies of Erasmus University, Dec. 2014, pp. 1–30, hdl.handle.net/1765/77403.

———. "Global Surrogacy, Exploitation, Human Rights and International Private Law: A Pragmatic Stance and Policy Recommendations." International Conference on Social Science, March 2014. Presentation.

———. "Guatemala City: Hunger Protests amid Allegations of Child Kidnapping and Adoption Fraud." *Social Work and Society News Magazine*, Aug. 2009, www.socmag.net/?p=540.

Rotabi, Karen S., and Nicole Bromfield. *From Intercountry Adoption to Commercial Global Surrogacy*. Routledge, 2017.

Rotabi, Karen S., and Carmen Mónico. "Intercountry Adoptions: Legal and Policy Issues Affecting Adoption Practice." *Transracial and Intercountry Adoptions: Cultural Guidance for Professionals and Educators*, edited by Rowena Fong and Ruth McRoy. Columbia UP, 2016, pp. 15–33.

Rotabi, Karen S., and Beatriz San Román. "Rescue, Red Tape, Child Abduction, Illicit Adoptions and Discourse: Intercountry Adoption Attitudes in Spain." *International Social Work*, 24 July 2017.

Selman, Peter F. "Global Trends in Intercountry Adoption, 2003–2012." *The Intercountry Adoption Debate: Dialogues across Disciplines*, edited by Robert L. Ballard et al. Cambridge Scholars, 2015, pp. 9–48.

Siegal, Erin. *Finding Fernanda: Two Mothers, One Child, and a Cross-Border Search for Truth*. Beacon, 2011.

Smolin, David M. "Child Laundering: How the Intercountry Adoption System Legitimizes and Incentivizes the Practices of Buying, Trafficking, Kidnapping, and Stealing Children." *Wayne Law Review*, vol. 52, 2006, pp. 113–200.

———. "Intercountry Adoption as Child Trafficking." *Valparaiso University Law Review*, vol. 39, 2004, pp. 281–325.

———. "Intercountry Adoption and Poverty: A Human Rights Analysis." *Capital University Law Review*, vol. 36, 2007, pp. 413–53.

"Saviours or Kidnappers? International Adoption." *The Economist*, 6 Feb. 2010, www.economist.com/node/15469423. Accessed 10 June 2010.

United States, Congress, House of Representatives, Committee on Energy and Commerce. *Sexual Exploitation of Children over the Internet: Follow-up Issues to the Masha Allen Adoption: Hearings Before the Subcommittee on Oversight and Investigations of the Committee on Energy and Commerce of the House of Representatives.* Government Printing Office, 2006.

United States Department of State. 2001. "Guatemala." *Country Reports on Human Rights Practices*, Bureau of Democracy, Human Rights and Labor, 23 Feb. 2001, www.state.gov/j/drl/rls/hrrpt/2000/wha/775.htm. Accessed 15 May 2017.

United States Government Accountability Office. "Foreign Affairs: Agencies Have Improved the Intercountry Adoption Process, but Further Enhancements Are Needed." *Report to the Chairman*, Government Printing Office, Oct. 2005, www.gao.gov/new.items/d06133.pdf. Accessed 15 May 2017.

2

On Cruelty and Care

Motherhood and the Crisis of Futurity

Kumkum Sangari

If the inherent unevenness of capital is extended and taken as a figure that combines economic inequality and social discrimination, then the uneven temporal relation between near future dystopias and contemporary polities, between fictive and real future imaginaries, provides a significant entry into the dislocation and de/renationalization of the figure of the mother. In Hasan Manzar's "A Requiem for the Earth" (1981) and P. D. James's *The Children of Men* (1992)—near future dystopias—the mother materializes as a guarantor of orderly social reproduction, species-sameness, survival, and futurity that is freighted with anxiety and subject to tendentious emplacement. Reading near future fiction retrospectively compels a turn to the present. These relatively denationalized fictional future imaginaries emerging from Pakistan and England resonate, retrospectively, with contemporary misogynist and sectarian social imaginaries centered on son selection, surrogacy, fertility, and motherhood in India. Both imaginaries, as I will show, revolve on common axes of partial depletion or extinction, de/renationalization, social reproduction and care, local and global surveillance, eco-destruction, enclavization, and the production and repression of heterogeneity. Two recent and contested bans on commercial surrogacy and cow slaughter in India, which have been under public and legal scrutiny for their unconstitutional clauses, dubious legality, and material effects, can be read as social texts, texts that seek to instantiate fictive social imaginaries, put into play a regulated legal space imbricated in extralegal violence, and shape present scenarios. Both are apparently renationalizing bans that destroy lucrative markets, seem to go against the grain of neoliberal state policies, and build on the figure of the altruistic surrogate and the cow as a collective mother. Motherhood is a material signifier of social reproduction, which as JaneMaree Maher notes refers not only to biological reproduction and social and emotional care, but has broader communal and national significance.[1] Motherhood has also become the pivot of cultural, legal, and literary imaginaries as they twist and turn on the ground and open, unexpectedly, into sites of human-animal indeterminacy.

Scenes of Extinction

In 1981, just as prenatal diagnostic techniques of sex detection followed by son selection were making an entry in India, Hasan Manzar, who moved with his family to Pakistan in 1947, published "A Requiem for the Earth" ("Zamin ka nauha"), a story about the global disappearance of women. A new biological inhibition occurs, women cannot reproduce their own sex, and sometimes they give birth to mutant "litters" that "do not resemble human babies": "Pink, like newborn cats or rabbits, hairless, eyes closed" (209).

The narrative, circling around cause and consequence, attributes this strange onset of sex-selective infertility to an ongoing destruction of nature by geopolitical rivalries and the techno-invention of weapons of total extinction. It indicts clandestine nuclear tests and nuclear radiation, the military-industrial production of poisonous insecticides, food preservatives, the destruction of marine life by oil spills, factory effluents, and ocean acidification. (As an eco-critique, the story falls into the thematic of Rachel Carson's *Silent Spring* (1962) where agricultural pesticides bring on strange diseases and toxic environments emerge as if by-products of atomic bombs.) The narrative gradient ascends from the disappearance of infant girls, children, young women, middle-aged to old women and the total disappearance of women exactly when a scientific cure is discovered. The hunt by the global Save Mankind Centre for the last woman on earth yields a dying woman on a remote mountaintop, a schoolmaster's wife and mother of two young sons who had died suddenly of a blood disease. Her husband refuses the cure, accuses the international saviors of plundering and despoiling the earth, and buries her, his "most beloved possession," in the still "good" and "beautiful" earth (220). The last woman is silent. Women become a composite body overtly fused with a fecund nature/earth and have neither an individual presence nor a narrative voice.

Manzar's infertility narrative deregionalizes its referents in order to encompass the world. The frequent references to Pakistan and India situate them not as Third World isolates but either as pawns in a larger geopolitical game or as part of a common planetary destiny. The prospect of extinction seems to reverse daughter dispreference. As the number of women decrease, several boundaries weaken and vanish. The homogeneous and endogamous enclaves of heterosexual marriage melt under the pressure of male demand. Matrimonial advertisements for brides relegate specific requirements of caste, sect, race, religion, region, nation, as well as the criteria of youth, education, modesty, virginity, piety, beauty, fair color, and "wheatish complexion." "Wife-hungry Dutch and German males" advertise in a Malayalam newspaper, men from Trinidad and America advertise in Urdu papers, global marriage bureaus set up shop. "It did not matter if a girl was a Christian or a Muslim or a Hindu" and "No one objected if the girl happened to be an untouchable" (207–08). The story reconfigures extant daughter dispreference in India and Pakistan into a limit situation that foreshadows how some women understand son selection today: "hum thodi ho jayengi to hamaari keemat badh jayegi" (when our numbers become fewer, our value will increase).[2]

Pollution, new diseases, degradation of habitats, and species extinction are uneven but not local, and presented as globally consequential. The world unifies across existing lines of power and predation in finding a wife, saving the women/earth, and looking for salves or explanations. Men who still desire to marry drift into opium-induced entropy. Older people shout in their sleep: "A great hole has appeared right through the globe and as a result the waters of the Ganga–Jamuna are pouring into the Missouri–Mississippi, and the Missouri–Mississippi into the Ganga–Jamuna" (213). In this collective nightmare, the flow of (life-giving) water becomes gravity-defying and bidirectional, mingling India and North America in a fatal indeterminacy of substance.

According to Justin McBrien, "The death wish of the deep ecologists and the death drive of capital lies in the same misanthropic fantasy of a world emptied of ourselves—the former in a masochistic longing to erase our sins, the latter in the hope to become pure abstract value unmoored from material entropy and death" (135). In returning his wife to the earth, the husband of the last woman chooses species death. The extinction of humans to save the earth is an intense political rejection of survivalism devoid of ethics, and punitive rather than misanthropic. Better if humans cease to exist before they destroy their progenitor: humans belong to the earth, the earth does not belong to humans. This pyrrhic victory in taking down those the husband holds responsible for the end of female fertility suggests that the hubris and cruelty of capitalism can only be abolished by human extinction while the ontologically independent earth and nonhuman reproduction will continue after capitalism. The denouement is paternalist since the extinction of women precedes that of men who must oversee it. Yet, given the connection between the crisis of fertility, toxic nuclear tests, and eco-destruction, the female reproductive body is neither macro nor individual but extensive across and constitutive of diverse human and nonhuman domains and partakes of what Michelle Murphy calls "the dispersion of sexed living beings into their infrastructural and political economic milieu" (22).

"Requiem" accomplishes an implicit denationalization of son selection in the worldwide extinction of women and thus of future procreation and insists on the ethical, political, and economic responsibility of humans; yet the narrator ignores other aspects of social reproduction. P. D. James's dystopia, *The Children of Men* (1992), a male infertility narrative that charts the lost motility of sperm, also heads toward the extinction of the human species but textures it through care work. In "Requiem" human extinction is simultaneous with the demise of capital—capital is not an abstraction but the sum of material human agency and disappears with it; in *Children* the impending extinction is governed by the social relations of capital and filtered through a bubble of hedonistic privilege. Asia is subject to predatory geopolitics in "Requiem" while in *Children*, a shrinking England depends on and is subsidized by the Global South, which reproduces the British workforce and offsets demographic decline, maintains northern standards of living, yet remains fungible and disposable.

The narrative tension in both texts rests on waiting for a foreknown near future. No child has been born in the world for twenty-five years, even frozen sperm has lost its potency in *The Children of Men*. The narrative, set in 2021, does not assign a cause or admit human implication, and in the end fertility is almost miraculously restored. The male historian narrator, an Oxford don, awaits the impending extinction and relays it through a partly autobiographical exercise. Though extinction will erase the entire human species, it is nationalized. Other countries seem to exist only as rivals who might find a cure before England and refuse to reveal it. The wait for species extinction is supervised by an autocrat who annuls democratic governance, installs a paranoid policing state, makes a special offer to remaining citizens who can await it free from boredom, want, and fear, and promises to prepare these sterile subjects for a secure and painless end. This willful national enclosure in which the prospect of extinction intensifies securitization could signify a recessive postimperial England without colonies or an enforced renationalization of survival.

Even with the near certainty of extinction, a neo-Darwinian, utilitarian, and eugenic model of genetic fitness underwrites the dictatorial dream of an improved population. The regular sperm and gynecological testing of healthy men and women becomes a state-mandated norm. Nonfunctional lives that do not deserve to live anymore (old, diseased, disabled) or to live in the same way (criminals, migrant labor), inhabit a "zone of indistinction" (Agamben 1). The disappearing species is an ageing species. Care for the British population is provided by a still existing class of waged domestic workers—women who come in for a few hours every week—and for a select elite by a migrant labor pool, the Sojourners. The Sojourners are imported from less affluent countries in fixed quotas designed to keep out "the invading hordes" coming to Europe (97); they look after the old and incontinent, mend roads, clean sewers, collect rubbish; they are underpaid, have to be healthy, live in camps, women separate from men, and are deported to their home country at the age of sixty—before they might themselves need care. Since they cannot claim family reunion or citizenship, the provision of care depends on the invisible reproductive labor of the Global South and families broken by labor migration.

The narrative lingers on the vulnerability of old persons, their unmet needs in the absence of children, grandchildren, and state-provided care. Twenty percent of the population is over seventy. Many commit suicide and the state pays "handsome pensions to the relations of the incapacitated and dependent old who kill themselves" (8). For others mass suicide—"Quietus"—becomes compulsory and is state-enforced. An old husband who takes care of his sick wife worries that if he dies she will be sent to a Quietus. There is a chilling scene of a state-orchestrated Quietus as a group of old women, possibly drugged, ankles weighted and shackled, and in a symbolic severance from national territory are towed out to sea to drown. The one woman who tries to escape is bludgeoned.

The counterforce in "Requiem" is limited to the acidic narrative voice, whereas in *Children* it materializes as a salvific Christianity and a fusion of paternity with nationality. Rescue of the planet/England, at least hopefully, comes from its imperfect and relegated margins—a disabled woman and an epileptic priest—"religious idealists" (60) who want "to die as human beings" protecting the "dignity of others" (108–09) and insist on the restoration of democracy, an end to forced suicides, and humane assimilation of migrant workers. This birth is witnessed as a near sacred event; the explicitly Christian denouement wraps motherhood in faith and fecundity. The unstated yet vivid terms of the eligibility to be a mother are that she will pass on old beliefs (Christian) and correct values (democratic) to a new generation. The pregnant women is valued and saved at the cost of other lives only for her fertility. The baby, a white child, is delivered by a black midwife who is killed soon after she fulfills her function: her agency becomes a synoptic image of the indispensability and expendability of the Global South. As most critics agree, the novel reconstitutes a white, heteropatriarchal, nuclear family unit, a homogeneous racial formation, and a national womb that quells white European demographic anxiety.

An imaginary of stable copulative heterosexual procreation dominates both texts—neither proposes a new reproductive technology to reverse the macronarrative of infertility or reproductive failure; the one ends on a medical cure that comes too late to be tested, the other in the unexpected and possibly redemptive birth of a child after a punitive pause. Both texts conjure the same specter of the erasure of cultivated, upper-class patrimonial transmission. In "Requiem," among the social and cultural effects of the gradual disappearance of women are the waning of heterosexual desire and interest in love poetry, fiction, cinema, familiar plots, even adventure stories. In *The Children of Men*, the disappearance of children produces entropy, a growing neglect of property, a loss of interest in arts, culture, and national history. The prospect of no future weakens heterosexual desire, which seems to depend on uninterrupted transmission. The birth of a *son* might stall this rupture: a daughter would only become the last human on earth, while a son could begin to impregnate women in twelve years. Species future rests on potent sperm. The mother is a conduit for the future generation as provider of labor power and care, the barrier against species extinction. Somewhat like son selection in India, in *Children* the son born through a mother is nominated as the object and subject of a futurity held in place by patrilineal transmission.

The Stakes of Renationalization

In "Requiem" and *Children*, the human species, as it awaits its demise, remains locked within the inherent logic of capital that expands through uneven differentiation of sectors, geographies, and labor forces. The articulation of northern and southern economies produces intertwined contradictions and different roads to extinction. The labor markets at the inferential edges of *Children*, the valorization of the mother as an indispensable vector for the future (child), become volatile in transnational commercial surrogacy—in the micronarratives of infertility and biogenetic continuity. The renationalization of motherhood in India through the proposed and enacted ban on commercial surrogacy could be unpacked in the context of the unevenness and heterogeneity produced by transnational capital, the crisis of social reproduction in which familial, market, and state gender regimes are reassembling in self-divided or internally contradictory ways,[3] as well as the state's negotiation of the friction between market and familial regimes.

As the material base of familial patriarchal regimes is patchily eroded or recomposed by state or market interventions, there are concurrent moves to defamilialize *and* refamilialize,[4] and power oscillates between familial, state, and market gender regimes. In a market-led patriarchal regime, there is a greater market absorption of the services, work, and relationships hitherto supervised in the family; the family is more deeply and explicitly contractualized, while the market facilitates, determines, or even governs the exchanges that create or sustain marriage, procreation, parenthood, care of old and young, and domestic labor.[5]

With the proto-governance of fertility and infertility by the market in son selection and commercial surrogacy, biological reproduction ceases to be a simple synonym for "nature." The crisis of social reproduction, exacerbated by eco-destruction, is complicated by the fact that social reproduction is itself often sustained by normative and regulatory marriage, the control of sexuality, procreation, domestic services, and resources in familial regimes. Since social reproduction is at once inside the global accumulation process and outside the realm of market exchange, neither the state nor the market can ignore it even as they destabilize it. The crossable boundary between market exchange and biological/social reproduction, and the partial integration of procreation and childbearing into production subject existing familial regimes, differentiated on lines of caste and class, property and subsistence, to new processes and pressures, especially through the unsettling of conventional, stereotypical, and symbolic motherhood in the linked practices of son selection and commercial surrogacy.

Commercial surrogacy in India, which I have analyzed and critiqued in *Solid:Liquid: A (Trans)national Reproductive Formation*, is a transnational and post-Fordist practice, egregiously used for son selection. Surrogates are drawn from a survival-oriented labor market where women may be primary wage earners; their choice is circumscribed by their menialization, indebtedness, and distress recast as a voluntary exchange governed by written or unwritten contracts. The labor pool for commercial surrogacy is class specific and largely overlaps with sex work and waged domestic service. As is well understood, capital can displace or reassemble social norms, replicate or reformulate gendered regimes, while care and labor markets can maintain, reinstate, or exploit class, caste, ethnic, religious, racial, and other coercive hierarchies that downgrade and segment labor and depend on gendered subordination. There is a wavering and hesitant line between precisely what constitutes unevenness and what classifies as heterogeneity. Commercial surrogacy is itself a remarkable site for the production of deliberated and circumstantial heterogeneity that caters to various hierarchized preferences—sex, race, color, caste, religion, class, nationality—and assembles varieties of gametes, embryos, surrogates, clients, clinical providers in different geographical locations of the production chain. The Ganga–Jamuna and Missouri–Mississippi can flow into each other. Some years ago, the entrepreneurial Dr. Nayana Patel, pointing to pregnant women in her surrogacy clinic in Anand, Gujarat, said to a reporter—"So many American citizens growing here."[6]

Further, spatial and temporal heterogeneity is a historical question attached to different phases and instruments of capitalism.[7] In his characterization of the financial derivative in which "multiple nationalities and labour processes, multiple technologies, incomparable forms of living labour and ways of life . . . a host of utterly distinct and unrelated realities are . . . momentarily brought into relationship with each other" (118–19), Fredric Jameson positions it as "the very paradigm of heterogeneity, even the heterogeneity at the heart of that homogenous process we call capitalism" (119). Such amalgams that bring "qualitatively incommensurable" dimensions, spaces, populations, production processes, technologies, and histories into relationship suggest a succession of unique events (119). Commercial surrogacy, however, is embedded in ongoing structural changes in forms of manufacture and labor organization by the post-Fordist disaggregation of production and outsourcing of services, and predicated on the *simultaneous* production of heterogeneity and unevenness. Neither allows for an ethical pluralism.

Banned in many countries and legal or unregulated in a few, commercial surrogacy is a shifting transnational formation, a mobile practice in search of countries without regulation, and finds new trade routes in an undulating race to the bottom. In 2002, commercial surrogacy became a neoliberal development strategy in India with the Bharatiya Janata Party–ruled state of

Gujarat at its epicenter. From 2012, the Congress government at the center redirected commercial surrogacy toward heteronormativity by barring single persons, unmarried couples, homosexual couples, and foreigners but made it easier for diasporic married couples of Indian origin who could fly in without a visa. The current BJP government, contrary to its earlier enthusiasm for the practice, debarred all foreigners.[8] Responding to the Supreme Court's queries, it declared its intent to allow only altruistic surrogacy, prohibit and penalize commercial surrogacy "to protect the dignity of Indian womanhood," and prevent trafficking and sale of children.[9] A surrogacy regulation bill was split off from the Assisted Reproductive Technology (Regulation) Bill (which has been under construction since 2008), approved by the Union Cabinet and introduced in the Lok Sabha in November 2016. In response to the regulations, the market along with doctors and surrogates moved from India to Nepal, then to Thailand, Mexico, and Cambodia and has been successively banned in each country.[10] Subsequently, Laos became a center for surrogacy procedures.[11]

Each new site "benefits" from the closing of a previous one, yet each ban has specific contexts and implications. The Surrogacy (Regulation) Bill of 2016, revised and passed in 2019 in India, was opposed by potential clients; medical lobbies on the ground that the ban on foreigners killed three-fourths of the industry, reduced medical tourism and lost foreign currency; and by surrogates who stood to lose their livelihood and demanded alternative employment, housing, and jobs for their husbands.[12] Yet the social imaginary of the 2016 bill is significant in its culturalist moves to nationalize the surrogate mother's womb and refamilialize surrogacy in an attempt to control heterogeneity, retrieve segments of social patriarchal control that are patchily moving out of the family and being reconstituted by the market, and produce not a national imaginary but a divisive nationalism that dovetails with older Hindu right projects. Since the Surrogacy (Regulation) Bill of 2019, did little to change this, I will refer to it only for significant differences.

Commercial surrogacy is said to be "against our ethos" and the ban is represented as ending the "commodification of motherhood."[13] The bill profiles the antagonists of this newly recovered Indian ethos. Altruistic surrogacy is allowed for heterosexual couples who are Indian citizens and of medically "proven infertility" after five years of marriage (4.c). A "surrogate mother" receives no monetary incentive or compensation except medical expenses and insurance (2.b). The egg donor or surrogate mother must be young (between the age of twenty-three and thirty-five), an "ever married woman" with a child of her own, and a "close relative of the intending couple" (4.iii). The import of gametes and human embryos for surrogacy procedures is banned (35.f). The bill indicates that homosexuals, single/unmarried persons or those in live-in relationships, foreigners, the Indian diaspora (variously categorized as Persons of Indian Origin, Nonresident Indians, Overseas Citizens of India), fertile couples, older couples past the age of reproduction, or couples with adopted and biological children are ineligible to be intending parents, while nonresident Indians (NRIs) are ineligible to be altruistic surrogates. The term "ever married" woman (to which I will return) seems to bar widows, divorcées, and single women from acting as altruistic surrogates. Prohibiting the import of gametes and embryos suggests that the genetic mixing of nationalities and production of "foreign" children will stop, and the heterogeneity produced by capital will be limited to a national repository of unmixed "Indian" paternal or maternal genetic lines.

Curiously, by going against the grain of neoliberal policies and downsizing the fertility tourism industry, this renationalizing bill sets the stage for a refamilialization that might offer other symbolic and material gains. It seems to work against domestic and transnational profit to restore surrogacy to a familial gender regime and thus promises to resolve the contradiction between capital accumulation and social reproduction. Yet as the state conscripted by finance capital supervises the neoliberal transition and also retracts from social welfare, it acquires a higher stake in allowing familial regimes to continue and returning tasks of social reproduction to a refoundationalized family.

The Close Relative

The practice of commercial surrogacy splits conception from gestation and restructures maternalism. By asserting the regulatory power of the state in the constitution of the legal family and pulling motherhood out of a monetized terrain, the bill can bundle and reject so-called nontraditional life styles and families. Yet the bill and official explanations polarize the heteronormative family. The family of the commercial surrogate is seen as always potentially coercive, while the intending couple and the altruistic surrogate are presented as belonging to a cooperative and idyllic family.[14] According to the health minister, the bill proposes close relatives only to ensure that "the surrogate mother is not exploited and that it is truly altruistic . . . she will be part of the larger family, and will go for surrogacy out of concern and goodwill."[15] The stated reason for excluding the Indian diaspora (OCI, PIO, NRI), otherwise hailed as members of a "global Indian family," is that "divorces are very common in foreign countries."[16]

In a double optic of condemning and retaining kin control, the family is coded as bad if it is eager for financial gain and pushes surrogate mothers into the market economy, unreliable if it is divorce prone like the Indian diaspora, uncoercive and impelled by goodwill if the altruistic surrogate mother is a close relative. Evidently the family has to be restored as an altruistic unit to counter the encroachment of a market regime in which it is losing its conventional monopoly on the initiation of lifelong bonds and sacrificial, servicing, altruistic affects as market transactions mediate the creation of conjugal and parental attachment. In fact, familial regimes press equally on commercial surrogates and wives who cannot be mothers of sons/children, and altruistic surrogates would be no exception. Ironically, the altruistic surrogate conjured in the bill has demystified the idealized kin relations it proposes as well as unraveled altruism both as an "ideology of unequal exchange" and as an industrial apparatus (Sangari 123–28). Doctors and other supporters of commercial surrogacy no longer invoke the altruistic maternalism of commercial surrogates but point to the physical absence (more nuclear families), shortage or unavailability of close relatives (more working women), as well as the unwillingness of close relatives to agree to be surrogates without financial gain.

The definition of the surrogate mother as a "close relative" and an "ever married woman" in the bill indicates its heteronormative thrust. The term "relative" can include families related by marriage and not blood. The "ever married" woman translates in Hindi into *sada suhagin*—a not-unmarried, not-divorced, still-married, not-widowed woman. Both definitions have stabilizing, restorative, and policing functions.

The recourse to an "ever married" close relative could help stabilize the figure of the wife/mother, which in commercial surrogacy is premised on the circulation of a married woman's reproductive capacity, and can interrupt spousal and familial possession. The ability to transact wombs segregated from ownership of the surro-child offers a temporary market individuation that must be recalibrated with spousal and familial propertarianism. However, the altruistic relative, like the commercial surrogate, must still perform an "abnormal" surrender of the child she bears, while the intending mother, like the commissioning mother, has no gestational link to the child.[17]

The close relative could loosely suture the fragmentation of genetic and gestational motherhood by redistributing motherhood only within the narrower confines of a kinship circle. It could also reinforce the established connection between surrogacy and son selection that was unremarked in public discourse and not directly addressed in the 2016 bill.[18] The 2019 bill, however, explicitly prohibits sex selection (2.3.viii).

The mandatory heterosexual marital status of the intending parents and the surrogate mother embeds them all into a familial matrix that seems to devalorize contract pregnancy and restore childbearing as a normative task of procreation within a familial enclosure. Positioning the unpaid birth mother and intending mother in the same family would seem to dissolve the contradiction posed by contract pregnancy between doing the same procreative work for a wage as well as without a wage. The commercial surrogate exemplified this contradiction by engaging at once in commodified and noncommodified work: her reproductive labor becomes (devalued) waged work yet also remains "not work" in relation to her own biological children. The close relative would also support the valorization of indissoluble marriage encoded in the "foreign" irresponsible divorcée and edge toward defining the family as a noncontractual domain aligned to Hindu nationalism.

Yet altruistic surrogacy is not a return to an Indian or a "Hindu" ethos even if the import of clients, gametes, and embryos are banned, since it still imports and repurposes significant components of the surrogate industry: a new propertarian genetic imaginary for the "intending" couple, a contract pregnancy in thin disguise, and the ethnicizing of gametes and wombs.

Though confining procreation and social motherhood within the larger family is the aim, the long-standing practice of intra-family adoption is not invoked in the bill. Rather, the genetic materials of the heterosexual intending couple matter. The surrogate mother cannot provide her own gametes. An "order concerning the parentage and custody of the child to be born through surrogacy" has to be passed by a court "on an application made by the intending couple and the surrogate mother" (3.a.II), the surrogate must agree to hand over parentage and custody (3.a.II), and her written consent on a "prescribed form" is required (3.6.ii). Despite the attempt to decontractualize the family by pulling surrogacy out of the market, a legal intra-family agreement is proposed in which the process of procreation and gestation might be shared between two women but genetic property in the surro-child and property transmitted to the surro-child are not shared (3.7). The 2019 bill simply states that the surro-child "shall be deemed to be the biological child of the intending couple" and entitled to all the same rights and privileges (3.7). This attention to the legality of the agreement alongside the proclaimed reliance on the goodwill of the close relative show that altruistic surrogacy remains within the contractual premises of commercial surrogacy. The close relative, presumably acting upon obligations or obeying the compulsion of familial bonds, must nevertheless be bound by a legal order. Two acknowledged mothers would henceforth be entwined in the life of the surro-child but only one would have a legal claim. And altruism—in the mandated refusal of the role of social mother by the surrogate—could be legally enforceable.[19]

In the practice of commercial surrogacy in India, genes, gametes, wombs, and blood have often been perceived as marked by caste and religion. By conflating the biological and the social, caste and religion can be recoded as genetic and "scientific." How then could higher-caste Hindu genes nest in a lower caste woman's womb? Would they be contaminated or polluted? Can the gene be an impermeable barrier between the fetus and the surro-mother? Despite the superior claim of genetic kinship in commercial and now altruistic surrogacy, both tacitly accept gestational kinship—that is, the significant role of the surro-mother's womb and blood. At this level, genetic and gestational motherhood are no longer antagonistic in the bill: they are allies, close relatives. Together they will produce the correct progeny, nurtured in the appropriate wombs. Each caste and religion can find its own close relative. In the new reproductive futures whether curtailed in son selection or enhanced in altruistic surrogacy, the child and parents must match. The Hindu right is not worried about intervention in "nature," noncoital conception, or recombinant paths to procreation but about maintaining a family form where the wife-mother does not circulate commercially and about dilutions of caste endogamy and religious distinction. "Our ethos" thus translates into exclusivist caste endogamy as the central node where caste and communal discrimination come together, now on a *new* technoscientific terrain of assisted reproduction and a genetic imaginary that segregates along the axes of property, caste, and religion, an imaginary that has an ancestor in scientific racism.

The close relative is a border patrol (or herself a border?) pitted against wrong wombs/mothers and any genetic mixing across nations, castes, and religions; she upholds heterosexual marriage, caste endogamy, and the separation of religious and caste groups. If the close relative can herself be distanced by the barrier of property, caste endogamy can do the work of dividing close *jatis* (subcastes). As Étienne Balibar argues, "the interference of family politics, more generally a politics of genealogy, with the definition of the national 'community' is a crucial structural mode of production of historical racism" (*We* 123).

Confining altruistic surrogacy to the same caste and community by familializing it through the close relative is a soft replay of what is *already* an ongoing enforcement of caste endogamy and enclavization of religious minorities through "love jihad" campaigns and punitive acts by Hindu right vigilantes against self-arranged intercaste and interreligious marriages. The ban on commercial surrogacy arcs from the legal terrain to meet the extralegal and violent imposition of regulatory marriage. Beneath this commitment to exclusive caste and religious identities lies the imperative to conserve obligatory family relations and regulatory marriage as *forms* that encapsulate the unwaged labor of social reproduction. The renationalization of surrogacy is not merely a "nationalist" homogenization to keep out foreign elements, rather it is a sectarian project of internal caste and religious enclavization in India in which, ironically, motherhood not only remains divisible but becomes divisive.

Altruistic surrogacy retains technological enablement but pares down its scope, softens the impersonality of the contract by making it a mutual legal agreement between familiars rather than strangers, absorbs the contract within the family in the language of consent, thus embedding both contract and consent within remodulated concepts of family and endogamy. As it accelerates the transition to neoliberalism, the state battens on familial patriarchal regimes that produce governed and supposedly altruistic laboring subjects and ensure unwaged social reproduction.

Renationalization, then, does not establish national unity; it produces separate homogeneous enclaves and reclaims a divisive sectarian nationalism on neoliberal ground. Taken together, renationalizing and familializing surrogacy are part of a larger attempt to regain control over material and symbolic maternity to underline the hierarchization of citizenship, and to *cordon* affiliations, affects, and attachments. The bans on cow slaughter explicitly deploy maternal affects and attachments as a weapon against religious minorities and Dalits. But first I want to note that enclavization, paradoxically, also produces a Hindu majority. Enclavization can be defined as a process of differentiation and enclosure of similar selves *and* others by majoritarian groups. This is a repressive process of constitutive exclusion in which the generation of differential citizenships with graded entitlements can coalesce with the increasing standardization of phobic politics. The erasure of some types of heterogeneity and the production of other distinctions may comprise a single move when a neoliberal economy and formulaic phobic politics come together.

Neoliberalism needs some practical forms of economic standardization—individuals must learn to repay debt, to live with less or very little, be responsible entrepreneurs, and so on. It also needs a regular supply of alterity on the basis of which public assets can be corralled and distributed upward to the deserving few, and undeserving groups with fewer rights and entitlements can be hived off either as minoritized second-class citizens on different scales or as servicing underclasses by legal and bureaucratic means as well as by sanctioned violence and private militias. This canny recognition that the class privileges of the few cannot be maintained if the demands of the many for substantive dignity are met is generating a mutually reinforcing and standardized politics of state-sponsored ressentiment against specific groups in India and other countries. The process of devaluation of peoples generally tends to cheapen labor, act as a rationale for economic exclusion and social segregation. In India, enclavization on the basis of occupational, culinary, religious, and caste difference can be a prelude to targeted majoritarian violence; though these divisive renationalizations go against the grain of the neoliberal export-oriented agenda, they resonate with other aspects of neoliberalism. Or as Silvia Federici puts it, "the production of a population without rights . . . remains a structural necessity of capitalism" (105).

Collective Mothers

Given scenarios of selecting sons partly to guarantee old age care, the disaggregation of biological and social motherhood and wider geographical redistributions of reproductive labor, the futurity of motherhood is entangled in fictive social imaginaries and a subterranean site of anxiety. "Maternalism is blocked *and* exaggerated" in son selection and surrogacy (Sangari 122–23). Both are practices of conditional motherhood: in one a woman must refuse to reproduce her own sex, in the other she must refuse to own the children she bears. As the attributes of motherhood become subject to divisibility, legal contract, and biopolitical control, both practices jeopardize the conventions of social reproduction and turn away from the mother as a conventionally idealized figure of embodied nature, unstinting nurture, and unqualified love. The affective power of motherhood that stems from its vaunted *unconditionality* may thus need to be recouped from other human/nonhuman terrains. At present, the cow mother (*gaumata*) is positioned as a political weapon against minorities. Is it also subject to a populist and tendentious displacement that seeks to consolidate a collective mother that, ironically, further instrumentalizes the figure of the mother?

Colonial campaigns to protect and install the cow as a universal mother were largely aimed at uniting "Hindus" and demonizing Muslims and Christians. Later the constitution directed that cow protection should not be coercive.[20] In the recent resurgence of this much-legislated history, the cow—coded as a reproductive, pastoral sign of nurture and routinely described as "our mother," "symbol of faith," and cultural heritage by her protectors—is once again represented as a mother in jeopardy and has acquired a new conjunctural force. The cow as the sacred mother of a Hindu nation involves a material and symbolic renegotiation of a motherhood already *in* the market. Dairy cows are integrated into the domestic and transnational market via the import of more profitable breeds and their sperm, and the export of leather and bovine meat.[21] Pulling these mothers out of lucrative markets has deliberately created massive unemployment for Muslims and Dalits as well as "collateral" damage for several agricultural, tribal, and artisanal groups, small traders and local markets, and is now viewed as an attack on the entire agrarian economy in which the production of milk, meat, and leather interlock. Existing, reactivated, and newly minted laws that ban the possession of beef, trading, transport, export, purchase, sale, and disposal of cows, calves, and almost all other cattle for purposes of slaughter have spread across several states and been enhanced in some with formidable punishments such as life imprisonment and indictment under the National Security Act.[22]

Feralization in the name of a collective mother by a majoritarian state regime escalates already existing violence against minorities. The renationalized and weaponized cow primarily serves to attack the so-called enemies within. State-supported, -sponsored, and -rewarded vigilantes monitor the bans, storm and seal restaurants and abattoirs, burn vehicles and homes, expel minorities from their homes or villages, do not hesitate to flog, bludgeon, lynch, and kill men and women *without* evidence, merely on the basis of rumors, allegations, and accusations of beef possession or cattle theft.[23] The perpetrators are usually not arrested despite video documentation or let off in trials while legal cases are filed *against* those injured and killed by vigilantes. The claim to *gauraksha* has become a mercenary activity that involves personal vendettas, commercial rivalry, ad hoc fines, protection money, organized extortion, confiscation of cattle, land grab and land encroachment, as well as demands for allotment of land for cattle shelters by the state. The legal bans are intended to activate extralegal violence and double as guarantees of immunity for vigilantes who both supplement and erode state authority.

Is the cow a milk-providing foster mother, the loved mother who will materialize a future united Hindu family, the revered collective mother to be saved, the mother who will redeem her self-anointed children, or also a reminder of "unsaved" daughters (future mothers)? Is it (co)incidental that the unconditional parental love of all present and future progeny, undermined or even withdrawn through son preference and son selection, is now seen to flow from the cow mother? Whether or not cow protection is an attempt to restore motherhood, it institutes a shadow familial regime on a political field that gains consent for and spreads the entitlement to majoritarian violence.

Print and visual media relay affective discourses and narratives of extinction, action and forensic detection. In official Hindu right proclamations, the affective discourse of love for "our mother," and the pious discourse of *gauraksha* as *dharma-raksha* fuse with a spurious dystopic narrative of the impending extinction of a threatened species subject to illegal slaughter. In this old colonial and majoritarian victim narrative, cows as a dwindling species are still a metonym for Hindus.[24] Stories of ill-treated, underfed, starving cows on roads or cattle shelters and cows imprisoned for their own protection are national news.[25] Vigilante dossiers upload photos and videos of flogging and lynching, intercepted vehicles, seized "cow meat" and animal/bovine hides, victorious cow rescuers and beaten "perpetrators" on Facebook and What's App groups as "live proof" of "*gauraksha* events."[26] A forensic detection narrative is consolidating around the plot devices of a police procedural: rumors of beef possession, missing or dead cows, secret tips by informers, planned vigilante action, police arrests, and autopsies. There is a structured unverifiability in this narrative—it seems cow hide cannot be distinguished from other bovine hides, slaughter from natural death, or cow from buffalo meat (which is not banned in all states). The evidence is sent to friendly forensic labs, government vets, or doctors associated with vigilante organizations who immediately certify that the samples are beef/cow meat. All samples are destroyed or "buried" by vigilantes before they can be retested, making it impossible for those accused of possessing bovine meat to defend themselves (Pisharoty).

Yet some internal contradictions are emerging between the sacred and the functional cow, between faith and anthropomorphic renditions of the cow, between worship and care, between the human and nonhuman, and the (in)fertile animal body as it enters the scene of neoliberal aspiration and destabilization. Can the symbolic and economic value of the cow be fixed if the symbolic order of motherhood is mutating and the logics of capital inhabit the cow?

There is a clash between sacralizing the cow and functionalizing the cow in order to buttress sectarian rationales for cow protection. The cow as dairy and agricultural animal that produces market value made a legal appearance in the 1950s, a value that could also double as a rationale for its sacredness.[27] Yet the affective status and nonmarket value of the milch cow—as a nurturer who gives without demanding, as a nonhuman outside wage relations who requires no more than subsistence—do not synchronize with her market value. The animal sameness of the cow as a collective noun is differentiated by reproductive capacity and yield. The cow's procreative years and lactation periods comprise only about half of her life span of fifteen to twenty-five years (Kumar). Given that nonlactating cows can be an economic liability if the market value of dung as fuel and fertilizer is much less than the cost of feed/upkeep, the lifelong protection of the cow has to be unconditional and subsidized with food, shelter, and health care. Hence the productive role of the cow, the nutritional and market value of milk, the medicinal value of cow urine, the value of dung as fertilizer and fuel after a cow ceases to be a dairy animal have had to be proved and calculated again and again. For instance, the functionality of cow urine as a rationale for cow protection has been remarkably extended: "Cow urine helps in anger control. It helps attain a 'cow-like calm nature' and can prevent people from committing crimes like assault and murder."[28]

There is an unresolved tension between the cow established as a maternal sign of reproduction pulled out of food and leather markets and the cow as worth protecting because she is functional and continues to generate market value even when no longer milk-producing. Thus the *unconditional protection of the nonfunctional* mother surfaces as a question in itself and as a question about state care of apparently nonfunctional humans and animals.

Another sharp tension is emerging between the cow as collective mother based on faith and an anthropomorphic understanding of the cow as ban-supporters struggle to reconcile its different aspects. If this nonhuman actant is a mother on the ground of faith, should she not be treated as one and given old age care and unconditional support? The humanization of the cow which, ironically, seems necessary to induce *both* protective feelings and violent acts, dehumanizes the Muslims and Dalits whose livelihood depends on cows/cattle but, oddly, also makes bovine and human mothers fungible. A chief minister asked farmers to look after dry cows like "your aged parents."[29] The affective transpositions of the body-in-need-of-care across human mothers and cows can become unwieldy. If useless cows who cannot work for a living should be treated like living human mothers with the same care and compassion, then should old human mothers be treated with the same unconditional care and compassion as useless cows? And should this treatment be reserved for Hindu mothers or extended to all Indian mothers if the cow is to become a national concern and a "national" mother?

If the cow is understood in its contemporary anthropomorphic shapes, then at least three apertures become visible. The first is the basis of nationality. Cows are heterogeneous but in the legal bans they are undifferentiated by origin, import, and mixed breed, that is, the renationalized cow is already hybrid. If the cow is a composite of multiple origins/breeds through the import of bulls and semen from the 1960s and Indian largely by virtue of residence, and as such an indivisible national mother, then should not every human resident of India have a claim to substantive citizenship regardless of caste and religious distinctions or country of origin? Cow protection is claimed "to save the whole world from moral and spiritual degeneration. . . . To Indians the cow symbolizes all other creatures. Cow is a symbol of the Earth, the nourisher, the ever-giving and undemanding provider."[30] Does casting the cow as a universal exemplar undermine its nationalization? In Satya Sagar's "Ruminations of a Holy Cow," a first-person animal narrative, a dispassionate cow critiques the myth of the "Indian cow" since many breeds are not native but brought by nomadic cattle herders from all over Asia in the past and more recently imported by dairy farmers from Europe. She asks if "European and Pakistani cows [are] also sacred to the Hindus?" and if not, will foreign cows be deported? Since ancient prescriptive texts did not speak in terms of the cow's "nationality" or "breed," perhaps all the world's cows are "holy."

Second, if the cow can only be understood and protected by virtue of such anthropocentrism that seems to close the gap between human and animal, then can the human be understood via the cow—as at least equally and unconditionally deserving of care and dignity regardless of distinctions? Though the renationalization of cows as collective mother of Hindus can repress their heterogeneity and increasing hybridization, it does not produce homogeneity.[31] Instead it exacerbates unevenness on economic, caste, and religious grounds and so widens the gap between human and human. Like son selection, value is finite in cow protection: to increase that of the son or the cow it must proportionately decrease that of daughters and minorities. Like the close relative, the cow marks the terms of eligibility and singles out those humans who are unworthy of protection. Can an inhumane subdivision of humans be the basis for instating the value and care of nonhumans, and recognizing animals as relational cospecies?

The third significant aperture opens on the question of subsistence in a neoliberal era. The cow oscillates between the most revered and most *needy* animal. In strictly anthropomorphic terms, the familial status of the cow is amorphous and teeters between many subject positions. Does she constitute a parent-child unit with her calves and so become an analogue for the "Hindu" family and "Hindu" nation? This image of familial maternalism crumbles since, unlike sons or surro-children conceived as a hedge against unprotected old age, the milch cow has no animal guarantor for future care. Male calves, her biological sons, can be seen as unproductive wherever bulls are being displaced as draught animals by the tractor and mechanized agriculture, and when few are needed for procreation because semen for artificial insemination is locally purchased or imported (Kumar). As the biological mother of increasingly outmoded and nonfunctional sons, she seems to be a mother without family support.

The wide gap between faith and filial care is becoming apparent as abandoned cows proliferate after the bans on trade and transportation. Hungry and angry, they attack crops, turn into a threatening species—an entirely animal cohort—and have become objects of violence. Hindu farmers chase them with sticks, stones, and acid-sprayers.[32] Demographic intervention by state governments through subsidies and by private entrepreneurs through collaboration with European companies are under way; they plan to produce mainly female calves and prevent the birth of unwanted male calves by importing sorted sperm from the USA.[33] As in commercial surrogacy, the Missouri–Mississippi seems to be flowing faster into the Ganga–Jamuna. Inducing selective procreation amounts to a selective elimination of a supposedly endangered species, and it is rationalized as protecting male calves from abandonment or from beef and leather markets. Paradoxically, this femalecentric reproductive futurism repositions male calves in a cost-benefit calculus that devalues them and saves future expense for prosperous farmers and the state. Like the shortage of altruistic close relatives, filial human sons may be in short supply or not disposed to be altruistic without financial incentives. As the prospective subject of prenatal sex selection, the dairy/milch cow is no longer a figure of regenerative nature but signals the joint control of state and market and their mastery of conceptive technology; she is subjected to a Foucauldian biopolitics—sex selection, genetic manipulation, demographic reduction, and enforced care.

At any rate, infertile, ageing, and abandoned by farmers, the self-supporting cow seems to occupy a nonentrepreneurial subsistence economy, ingesting accumulations of human-produced waste and debris—bottle caps, iron nails, coins, blades, safety pins, stones, temple waste, and plastic. She can scavenge on the street, forage on crops under cultivation, and be chased away or die of starvation in an overcrowded cattle shelter. Prior to the bans, undemanding cows depended on their own enterprise, private charity, and a few state-supported shelters. After the bans, the *state* had to become filial and paternalistic, instate the cow simultaneously as symbolic mother and a welfare subject, and ensure lifelong provision.

In other words, the bans invigorate a *contrastive* discourse of human and nonhuman in its violence, a *comparative* discourse of the lack of care/provision for humans and nonhumans, and a *leveling* discourse in putting humans in competition with cows for the same medical and nutritional resources.[34] The very weaponizing of cow protection, which also casts the cow as dependent on her symbolic human children, raises the question of state provision of welfare from below. The renationalization of the cow as an incitement to majoritarian violence, ironically, also kicks in a national discourse on the conditions of cows—uncared for or aging in old age homes that are like death camps, the animal counterparts of the Quietus for old persons in P. D. James's dystopia. Both human and nonhuman life-cycle needs rest on a substrate of dependency and vulnerability. As a neoliberalizing state sheds several social, labor, and environmental protections, the renationalization of cows brings each one of these to the forefront. The politics of othering exposes neoliberal policies in unexpected ways. The plastic-ingesting cow as abandoned mother becomes a spectral figure for the erosion of subsistence economies, the eco-crisis, anthropogenic resource depletion, corporate appropriation/enclosure of common and grazing lands, pastures, and forests, the shrinking rural land base for humans and nonhumans alike. The rural workforce and agricultural animals can both be subject to distress migration, marginalization, and replacement by mechanization. Disease, disability, old age, and death become the *"nonproductive" sites* of human-animal indeterminacy.

The severest contradiction is between sacralizing the cow and the economic liability of a neoliberal state. The more strident the sacralization, the more the faith mother becomes an anthropomorphized neoliberal subject of demographic control and surveillance. Suggested and implemented strategies seem to be underwritten by the sovereign power to decide *who* manages the cow's life cycle, *who* controls her reproduction, and *who* controls her death. The central government has fixed the duty of cow protection, responsibility for abandoned cows, and special care of cows beyond the age of milking on state governments,[35] and states are looking for ways out. For instance, in a Madhya Pradesh State Assembly discussion of stray cows raiding agricultural lands and the monetary reasons why they were being abandoned by owners, a BJP member of the legislative assembly said a law should be made to force every below the poverty line (BPL) cardholder to rear at least one cow, and if they don't, their ration and other BPL "facilities" should be withdrawn.[36] Another suggested that cows should be tagged to establish their identity and those without owners should be given the status of "wild animals" and kept in enclosures in national parks or forest lands.[37] Special taxes, subcontracting, or putting the onus of housing cows on schools, hospitals, prisons, and NGOs are also presented as solutions.

As a beneficiary of state welfare and protection, the cow too joins emerging surveillance and digitalization regimes of neoliberal governance. The central government promised a unique identification for an estimated forty-seven million indigenous and cross-bred cows that will have age, breed, sex, lactation, height, weight, body, color, horn type, tail switch, and special marks and help to track their movement and productivity (SenGupta). While the biometric Aadhar card standardizes human identities for state surveillance, market convenience, and easy targeting of minorities, cow identities are to be enumerated and standardized to keep them out of market. Will such an identity card reterritorialize the cow untethered by (trans)national markets? Digitized tags are intended to prevent farmers from abandoning cows while a cow's identity is to be registered on her owner's Aadhar card and, if sold, transferred to the next owner. This tethering of a cow's identity to her owners also monitors them.[38] Here too the surveillance state interlocks with vigilantism: like the altruistic surrogate, the external enemies act as conduits to internal enemies.

The bans turn the cow into a multivocal sign. As a collective mother who cannot assert or demand, the cow is a nonagential, submissive female body that depends on male protection and is subject to unilateral representation and manipulation; somewhat like the last woman in "Requiem," she is weak, helpless, and has no voice. At the heart of this locution of motherhood lies the dream of female docility, a docility that can be the ground and the trigger of masculinist feralization and the cultural/corporeal extermination of others. The cow is positioned as a sign of selective animosity, incitement, and instantiation of violence and at the same time as the animator of a reverent, antimarket, and affective disposition toward the maternal. Both moves founder on market rationales: they threaten to drain the cow of the very maternal qualities that are sought to be recouped and turn the cow into another precarious neoliberal subject.

The cow as a destitute scavenger is de facto Dalitized and minoritized, that is, embodies the caste and religious differences sought to be excluded by a Hindu nation-in-the-making. If Muslims and Dalits/minorities are the constitutive outside of majoritarianism, after the hyperactivated bans this outside is revealed as internal to the current life cycle of dairy cows in the agricultural economy. The cow as corpse becomes untouchable on her death.[39] Yet the reluctance or refusal of higher-caste Hindu sons to dispose of the corpses of their collective faith mothers showed that dehumanized Dalits were indispensable, and that they could withdraw their labor.

The multivocality and anthropomorphism of the cow as a mother, the refusal of some Dalits to remove bovine carcasses, binds the human and the nonhuman in a single servicing economy of care, a care that depends on the servicing labor of excluded others even after death.

Conclusion

The actually existing present is dystopic in these violent, symbolic, and serrated restorations of the mother on phobic social and political fields. Cultural nationalism and neoliberalism feed each other; neoliberal capital produces heterogeneity but not an ethic of plurality. In P. D. James's novel, the British welfare state morphs into an authoritarian state that controls the termination of the lives of the elderly in the prelude to a species extinction over which it has no control. The Hindu nationalist state asserts its political sovereignty over humans and animals, sets out to control procreation, reproduction, and the lives of others through ongoing violent episodes of extermination, and offers *these* as a fractal renationalization of transnational markets (for surrogacy and bovine products) even as it remains subordinate to global capital. The "close relative" in altruistic surrogacy and the cow revered as a collective mother can become, ironically, neoliberal subjects who work to intensify contemporary logics of the forcible enclavization and underclassing of minorities. The alterity of the present preempts the alterity of the future. Unlike fictional sterility/infertility narratives where the mother configures a passage into a future and can bind the present and future within the child she bears, the social imaginary of motherhood in son selection, surrogacy, and cow protection represents the crisis of futurity.

Read retrospectively, the near-future fictions of Hasan Manzar and P. D. James condense existing social and ecological trends into singular apocalyptic events of sterility. They compress and quantitatively massify the negativity of reproductive futures already in the present. Given the presence of malignant fantasies and persistent violence, the impending catastrophes of these fictional dystopias lose their force both as prophesy and as warning. Their critical energy is also dissipated by their narrative closures. At this level, the dystopic near future rendered as racialized, gender selective, and unequal, loses the shock of spotting the emergent, loses its novelty and its temporal border, becomes continuous with the present, and sinks into the dismal exhaustions of the already known. The present, however, continues to unfold in scenes of surveillance, prohibition, and violence that carry volatile contradictions and may release agential possibilities.

Reading sequentially from realist dystopias to the dystopian real, the fictional dystopias seem to move relentlessly from the near future into a near-certain future, from what might be to what will be, enter the present, and in the last move, given the still germinating seeds of the future in the present, to a fear of what *can be*; that is, the traumas of instantiation and anticipation come together and foreshorten futurity. Yet, what might the present subjects of continuing violence have to lose in the future? Can a fear of universal female or human extinction take hold in a present that regurgitates slow *and* instant intra-human violence under varied social and (trans)national incitements? Perhaps no propulsion into a future of care and compassion takes shape without a struggle against the cruelly extractive present and its cognitive and political enclosures.

Notes

1. Maher 16–17. Though some feminists separate social from biological reproduction, here I follow a common definition of social reproduction that includes daily subsistence and domestic labor, intergenerational care, socializing children, reproduction of labor force, emotional labor, care work, maintenance of family, neighborly and community ties, as well as biological reproduction that includes procreation, mothering, and nurture. .

2. See interviews in Dahiya.

3. On this crisis and the damaging effects of the reprivatization of social reproduction for the majority of the world's population, see Bakker and Gill 27, 34–36.

4. In a study of welfare state restructuring, Bezanson defines refamilialization as pushing social reproduction onto family/households and defamilialization as elevating the individual citizen worker and making women more like men (174).

5. For details on when a patriarchal regime could be termed market-led, see Sangari 136–38.

6. Cited in Williams and Cress.

7. As Balibar notes, "the elements combined by the capitalist mode of production have different and independent origins" (1975, 281).

8. In 2012, the quarterly *Gujarat*, official mouthpiece of the Gujarat government, in an article titled "Where the Storks Dare to Fly," hailed it as an embrace of "humanist ideas by facilitating reproductive tourism" that empowers surrogates and brings enormous revenue to the state (cited in Nair).

9. Cited in *Indian Express*, 2 Nov. 2015.

10. Mexico followed the Indian model and banned commercial surrogacy for foreign couples and gay men and restricted it to infertile heterosexual couples of Mexican origin.

11. Doctors from India and Thailand went to Ukraine, Kenya, and Cambodia; and the surrogates were from Thailand, Cambodia, and India (*The Hindu*, 19 Sept. 2016). Cambodia emerged as a new hub where clients, doctors, and surrogates from India and Thailand converged. After the ban in Cambodia, surrogacy procedures were performed in Laos but the babies were often born in clinics in Thailand.

12. Both feminist opponents and supporters of the ban on commercial surrogacy have critiqued the language, discriminatory exclusions, and heteronormativity of the 2016 bill. The opposition to the ban is mostly on the same lines as earlier feminist support for the practice: commercial surrogacy as an arena of choice and reproductive autonomy, as an agential practice, and a form of labor preferable to waged domestic work or sex work that only needs better regulation. Medical lobbies present similar rationales and also claim that commercial surrogacy is just a paid service. I have discussed these rationales extensively in Sangari 7–8, 79–80, 90–92, 98–103, 108–09.

13. External Affairs and Overseas Indian Affairs Minister Sushma Swaraj, cited in Dhar; BJP leader Vani Tikoo, cited in *The Hindu*, 28 Aug. 2016.

14. The bill states that in a case of commercial surrogacy "it will assume compulsion by husband, intending couple or any other relative" (39). Conversely, doctors and other supporters of commercial surrogacy set up the commercial surrogate as a free agent unconstrained by her family, while the altruistic surrogate is said to be vulnerable to familial coercion, emotional blackmail, or stigmatization since traditional families will not accept surrogacy.

15. J. P. Nadda, cited in *Indian Express*, 3 Sept. 2016.

16. Sushma Swaraj, cited in *Indian Express*, 8 Jan. 2015, and 25 Aug. 2016.

17. In the United Kingdom motherhood is construed as the compound of a genetic link, a natural urge or desperation, and the intent of the commissioning parent. The surrogate mother must refuse social motherhood and thus stands outside the "normal" bounds of motherhood in her willingness to alienate the product of her labor (Ashenden 212).

18. On the connections between these practices, see Sangari 70–71. Prenatal son selection is usually clandestine.

19. In this respect, the bill differs from the United Kingdom, where altruistic surrogacy agreements are legal but not binding. As Ashenden notes, the birth or surrogate mother is the primary parent whose status must be extinguished by a parental order after the birth of the child. Even though kinship becomes a matter of choice, in practice the genetic link become *the* biological link at the expense of the equally biological processes of gestation, birth, and weaning and is regarded as fundamental to kinship (201–07).

20. Noorani shows that the protection of cows in the directive principles of the constitution was intended to be noncoercive and balanced against the economic disadvantages of feeding and maintaining unserviceable cattle—until court rulings in 2005. However, the existing laws were seldom implemented. See Chigaleri on the legal history of bans on beef, cow, and calf slaughter, the challenges to fundamental rights at stake—rights to life, equality, occupation, trade, to eat, to privacy of food consumption, and freedom of religion—and Supreme Court judgments.

21. American and Danish breeds such as Holstein Friesian and Jersey as well as cross-breeding with Danish and Israeli breeds have been introduced for quicker and higher milk yields.

22. Some states have opposed the bans as an antisecular criminalization of food habits and entire communities, and as a large-scale disruption of the livelihood of cattle-rearing families, nutrition security, and the economy. The universalization of the ban is an old RSS and VHP agenda and was a campaign promise by the current prime minister, Narendra Modi. Despite Supreme Court injunctions against mob violence and cow vigilantes and widespread condemnation, the mob lynchings have not stopped.

23. Most of the major incidents of vigilante violence in the past few years occurred in BJP-ruled states. Helplines were set up where people would be asked to report any suspicious trafficking of cows (SenGupta). See Jaffrelot on state outsourcing of violence to vigilantes.

24. RSS chief Mohan Bhagwat continues to stoke demographic paranoia and global Islamophobia: he claims that the number of Muslims and Christians will increase in India, Hindus will cease to be a majority in 2025, while Europe will become a Muslim continent in a few decades (cited in *Indian Express*, 22 Aug. 2016).

25. The BJP government in Haryana has decided to build *gaushalas* in state-run prisons for cow protection and to make milk available for prisoners who will help to maintain the sheds (*The Hindu*, 12 Jan. 2017).

26. *Indian Express*, 31 July 2016, and 23 Aug. 2016.

27. A total ban was seen as unreasonable until a 2005 judgment in Gujarat in which the "usefulness" of draught and milch animals was extended throughout their lives as their urine and dung could be used for manure and biogas. Chigaleri

shows that the legal language of scientific rationality reflects "Hindu sentiment" while purportedly not doing so. See also Jaising et al.

28. Remedies from "Aarogya Geeta," an advisory on the website of the Gujarat Gauseva and Gauchar Vikas Board of Gujarat's Department of Agriculture and Co-operations (cited in *Times of India*, 11 Oct. 2016).

29. Yogi Adityanath, chief minister of Uttar Pradesh, cited in *The Wire*, 9 Sept. 2017.

30. Chief Minister of Gujarat, cited in *Scroll.in*, 31 Mar. 2017.

31. On the increase in cross-breeding and promotion of imported cattle, see Mazoomdar. Baba Ramdev's company Patanjali is planning to artificially inseminate cows with frozen bull semen from Brazil (Abraham). Yet, the Haryana government is planning to make cow hostels only for indigenous and not cross-bred cows (*Indian Express*, 30 July 2017). There seems to be a prejudice among cow protectors against Jersey cows and calves as impure, inferior, not indigenous, even not cows, and undeserving of protection because they are a breed imported from America. See Narayanan, "Cow Protection" 344–46.

32. *The Wire*, 9 Sept. 2017.

33. The Punjab Gau Sewa commission chief announced that the government, looking for ways to reduce the number of stray cattle, was "working on viable methods like importing of semen from the US to produce only female cattle, which farmers don't abandon" (Kimti Bhagat, cited in Goel). The Bihar government is offering a 45 percent subsidy to farmers who adopt insemination with sorted sperm to ensure the birth of female calves and reduce the number of male calves that farmers don't want (Singh). Baba Ramdev's company, Patanjali, is planning to produce 92 percent female offspring for cows with the help of a Dutch company (Abraham).

34. There are state-conducted seminars on cow conservation, cows as urban foragers, unsorted garbage, open drains, plastic ingestion as reducing milk production capacity, and official plans to distribute free fodder. The Uttar Pradesh government is reported to have started an ambulance service for ill and injured cows.

35. Ministry of Home Affairs advisory to all states, cited in *Indian Express*, 10 Aug. 2016; and SenGupta.

36. Murlidhar Patidar, cited in Ghatwai.

37. Divyaraj Singh, cited in Ghatwai.

38. See *The Wire*, 9 Sept. 2017; and *The Financial Express*, 2018, cited in Narayanan, "Jugaad" 1531.

39. Carcass collection and disposal of dead animals are linked to caste and customary obligation in rural areas—caste-determined practices are what keep labor costs low. In a protest against the flogging of skinners in Una, Gujarat, Dalits carried the slogan: "You love your mother keep her" (Damodaran). In some regions, Dalits refused to dispose of dead cattle, whether owned or stray (*Indian Express*, 28 July 2016, and 26 Aug. 2016).

Works Cited

Abraham, Bobyn. "'Desi' Patanjali Plan Import Brazilian Bull Semen to 'Make Indian Cows More Productive.'" *indiatimes.com*, 15 Oct. 2016.

Agamben, Giorgio. *Homo Sacer: Sovereign Power and Bare Life*. Translated by Daniel Heller-Roazen. Stanford UP, 1998.

Ashenden, Samantha. "Reproblematizing the Relation of Agency and Coercion: Surrogacy." *Gender, Agency and Coercion*, edited by Sumi Madhok, Anne Phillips, and Kalpana Wilson. Palgrave Macmillan, 2013, pp. 195–218.

Bakker, Isabella, and Stephen Gill. "Ontology, Method and Hypothesis." *Power, Production and Social Reproduction: Human In/security in the Global Political Economy*, edited by Isabella Bakker and Stephen Gill. Palgrave Macmillan, 2003, pp. 17–42.

Balibar, Étienne. *Reading Capital*. New Left Review, 1975.

———. *We, the People of Europe? Reflections on Transnational Citizenship*. Translated by James Swenson. Princeton UP, 2004.

Bezanson, Kate. "The Neoliberal State and Social Reproduction: Gender and Household Insecurity in the Late 1990s." *Social Reproduction: Feminist Political Economy Challenges Neo-Liberalism*, edited by Kate Bezanson and Meg Luxton. McGill-Queens UP, 2006, pp. 173–215.

Chigaleri, Shraddha. "Bombay High Courts' Beef Ban Judgement Marks Triumph of Privacy Rights over 'Hindu' Sentiment." *The Wire*, 5 May 2016.

Dahiya, R. S. "Declining Sex Ratio in Haryana." Paper presented at the seminar The New Paradigm of Development and Sex-Selection, Nehru Memorial Museum and Library, New Delhi, 2004.

Damodaran, Sumangla. "Gau rakshak vs. Make in India." *Indian Express*, 23 Sept. 2016.

Dhar, Aarti. "India to Ban Rent-a-Womb." *The Wire*, 24 Aug. 2016.

Federici, Silvia. *Revolution at Point Zero: Housework, Reproduction and Feminist Struggle*. PM Press, 2012.

Ghatwai, Milind. "MP House Debates Stray Cows, BJP MLAs Say 'a Problem.'" *Indian Express*, 23 July 2017.

Goel, Divya. "At 'Cow Hospital' in Jagraon, Signs of Sword and Acid Attacks on Bovines." *Indian Express*, 14 July 2017.

Jaffrelot, Christophe. "Over to the Vigilante." *Indian Express*, 13 May 2017.

Jaising, Indira, Amritananda Chakravorty, and Meher Dev. *The Wire*, 18 Aug. 2016.

James, P. D. *Children of Men*. Vintage, 2006.

Jameson, Fredric. "The Aesthetics of Singularity." *New Left Review*, no. 92, 2015, pp. 102–32.

Kumar, Seshadri. "Milking the Holy Cow." *Frontline*, 17 Aug. 2016.

Maher, JaneMaree. "Motherhood: Reproduction and Care." *The Globalization of Motherhood: Deconstructions and Reconstructions of Biology and Care*, edited by Wendy Chavkin and JaneMaree Maher. Routledge, 2010, pp. 16–27.

Manzar, Hasan. "A Requiem for the Earth." Translated by Salimur Rahman. *The Penguin Book of Classic Urdu Stories*, edited by M. Asaduddin. Viking, Penguin Book India, 2006, pp. 207–20.

Mazoomdar, Jay. "The Desi Cow—Almost Extinct." *Tehelka.com*, 2 Feb. 2012.

McBrien, Justin. "Accumulating Extinction: Planetary Catastrophism in the Necrocene." *Anthropocene or Capitalocene? Nature, History and the Crisis of Capitalism*, edited by Jason W. Moore. PM Press, 2016, pp. 116–37.

Murphy, Michelle. "Distributed Reproduction." *Corpus: An Interdisciplinary Reader on Bodies and Knowledge*, edited by Monica J. Caspar and Paisley Currah. Palgrave Macmillan, 2011, pp. 21–38.

Nair, Avinash. "Gujarat Govt's Magazine Bats for Surrogacy." *Indian Express*, 21 May 2012.

Narayanan, Yamini. "Cow Protection as 'Casteised Speciesism': Sacralization, Commercialisation and Politicisation." *South Asia: Journal of South Asian Studies*, vol. 41, no. 2, 2018, pp. 331–51.

———. "Jugaad and Informality as Drivers of India's Cow Slaughter Economy." *Economy and Space*, vol. 51, no. 7, 2019, pp. 1516–35.

Noorani, A. G. "The Ban on Cow Slaughter." *Frontline*, 8 June 2016.

Pisharoty, Sangeeta. "Muslim Residents Fearful after Gurgaon Police Make First 'Beef' Arrests." *The Wire*, 2 Apr. 2016.

Sangari, Kumkum. *Solid:Liquid: A (Trans)national Reproductive Formation*. Tulika Books, 2015.

Satya Sagar's "Ruminations of a Holy Cow." www. countercurrents.org/sagar271014.htm, 27 Oct. 2014. Accessed 17 Dec. 2015.

SenGupta, Subhajit. www.news18.com/news/india/bovine-intervention-here-comes-a-inique-id-number-for-cows-1302049.html. Broadcast on 24 Apr. 2017.

Singh, Santosh. "Bihar's Plan to Ensure Cows Birth Mostly Female Calves." *Indian Express*, 18 May 2017.

The Surrogacy (Regulation) Bill. 2016. www.prs.india.org.

The Surrogacy (Regulation) Bill. 2019. www.prs.india.org.

Williams, Ian, and Rory Cress. "A Baby Mall in India: A Couple's Dream Come True." *Health*, 28 May 2012, www.todayhealth.today.com/_news/2012/05/28/11883566, p. 1. Accessed 11 Nov. 2014.

3

Promissory Futures

Medicine and Markets in Speculative Fiction

Sherryl Vint

> The theoretical problem of this volume is not to come up with the "theory of" life or capital or governance or globalization or markets or neoliberalism, but is rather to come up with *forms of inquiry* that are adequate to studying a contemporary conjunction of the life sciences and capital.
>
> —Kaushik Sunder Rajan, *Lively Capital: Biotechnologies, Ethics, and Governance in Global Markets*

This chapter brings together three strands of inquiry: work by science and technology studies (STS) scholars examining the intersection of life with capital, especially the commodification of body parts or bodily functions such as gestation; work about the role of the imagination as a social force, drawn largely from utopian studies, premised on the idea that how we tell stories about our possible futures shapes the ones that materialize; and finally the work of speculative fiction authors and directors, who use this genre to interrogate and respond to the confluence of medicine and the market in contemporary biotechnology. My focus is especially on science fiction (SF) texts that examine the border as a fraught space for negotiating the economics of bodies and health, whether these are the transnational borders relevant to transplant and surrogacy economies, or the borders established between communities of the privileged and the dispossessed, used to distribute unevenly conditions of health or deprivation. The status of immigrants and their heightened vulnerability to exploitation via biomedical practices is a theme that recurs across texts I analyze in this chapter; all are recent, and the short films are part of the PBS series *Future States*, which asked filmmakers to imagine the United States into the near future. The prevalence of titles within this series that investigate what happens when health care, the market, and politics collide reveals the urgency of addressing this topic.

A number of recent works in sociology and anthropology of medicine offer new tools for understanding this conflation of medicine, markets, and borders. In her book *Life as Surplus*, Melinda Cooper argues that neoliberal biotechnology reinvents life beyond material limits by wedding biological processes to capitalist accumulation, a project of consuming in the present value that can be created only in the future. In *Biocapital*, Kaushik Sunder Rajan suggests that we should understand the discourse of venture capital as "promissory futuristic discourse," hype that "constitutes the discursive grounds on which reality unfolds" (116). Such creations of economic value by colonizing our imagination about the future mimic SF, and fiction can return fuller depictions of social reality to these abstractions, helping us to understand how inequity is created and perpetuated. More recently, Cooper and Catherine Waldby have theorized the emergence of what they call "clinical labor," arguing that post-Fordist capitalism puts life itself to work, in sites such as surrogate pregnancies, sales of gametes, and participation in clinical trials. They argue that we should consider such practices as biological *labor* because they often constitute the only form of income for certain populations, even if this is income in-kind (such as the provision of shelter, etc.). Given that in the United States compensation for labor includes benefits such as health care, they believe that refusing to theorize some people's dependency on participation in clinical trials to gain access to health care at all is a failure to comprehend the consequences of these practices for labor and social justice.

As the epigraph from Kaushik Sunder Rajan points out, new "forms of inquiry" are needed to grasp this historically unprecedented situation. I argue that speculative fiction is precisely such a form of inquiry, a way of extrapolating from specific technological capacities through to the changes in social relations that they might entail. To be clear, this is not an argument for technological determinism, and indeed precisely the point of fusing sociotechnical practice with speculative fiction is that technologies will influence social life based on the political and social structures and values attendant on their emergence. The fiction foregrounds these cultural forces, and SF often enables us to see how otherwise neutral or even benevolent technologies could have dire social consequences if issues of equity are not addressed in how they are implemented. The prevalence of narratives that link medicine, markets, borders, and immigrant vulnerability signal this nexus as a site of intensified anxiety when we speculate about the futures of health care. At its best, SF can help us envision and materialize alternative futures that seek to transform rather than intensify these forces.

In their recent book *Dreamscapes of Modernity*, Sheila Jasanoff and Sang-Hyun Kim investigate the role that the imaginary plays in shaping, inspiring, directing, and channeling technocultural change. While they seek to show how doing politics is a kind of storytelling practice, I want to suggest that telling certain kinds of stories is a political one. She argues for the importance to STS scholarship of a concept of the sociotechnical imaginary, which they define as "collectively held, institutionally stabilized, and publicly performed visions of desirable futures, animated by shared understandings of forms of social life and social order attainable through, and supportive of, advances in science and technology" (Jasanoff, "Future Imperfect" 4). This transformative impulse—visions of desirable futures, enabled by forms of social life—is similar to the utopian impulse that scholars such as Darko Suvin and Fredric Jameson argue is foundational for SF as a genre. Jasanoff argues that thinking with and through sociotechnical imaginaries reminds "both observers, and observed that the seen reality is not the only one about which we can dream" ("Imagined" 340). Jasanoff recognizes SF as "a repository of sociotechnical imaginaries, visions that integrate futures of growing knowledge and technological mastery with normative assessments of what such futures could and should mean for present-day societies" ("Imagined" 337). Utopian studies scholars argue even more vehemently that the purpose of SF is to cultivate futures beyond the "seen reality," especially more inclusive ones. Thus, SF has a role to play equal to that of STS theorists and medical anthropologists in responding to how markets are shaping medicine and showing how politics frames medicine, especially around issues of borders.

Sabrina Vourvoulias's *Ink* (2012) depicts a world of intensified anti-immigration sentiment and surveillance technology, in which one's immigration status becomes a tattoo infused into one's skin. The system is color-coded and clearly targets people of color, especially Latinos (speaking Spanish is illegal), including those who have taken US citizenship—they wear blue tattoos, compared with the green ones for people with permanent resident cards, and the black ones for those with temporary visas. The tattoos contain GPS trackers that enable heightened social control, and the fact that the tattoo encodes information that links to a database also heightens vulnerability for these "inks," since its data can quickly and easily be modified to change their status. One of the novel's four main characters, Mari, is an immigrant from Guatemala who came to the United States as a child (rescued from civil war violence); her blue tattoo, evidence of her US citizenship, is described as lines that "don't look remotely like blood, but they make me wonder if this is the kind of wound that never stops bleeding" (10). Indeed, when the anti-immigration sentiment surges into vigilante violence, Mari is swept up in an attack and dumped across the border with several others: her brown skin and Spanish fluency render her citizenship invisible to those who attack her. Another main character, Del, a white citizen sympathetic to the immigrants, describes working with them on a job at which those with black, temporary tattoos are rotated out and replaced every six months, leading the foreman to call these men by their country or region of origin—Jalisco, Honduras, Salvador, Oaxaca, and so on—rather than take the time to learn their names. Although not maliciously motivated, this practice shows the slippage between structure and ethos, reinforcing the men's fungibility and thus further dehumanizing them.

Medicine is pertinent to the novel as the state takes steps against the "ink" population. Rumors circulate that they are more susceptible to certain disease outbreaks, and sanatoriums are built, theoretically to establish quarantine and treat the ill. In reality, as many characters admit, the specter of pandemic is used to further alienate immigrants from public sympathy. Abby is another main character, half-white and half-Mohawk, and her white mother runs one such sanitarium. Although she is not hostile to its inmates and does not treat them badly, she also refuses to take a stand against what she recognizes as a false narrative imprisoning them there. When Meche, another inked citizen, confronts her and points out that the quarantine is "really a way to make it more palatable to see so many people locked up" (73), she does not argue the point, but rather reveals her own lost dreams of becoming a doctor, instead of such a debased practitioner, along with other sacrifices she has had to make: "What's sentiment when your kid's freezing in a cold house?" Abby takes a more radical view, breaking Meche and Mari out of the sanitarium, becoming involved in the resistance that seeks to hide and protect immigrants, both legal and not, and having a child with a Latino gang member who is also involved in this resistance. Abby's Mohawk father and his reservation contacts help in this effort, offering treaty numbers to support some of the fake identifications the resistance uses, a storyline that further reinforces the ways that racism and anti-immigration rhetoric reinforce one another in the American imaginary.

The sanitarium's plan to sterilize all remaining inmates before it is closed, reminding us of the complicity of medicine with the eugenics movements of the early twentieth century. More crucially, however, this medical incarceration is used to delegitimize the civil status of its inmates, even once they have been "cleared" of disease. Those with black or green tattoos are deported by executive order, and those with blue tattoos have their citizenship status reduced, the extent of their remaining rights determined on a state-by-state basis, with their eligibility for full citizenship increased if they provide information that leads to the detention of those with green or black tattoos. In *Bioinsecurities*, Neel Ahuja argues that the politics of empire is embedded in the living bodies and planetary environments of subjects who become objects of inquiry for imperial science. Medical technologies, especially those directed toward managing outbreak, are a key sites of intervention used to galvanize racial fears and enact changes that reinforce settler colonial occupation. As he shows, the US historically has imagined disease as something originating in brown and black bodies from outside the country's borders. He uses the term "dread life" to describe "this racialized channeling of the fear of infectious disease into optimism about remaking life through technical interventions" (6). In *Ink*'s linking of disease control to selective sterilization, we see a domestic policy version of such imperial operations.

Barry Jenkins's short film *Remigration* (2010) similarly looks at the intersection of race, labor, and health care. Set in a near-future San Francisco, the story begins with two parents, Kaya (Russell Hornsby) and Helen (Paola Mendoza), calling for their child, Naomi (Avelina Salazar), as the soundtrack is dominated by someone's audible, labored breathing. They find her and return to their seaside home, where they are greeted by Jonathan Park (Rick Yune), who explains that he is from the San Francisco Redevelopment Agency and seeks their return to a city they left in 2013. The city has changed, he assures them, and recognizes its need for working-class people to staff key infrastructure jobs. If they agree to return, the agency can provide them with housing, medical care, and guaranteed tuition for Naomi, all if they agree to work at designated jobs on a ten-year contract. Suspicious, African American Kaya explains that they left the city to care for his ailing father, a man who "couldn't afford to convalesce in a city he gave his life to"; gesturing toward Latina Helen, he explains she lost her job as a teacher because a telepresence system to staff multiple classrooms with a single teacher was cheaper. Noting Naomi's asthma, Rick pressures the couple to return to "the grid" and get her access to care she needs.

The film transitions to scenes set in San Francisco, as the family travel to a hotel and meet with a group of about twenty people, mainly of color, who are gathered in its ballroom seated in a circle, almost as if in a support group. Rick explains that San Francisco is not alone in finding itself without sufficient workforce to maintain its infrastructure, and once again praises the importance of the working classes to urban centers. As he speaks we cut between him and a number of scenes of workers, again mainly of color, including a future Kaya working at a construction job and future Helen operating a tramcar; we also see an image of Naomi being treated at a high-tech medical center. The workers are suspicious, feeling betrayed by the city, but intrigued. In their hotel room that night, Kaya decides against the remigration program, while in the background Naomi watches a documentary about the 1960s civil rights struggle in the city. The next day the seminar continues. The potential workers, prompted by Rick's sales pitch for the remigration, explain how they and their ancestors contributed to a city that became so gentrified they were forced to leave, as the film cuts between them and photographs from midcentury San Francisco that depict vibrant neighborhoods of color. Repeatedly, people narrate experiences of loving and contributing to a city from which they were forced by economics.[1]

The film's climax is set that evening, at a gala reception where white-collar elites pose for television news crews, extolling the benefits of the remigration program, while the would-be workers marvel at the luxury. Kaya remains skeptical, but then Naomi has a severe asthma attack that he and Helen treat, as usual, with ice and soothing words. That evening in the hotel room, he breaks down and cries, remembering his grandfather being continually displaced from neighborhood to neighborhood as they gentrified. The next morning, they sign the agreement to return. Although Kaya and Helen accept typical working-class jobs—rather than the extreme forms of biolabor we see in the examples discussed later in this chapter—this film nonetheless might be read in terms of Cooper and Waldby's theorization of clinical labor. Despite their reservations, Kaya and Helen accept specific working conditions because part of the remuneration is health care for their child: potential debt servitude is the cost of health, at least for some. The border in this film is more notional, that is, zones delineating neighborhoods that are shaped by wealth, yet the film still speaks to ways that health and health care are increasingly bound up with a racial imaginary in political governance. Medical vulnerability can open one up to labor exploitation, just as lack of employment can make one vulnerable to medical exploitation. These issues are particularly dire in a US system where access to a for-profit healthcare system is contingent on employment. Moreover, given that the child's life is the one at risk, the film gestures toward the issue of reproductive futurity that haunts the intersection of medicine and capital: those with means can assure their future through their children, while those without may lose even their next generation.

Lisa Robinson's short film *Hollow* (2013) moves further into the future and uses more obviously science-fictional extrapolation to explore a similar but intensified scenario. Our Latina protagonist, Iris Moreno (Angelic Zambrana), is working as a janitor when she is told by a passing employee that the entire firm has gone bankrupt and her job has disappeared. Through a series of images of a screen that scrolls through data about Iris, we learn that she has a "restricted immigrant card," and, as she bicycles home, she receives a video-email recruitment offer from Neurolock, a corporation that promises to solve the risks of data hacking by allowing their clients to store and transmit essential data using a portion of a brain. Neurolock wishes to hire Iris for this procedure, and as the smiling woman in the recruitment video pointedly observes, "you are an immigrant with restricted work status; this is really the only job out there that could give you independence." Iris deletes this message, but once home she gets into a fight with her white girlfriend, Zana (Louisa Krause): they risk eviction, and Iris urges Zana, who has full citizenship, to find a job given her greater range of opportunities. Zana, clearly from a privileged background, prefers not to work, leading to a fight about her default of going to her father for money when they are under duress. They go out to the bar that evening, Iris remaining preoccupied by stories she has heard about the risks of the Neurolock procedure, including "memory corruption," and Zana becoming drunk and needing Iris to care for her.

We learn that the Neurolock procedure would require giving up some of one's memories to create the "space" needed for data storage, and Iris is further pushed toward contemplating this option when she learns that Zana has cheated on her, more than once. As they fight we see flashbacks to happier times in their relationship, the memories that Iris would give up. After receiving an eviction notice, Iris does further research about

Neurolock online, and with her we see a series of headlines that indicate problems such as a rushed approval process and uncertainty about long-term health risks. She and Zana fight once more as Iris leaves to undergo the procedure, and we follow her through the intake process, where she is told that if the procedure "goes badly" the company will take care of her. As she waits for her turn for download, wearing a hospital gown and in a room filled mainly with other women of color, Zana too enters, giving Iris a defiant look as if to counter their earlier argument about the differences between their financial options. As Iris undergoes the procedure, the cool blue tones of the clinical setting are intercut with warm greens and golds of her memories of Zana, the experiences overwritten by the data download. In the film's conclusion, we see that Iris survives the process mostly intact, and continues to work as a Neurolock courier, living in a slightly more upscale apartment but alone. As she reports in to work at Neurolock, the clerk helping her is Zana, who is friendly and tries to foster a social connection between them, but who clearly has no memory of Iris. Iris is polite but distant, and after this exchange she goes into the restroom and weeps. This film highlights the ways that certain populations, especially immigrants, are made more vulnerable to the exploitative and risky work of clinical labor.

Although the film's technology is speculative, the structures that compel Iris to put her memory—her identity—at risk mirror those of people who regularly participate in pharmaceutical trials because they lack other employment options. Cooper and Waldby note that in the United States "growing numbers of continent workers engage in high-risk Phase 1 clinical trial work in exchange for money" (7) and that "contract research organizations habitually recruit Phase 1 research subjects from among the underemployed, day laborers, ex-prisoners, and undocumented migrants, precisely those classes of worker who routinely endure the most hazardous and contingent of labor conditions" (17). The Neurolock technology makes clear that the issue is not merely ongoing risk for vulnerable workers, but further damage done to their humanity, symbolized by the loss of memories as a loss of part of oneself. In *Life Support*, Kalindi Vora analyzes how affective labor, understood as a vital energy, is detached from human bodies and transferred as a commodity through global neoliberalism, which regularly channels vitality from the Global South to the Global North: through surrogacy, organ transplantation, and the affective labor of call center workers. As Vora reveals, these structures extend patterns of colonial exploitation, wherein "cost-effectiveness mandates locating a labor process where it is cheapest, without concern for how that labor has been made to be cheap" (loc 138–39). She argues that affective labor practices "deplete individual and community life" (loc 982) because vital energies go to sustaining the commodity consumer's lifeworld, not that of the laborer. Iris's story is emblematic of this depletion: that she is both an immigrant and queer reinforces how certain subjects are made vulnerable. Vora theorizes this as a "conceptual violence" by which "the understanding or reading of a certain type of human as less human or not human at all" is "simultaneously naturalized, systemic, economic, and logical" (loc 327–30).

One of Vora's chief areas of analysis is the work of surrogates, and Tze Chun's short film *Silver Sling* (2010) explores how this practice targets immigrant women. The film opens with a voiceover from what we eventually learn is a promotional video for the Silver Sling surrogacy clinic: "human history is the history of revolution: industrial, political, sexual, and now reproductive," it announces, proceeding to tell listeners that they should not have to wait for anything in a world of instant consumer gratification. Silver Sling offers an "accelerated birth system" that suits such expectations, reproduction in a "timeframe appropriate for the fast-paced world of today." This voiceover is eventually matched with a woman speaking on a monitor, as we follow a white, blonde woman, Lydia (Julia Kots), through the city and into the Silver Sling office. She goes into an interview with an African American nurse, who notes that this will be her third accelerated surrogacy, conception to birth in three months, and tries to dissuade Lydia from taking the contact: after three accelerated pregnancies, a woman becomes sterile. Lydia insists that she must go through with it, and after she exits the clinic she argues with her boyfriend, Stepan (Jed Peterson) in Russian. Her brother, Pasha, is still in Russia and although his visa to enter the United States has been paid for, they lack resources to support themselves since Lydia just lost her job. This film once again shows that vulnerable immigrant populations are pressured into risky practices within commodity health care due to the lack of other sources of income.

Stepan and Lydia argue about how to best balance their current economic needs with their future prospects. Stepan wants to raise a family with her and refuses to accept that he must sacrifice their reproductive futurity for the sake of economic survival in the present. Lydia is saddened but prioritizes protecting her brother. Here the stakes of what Vora theorizes as the "life support" siphoned from some parts of the globe and used to sustain others are raised: it is not only Lydia's life energy that is directed toward other couples' futures, and not even that the "product" now transferred includes a material entity, the child, but most importantly the direct correlation the film establishes between Lydia sustaining other families' futures through clinical labor and her losing the chance for her own future family because of it. *Silver Sling* thus escalates the destructiveness of capital's commodification of life and biological processes. Cooper characterizes this acceleration of biology beyond natural limits—in examples such as shortened birth-to-harvest timelines for "broiler" chickens, or accelerated growth seasons for GMO crops—as the "delirium" of capital that involves the "breakdown and recreation of whole worlds" (20). The frivolousness of the accelerated pregnancies and lack of concern regarding its cost to the surrogates is another example of the way, as Vora argues, that neoliberal markets seek efficiency or "cost-effectiveness" without regard for the histories by which some are made vulnerable to risky employment. Silver Sling has no concern for the ethical costs of its mode of production.

The film concludes on an ambiguous note. Lydia returns to the clinic to interview with prospective couples. This scene of mixed-race surrogates and prospective parents is shown without dialogue, although we see that, as they chat, the prospective surrogates smile with animation. As one dryly notes to Lydia just before they enter, there are four clients and eight surrogates, "you do the math." Their various ethnicities index the fact that prospective parents often want a child whose ethnic features are similar to their own, and Cooper and Waldby note that Eastern European woman are often sought out for surrogacy services that involve egg donation, since they are a source of "fair-skinned biological capital" (76), as well as a population of economically vulnerable women. The film, however, does not seem to highlight this fact, since we see Lydia talking with an African American couple and eventually signing a contract with an Asian one. Only heterosexual couples appear as prospective parents, which was once the industry dominant, although single women and gay couples increasingly have access to surrogacy services (Almeling 33). This scene of smiling, accommodating surrogates each seeking to secure the contract contrasts sharply with the montage of scenes that follow, which show four of these young women, including Lydia, grimly removing their clothing and storing their personal belongings in plastic bags as they prepare to undergo the procedure. Lydia, in particular, struggles to restrain her emotion: her nurse once again tries to dissuade her, revealing that she (the nurse) completed three accelerated surrogacies in her youth and now regrets it. Lydia hugs, almost clutches at the nurse as she steels herself to undergo the procedure, but we never see her complete it: instead, we cut to a shot of a first-time surrogate undergoing her procedure, and then to one of Lydia walking rapidly away from the building. The possibility exists that she chose her own reproductive future over selling her life energy to survive in the present, but even if she made this choice, the film takes its meaning from the fact that she cannot securely have both.

In *Life as Surplus*, Cooper argues: "As long as life science production is subject to the imperatives of capitalist accumulation, the promise of a surplus of life will be predicated on a corresponding move to devaluate life. The two sides of the capitalist delirium—the drive to push beyond limits and the need to reimpose them, in the form of scarcity—must be understood as mutually constitutive" (49). *Silver Sling* offers a material image of precisely this dialectic: the accelerated, just-in-time children for an economic elite are produced in a way that eliminates the reproductive possibilities for the economically marginalized. It thus demonstrates how SF narratives can concretize such abstract flows of capital into specific, quotidian situations, and thereby make visible to a wider audience some of the harms of our biopolitical, bioeconomic present.

Mohammed Gorjestani's *Refuge* (2013) offers a more extreme example of what we might call commodity maternity and enhances our understanding of how certain people are made more vulnerable to such practices because of other ways in which they are restricted. Protagonist Sonia (Nikohi Boosheri) is an Iranian immigrant in the United States on a student visa in 2020. A cyber-attack on US systems mandates a review of all visas issued to Iranians, and the film opens with a scene of Sonia and other affected people attending a San Jose public safety hearing, where they are reassured—but without any of their questions actually being answered. The meeting is conducted in English, although a Persian translation appears on a screen, and Sonia seems to be one of few who can follow the exchange and respond in English. Bodily vulnerability is at stake, as she explains to the council, since she and many like her face imprisonment and worse if they are returned to Iran because of their dissident activities. *Refuge* takes care to establish that Sonia is a hardworking and contributing member of US society. As we follow her over the two days of the film's narrative, we see her continually engaged in productive activity: doing the dishes for her roommates as soon as she returns home, studying, working after class at tailoring.

After the meeting, Sonia is approached by Reza (Camyar Chai), who speaks to her in Persian, expresses admiration for her activist blog and tells her that he works for an organization that "could really help someone like you." When she follows up on his invitation to meet, Sonia discovers that it is not her intellectual capacities that his corporation, Nugene, desires, but simply her body. They seek surrogates to host genetically modified fetuses that Nugene wants to bring to term in its "genetic optimization" research program. Nugene exemplifies the conflation of surveillance state society, immigration, and border control with biopolitical markets in life. Reza must meet Sonia on a bench outside the facility, since she has not cleared security checks, and as she waits in the lobby, men in military fatigues walk past. Reza explains that he is able to offer the attractive incentive of a green card for her participation in the "maternity phase" of their research because of Nugene's close partnership with the Department of Defense, whose resources they require for their expensive research. When Reza explains that Nugene is a genetic research facility, Sonia seems open to commodifying her body through the sale of the stem cells or DNA, the requests she anticipates, but she balks at commodifying the social relationship of mothering, telling him, "I'm not the type of person who would do something like this," and politely declining. Reza warns her that he has reviewed her immigration case and knows she will be deported, but Sonia believes her documents are in order.

When we cut to Sonia's immigration hearing, however, she is indeed declined the visa. A tearful Sonia asks the judge, who has refused to make eye contact with her, to explain why she was denied, but no information is forthcoming. Finally looking directly at Sonia, the judge admits the decision was made at the federal level, that she is simply reading what is on the page before her and that for reasons of national security, "the NSA has decided to keep that information [the particulars of this decision] to itself." The film ends with Sonia returning to Nugene, a scene that is shown as the credits roll, without sound. In a steady medium-long shot, we see Sonia waiting in an austere and coolly colored room, with a staircase to the right of the screen and a walkway leading across a landing above. Reza comes down and meets with her, and then a woman in a lab coat enters the walkway. Alone, a stiff Sonia climbs the stairs and exits the visual field with this woman. The scene immediately before this one, when Sonia came to her decision, was filled with sound and music as she watched children play in her neighborhood, a complex scene in which the vibrancy of their lives contrasts with the relative poverty of their surroundings. This visualization of close communal ties comments ironically on Sonia's need to instrumentalize something as intimate as carrying another life in her body. Moreover, unlike the narrative in *Silver Sling*, in which Lydia had to give up a baby as a biomedical "product" but to the context of a family home, in this case the fetus to be implanted is fully and only a commodity, a tool for the military that is destined to experience a life even more dehumanizing and alienating than Sonia's.

In her work on the economics that underpin transnational surrogacy, Vora argues that the techniques by which we now exploit "the undervalued and often invisible reproductively of humans and other organisms and of their parts, such as tissues and cells, were present in the economies of colonialism and slavery in which dehumanized and unfree workers were also self-reproducing capital" (loc 152–53). In Sonia's story, we see these logics transformed under the post-9/11 configuration of American empire, such that Sonia's Iranian background exposes her to targeted recruitment by the US military as they seek to produce another system of living entities categorized as property. Transnational markets in body organs operate according to a similar logic by which some places on the globe are imagined as consumers for the latest medical advances in organ replacement while other areas appear as repositories of these organs, as scholars such as Nancy Scheper-Hughes, Lawrence Cohen, and Aslihan Sanal analyze. Transplant culture is itself haunted by two divergent metaphors, as Lesley Sharp explores in *Strange Harvest*: "Whereas transplant recipients are encouraged by hospital staff to depersonalize their new organs and speak of them in terms that can sometimes even approximate car repair, procurement staff regularly tell donor kin that transplantation enables the donor's essence to persist in others who are thereby offered a second chance at life" (14). The sociotechnical imaginary in SF responds to and unpacks these contradictions by imagining specific concrete worlds that might emerge from ways of negotiating them.

Tina Mabry's short film *Crossover* (2012) takes transplantation rather than surrogacy as the site of its investigation of mixing medicine with markets. The film remains within the US and concerns only those who are citizens, but the border it imagines is that between socioeconomic zones. The story is propelled by the different chances to thrive or perish that are concomitant with whether one lives in a gated community of economic privilege, the restricted-access zone, or is relegated to the space of collapse outside its borders. The film opens with Angela (Michael Hyatt) walking her daughter Jennifer (Alexis Matthews) into what we learn is the school in the unrestricted zone. The camera tracks at ground level across an overgrown landscape covered with litter, discarded police tape prominent among the trash. We cut to a much more orderly location, where well-dressed people walking on manicured streets approach a security guard, who carefully scans an implant in each person's wrist before allowing them to proceed. A caption tells us the year is 2028, and we hear a voiceover radio broadcast reporting the news that the Supreme Court has ruled that the new economically based separate-but-equal amendment has been deemed constitutional, thus segregation between "restricted access" and unrestricted schools will continue. In pointed sequence, the announcer continues, "In *related* news, a thirteen-year-old boy was shot last night in the unrestricted part of LA," concluding that no charges have been brought against the homeowner who killed the boy (emphasis added).

As the film continues, we are repeatedly reminded of the gap between opportunities in restricted and unrestricted zones. It firmly refuses any comforting myth about hard work or merit ensuring one's success. At Jennifer's school, disorder reigns. The teacher, Victoria (Lyn Alicia Henderson), struggles to take roll among distracted students, and she marks yet another on the long list of those who have dropped out: a derisive student observes, he "was just coming for the free food anyway." The lighting is dim, the facilities grim, and sounds of police sirens and gunshots just outside dominate the soundtrack. As the lights flicker and go out, a PA announces that rolling blackouts are predicted for the entire day and so classes are canceled. Jennifer's brother Quincy (Elijah King) takes a placement test, which will reveal he is autistic, while Jennifer does college-level mathematics with her teacher's encouragement. Angela and Victoria have a cryptic conversation about her need to keep her body "clean," one that makes sense if we realize that body parts can be thought of as commodities.

As we cut to a scene of the children at home, we get a sense of the larger social world: the news announces that "harvested bodies" were found in the unrestricted zone, and allegations that the separate-but-equal amendment has increased crime in the unrestricted area are denied by authorities. A cut to Angela arriving home shows her walking through flashing police lights. One of her neighbors, a man we saw earlier in the restricted zone working as a groundskeeper, is led by police past a vehicle labeled Organ Harvesting Unit, implying that the bodies of those killed in street crime are "made useful" by the state, and perhaps hinting that suspects are turned into bodies by authorities as well. Inside Jennifer tells Quincy he can emerge from a closet since the violence is "just normal," while the television news reports that thirteen children died in the San Fernando Valley from drinking tap water in their own homes, the second such incident within the month. Angela feeds her children but refrains from eating herself, presumably due to lack of food, and then she and Jennifer openly discuss her plan to sell her organs—"it's just a kidney, some bone marrow, and a little bit of liver," she reassures her concerned daughter—to raise the $500,000 needed to obtain access chips for the children to be educated inside the restricted-access zone. Angela insists this is the only way for Jennifer to get into the restricted sector and become an engineer, demurring that "only a year" of absence from her children's lives is a small price to pay for educational opportunity.

Crossover reveals the structural inequalities that create a situation in which some people are willing to serve as living organ donors. The film emphasizes not only the immediate economic needs that drive such a choice, but also the way economic resources shape all other opportunities in life. Without access to schools in the restricted zone, Jennifer will never have more than a menial career, no matter her intelligence. Within the restricted zone Quincy might be able to have a productive life aided by therapists and socialization support; because he spent his youth without such resources his autism now excludes him forever from crossing to the other side. The metaphor of crossing links the economic themes of the film to the US-Mexico border, another site where bodies are put at risk for economic opportunity. Although casting does not make everyone in the restricted zone white and everyone without a person of color, it does compel us to recognize that the legacy of structural racism means that socioeconomic difference tends to correlate with ethnic difference: most people within the restricted zone are white, and most without are persons of color, including Angela and her family, who are African American. The name of the socioeconomically based education amendment, separate but equal, ensures viewers note the connection to a history of racial exclusion.

In the film's conclusion, intercut scenes parallel two sacrifices Angela makes for her daughter's future. After Jennifer is injured by a stray bullet when Quincy opens one of the shutters on their windows, we see Angela searching through the dumpster to recover a card for an illegal chip, something she had discarded indignantly when told that Quincy could never cross. She can no longer refuse to separate her children, and she will lose Quincy just as she loses some of her organs for the sake of Jennifer's education. The film closes with intercut scenes of a crying Jennifer getting her restricted-access chip implanted in her wrist, as Quincy settles in with Victoria, and Angela passes into unconsciousness in the surgical theater. This future's economic hardships turn some citizens into mere spare parts, a posture not only imposed from the outside but also internalized by people such as Angela, who sees no way to protect her child's future other than to allow her body to be literally consumed. Further intensifying the uneven effects of healthcare markets that we saw in *Silver Sling* and *Refuge*, Angela here gives up not merely her biological capacity to reproduce, but parts of her material body.

The final film I will discuss, Julian Breece's *The Living* (2013), takes this logic the final step, portraying a future in which economic hardship and a medical market for body parts compel someone to give up all of his organs, in effect committing suicide. The film is set in a world in which a series of earthquakes and extreme weather incidents have destroyed many East Coast cities, displacing their populations into reservation camps. Once again, we see the invention of borders within the United States, here used to separate those who remain fully citizens because still in possession of their own homes, while others become dehumanized migrants, housed on reservations and dependent on whatever aid the state is willing to provide. Isaac (Brandon Scott) is a doctor sent to one such reservation, there to harvest the organs of an African American man, Luther (Sy Richardson), who appears in ragged clothes. Examination reveals he has a wound that will not heal on his leg, the consequence of untreated diabetes, but the only question Luther asks is whether it will "affect the agreement." Isaac assures the family that the procedure can go ahead as planned, that the Department of Treasury will put $120,000 in a trust in the wife's name as soon as it is complete.[2] Luther's daughter, Zion (Harmony Santana), refuses to shake Isaac's hand. More details of the institutionalized organ harvest emerge that evening when Zion and Isaac talk, after she comes to him for help with an injured friend, the nearest hospital being more than sixty miles from the reservation. She asks Isaac to role-play the procedure with her, an uncomfortable scene in which he asks questions about the patient's comfort, even though the procedure is one designed to kill this patient. Zion breaks into tears, upset by her father's sacrifice for the rest of the family, a decision fueled by the fact that "the government won't pay for him to get better" but will pay for Isaac "to cut his organs out and send them to someone worth saving, because he's not."

We see a similar dialectic here between surplus life for some, and devalued life for others, but ethnic difference is not as central to Breece's vision: Isaac is also African American, yet his different class status marks him as an outsider to this community. Isaac too lost his family and his partner during the New York earthquake. Another earthquake occurs during the night before the procedure, Zion comforts Isaac during the panic attack it provokes. He tells her of emerging into New York after the major earthquake to see piles of dismembered bodies: "our job was to save the living, but if you were there you'd have to redefine what that means."

The organ harvesting system in which Isaac is employed—his dreams of becoming a cardiac surgeon abandoned—is one way that the state has chosen to redefine what "the living" means, privileging the lives of those whose economic contributions make them "matter" more. The final scenes offer another way to think about this redefinition. The last voicemail Isaac received from this partner brackets the film: in the opening, we hear only part of it, "I can't shake this feeling that something is coming, that everything is about to change"; in the final scenes, we hear the rest. The partner claims that Isaac has been become withdrawn, and he wonders if Isaac is deliberating creating distance because of the looming dystopia. As we hear his final words to Isaac—"I love you. You can't just walk away, because for now we're still here"—we see Isaac return to the reservation and approach Zion's door. Previously Isaac expressed surprise that she remained on the reservation, but in this final shot he transitions from using his medical skill to serve what the state defines as "the living" and toward using it to serve the medical needs of those deemed irrelevant and warehoused in the reservation, the living who are "still here" despite the state's attempts to erase them.

Each of these fictions, set at the intersection of medicine, markets, and borders, enables us to see how these dynamics play out unevenly for differently positioned social subjects, and especially the way that immigrants and other economically marginalized people become test subjects for, rather than recipients of, new medical therapies. The overwhelmingly dystopian tone of these tales is balanced with their clear commitment to creating another kind of future, to recognizing, in Jasanoff's evocative phrase, that "the seen reality is not the only one about which we can dream" ("Imagined" 340). They are all examples of what Tom Moylan has described as the "critical dystopia," that is, a text that "self-reflexively takes on the present system and offers not only astute critiques of the order of things, but also explorations into the oppositional spaces and possibilities from which the next round of political activism can derive imaginative sustenance and inspiration" (xv).

In their various ways, these texts reveal the importance of activism that interrogates how the divisions enforced by borders—national, economic, or ethnic—shape vitality in distinct and specific ways, dependent on one's status vis-à-vis such borders, as citizens, legitimized occupants, immigrants, or the dispossessed and thus dehumanized. Collectively, they show the ways that biotechnology and medicine produce zones of what I call post-vital subjectivity, spaces in which subjects are alive but only as tools or resources to be deployed to sustain the vitality and futurity of others. The promissory discourse of new markets in medicine, new transplant therapies, and new possibilities for reproduction is haunted by these zones of the post-vital that it simultaneously creates. By telling stories about medicine and markets into these futures, embedded in concrete, quotidian, and diverse worlds, SF helps us to recognize the need for and encourages us to enact a different set of possible worlds.

Notes

1. No actor credits are listed for these performers, leading to the impression that they are real people speaking of their experiences.

2. The reality, of course, is that unhealthy bodies cannot donate healthy organs, and so the film takes some liberties to make a point about uneven resource distribution and its consequences for health and longevity. Indeed, the need for healthy organs often creates emotional crisis for medical teams, as Sharp discusses, due to the fact that they must at some point switch between regarding particular subjects as patients they are trying to treat and transition into regarding them as bodies they maintain until the organs can be harvested.

Works Cited

Ahuja, Neel. *Bioinsecurities: Disease Interventions, Empire, and the Government of Species*. Duke UP, 2016.

Almeling, Rene. *Sex Cells: The Medical Market for Eggs and Sperm*. U of California P, 2011.

Cohen, Lawrence. "The Other Kidney: Biopolitics Beyond Recognition." *Commodifying Bodies*, edited by Nancy Scheper-Hughes and Loïc Wacquant. Sage, 2002, pp. 9–30.

Cooper, Melinda. *Life as Surplus: Biotechnology and Capitalism in the Neoliberal Era*. U of Washington P, 2008.

Cooper, Melinda, and Catherine Waldby. *Clinical Labor: Tissue Donors and Research Subjects in the Global Bioeconomy*. Duke UP, 2014.

Crossover. Directed by Tina Mabry, performances by Michael Hyatt, et al., screenplay by Tina Mabry. Future States, ITVS, 1 May 2012.

Hollow. Directed by Lisa Robinson, performances by Angelic Zambrana and Louisa Krause, screenplay by Lisa Robinson. Future States, ITVS, Apr. 2013.

Jameson, Fredric. *Archaeologies of the Future: The Desire Called Utopia and Other Science Fictions*. Verso, 2007.

Jasanoff, Sheila. "Future Imperfect: Science, Technology, and the Imagination of Modernity." *Dreamscapes of Modernity: Sociotechnical Imaginaries and the Fabrication of Power*, edited by Sheila Jasanoff and Sang-Hyun Kim. U of Chicago P, 2015, pp. 1–33.

———. "Imagined and Invented Worlds." *Dreamscapes of Modernity: Sociotechnical Imaginaries and the Fabrication of Power*, edited by Sheila Jasanoff and Sang-Hyun Kim. U of Chicago P, 2015, pp. 321–41.

Jasanoff, Sheila, and Sang-Hyun Kim. *Dreamscapes of Modernity: Sociotechnical Imaginaries and the Fabrication of Power*. U of Chicago P, 2015.

The Living. Directed by Julian Breece, performances by Brandon Scott et al., screenplay by Julian Breece. Future States, ITVS, 1 Apr. 2013.

Moylan, Tom. *Scraps of Untainted Sky: Science Fiction, Utopia, Dystopia*. Westview Press, 2000.

Refuge. Directed by Mohammed Gorjestani, performances by Nikohi Boosheri and Camyar Chai, screenplay by Mohammad Gorjestani. Future States, ITVS, 1 May 2013.

Remigration. Directed by Barry Jenkins, performances by Russell Hornsby, et al. Future States, ITVS, 21 Mar. 2011.

Sanal, Aslihan. *New Organs Within Us: Transplants and the Moral Economy*. Duke UP, 2011.

Scheper-Hughes, Nancy. "Commodity Fetishism in Organs Trafficking." *Commodifying Bodies*, edited by Nancy Scheper-Hughes and Loïc Wacquant, Sage, 2002 pp. 31–62.

Sharp, Lesley A. *Strange Harvest: Organ Transplants, Denatured Bodies, and the Transformed Self*. U of California P, 2006.

Silver Sling. Directed by Tze Chun, performance by Julia Kots and Jed Peterson, screenplay by Tze Chun. Future States, ITVS, 8 Mar. 2010.

Sunder Rajan, Kaushik. *Biocapital: The Constitution of Postgenomic Life*. Duke UP, 2006.

———. "Introduction: The Capitalization of Life and the Liveliness of Capital." *Lively Capital: Biotechnologies, Ethics, and Governance in Global Markets*, edited by Kaushik Sunder Rajan. Duke UP, 2012, pp. 1–41.

Suvin, Darko. *Metamorphoses of Science Fiction: On the Poetics and History of a Literary Genre*. Reprint ed., edited by Gerry Canavan. Peter Lang, 2016.

Vora, Kalindi. *Life Support: Biocapital and the New History of Outsourced Labor*. U of Minnesota P, 2015.

Vourvoulias, Sabrina. *Ink*. Rosarium, 2018.

4

The Surrogacy Public Interest Litigation in the Indian Supreme Court

Marginalizing the Marginalized

Sital Kalantry

The surrogacy market in India flourished over the last few decades.[1] Some estimate that surrogacy has generated over two billion dollars for India (Shetty 1633). Gay male and infertile couples flocked to India, because their own country prohibits surrogacy, or perhaps because surrogacy is cheaper in India. India was an ideal host country for transnational surrogacy—it has state-of-the-art medical tourism facilities, English-speaking medical professionals, and a relatively large supply of poor women to provide gestational care (Witzleb and Chawla 167, 168). In a typical arrangement, the surrogate has no genetic relation to the child she gives birth to, but rather both intended parents are the ones that are biologically related to the child.[2]

All this activity has been occurring without any serious government monitoring or regulation. In February 2015, a senior lawyer, upset at what she saw as the exploitation of Indian women by foreigners, filed a public interest litigation (PIL) at the Indian Supreme Court, arguing that surrogacy violates surrogates' right to "life and personal liberty" (Wad). This PIL on surrogacy (Surrogacy PIL) prompted the Indian Supreme Court to haul top officials in the executive to the Court to question them about what they are doing to address surrogacy. At one of these hearings, the Supreme Court even went so far as to declare that surrogacy violates the constitutional rights of surrogates.

The year before the Surrogacy PIL was initiated, a new Hindu-nationalist party came to power in 2014. This government may have been more sympathetic to a prohibitionist approach to surrogacy. Soon after the Surrogacy PIL was initiated, the Ministry of Home Affairs unilaterally stopped granting foreigners visas for surrogacy purposes in November 2015 ("Foreign Nationals").[3] Thereafter, in August 2016, the cabinet approved a bill to ban compensated surrogacy altogether, even for Indian intended parents. On the other hand, the surrogacy bills that were proposed prior to the date the Surrogacy PIL was filed sought to regulate not prohibit surrogacy. Thus, it is only after the Surrogacy PIL was initiated that the executive pushed for a prohibitionist model.

The Surrogacy PIL was brought pursuant to a mechanism created by the Supreme Court in the 1980s, which allows any person to bring a petition directly to the Supreme Court or the High Courts claiming a violation of their own or someone else's fundamental rights.[4] The Court sometimes issues orders with wide-ranging impact in PIL cases. In one case, the Court froze new registration of auto rickshaws while promoting experimentation with cleaner fuel options, and it recently banned alcohol sales near major highways to address drunk driving (*Dr. Nayana H. Patel*; "One Lakh Fresh"; Anand). Even before issuing final judgments, the Court exercises enormous power by holding hearings and pushing for certain policy solutions.

Champions of public interest litigation argue that it gives voice to India's marginalized groups and allows courts to act where the legislatures have failed.[5] Critics of PIL contend that it is being misused by some people to further private gains rather than for the good of the public (Deva). Legal scholars have largely valorized PIL and when they critique it, it is to lament that the Court has taken fewer PILs in the 1990s than it did in the 1980s (Shankar). On the other hand, Anuj Bhuwania recently made a larger structural critique of PIL. Among other things, he argued that sometimes when hearing PIL cases, the Supreme Court and the High Courts marginalize petitioners' views and do not obtain the views of parties that will be impacted by the litigation (39–44).

Building from this vantage point, I argue that the Surrogacy PIL is problematic because it does not take into account the views of the very people whose rights it intends to vindicate. No current or former surrogates are petitioners in the Surrogacy PIL, nor have they been included as a party despite their attempts to participate. The surrogates that approached the

Supreme Court sought the right to provide gestational care for compensation. Similarly, the current and former surrogates we interviewed in India universally believe that they should have the right to sell gestational care.

Unlike the Court, when the Standing Committee of the Indian Parliament reviewed the Surrogacy Bill of 2016, they invited surrogates to testify before them. They rejected the executive's proposal to ban compensated surrogacy, and instead found that "preventing [surrogates] from being paid for their reproductive labor is grossly unfair and arbitrary" (102nd Report). The lawyer who brought the Surrogacy PIL and the Supreme Court both believe that surrogacy is "exploitative" of the women who undertake it. I believe that much of the exploitation in the process occurs because the compensation terms, health protections in case of complications, and other issues are privately negotiated between the medical clinic, intended parents, and the surrogate. There are vast educational, income, and social disparities between the fertility doctors and intended parents, on the one hand, and the gestational carriers, on the other hand. The privately negotiated contracts rarely provide surrogates adequate health protections in case of complications, do not guarantee postnatal care, nor do they allow surrogates to decide how many embryos are transferred (among other gaps). The government could address this asymmetry in bargaining power by requiring a minimum level of compensation, postnatal care, and other rights for gestational carriers through a strong regulatory framework.

In the first section in this chapter, I describe the various surrogacy bills that have been proposed in the Indian Parliament and explain that there has been a marked shift toward a more restrictive approach to surrogacy since the Surrogacy PIL was initiated. In the next section, I argue that the more restrictive approach can be traced, at least in part, to the Surrogacy PIL and the socially conservative political party elected in India in 2014. In the third section, I argue that the Surrogacy PIL is problematic because it marginalizes the very actors that it seeks to protect—surrogates.

In the fourth section, I point out that when current and former surrogates are asked about whether surrogacy should be legal, they all concur that it should be. Even though surrogates believe the practice should be legal, we should still ensure that they have adequate rights and protections, which I turn to in the fifth section. The private contract model that currently prevails does not give surrogates adequate protection and instead itself creates exploitative conditions. The fifth section concludes that a regulatory model rather than a private contract model can mitigate this potential for abuse. Finally, I conclude by proposing that both the Supreme Court and lawyers, when considering and bringing PILs, give voice to those affected by the litigation.

From Regulation to Prohibition of Surrogacy

The web of actors in the Indian surrogacy industry, including intended parents, medical fertility doctors, agents who recruit surrogates, and surrogates themselves, has been operating largely free of government regulation and oversight for decades. In 2005, the Indian Council of Medical Research (ICMR) issued guidelines on surrogacy, which are followed by many surrogacy clinics today but are neither binding nor robust (ICMR Guidelines). Since 2008, three draft bills have been proposed and have failed to pass in the Indian Parliament. While none of the prior bills banned compensated surrogacy, the Surrogacy (Regulation) Bill of 2016 was the first to prohibit compensated surrogacy altogether. Currently, the Surrogacy (Regulation) Bill of 2019 is pending in Parliament and is largely similar to the 2016 bill. Below I discuss each of these proposals and explain how a dramatic shift in regulation occurred in 2015.

ICMR Guidelines

The ICMR is a body funded by the government of India, responsible for the formulation, coordination, and promotion of biomedical research. In 2005, the ICMR, in conjunction with the National Academy of Medical Sciences, published the National Guidelines for Accreditation, Supervision, and Regulation of ART Clinics in India (ICMR Guidelines). Importantly, the guidelines neither impose restrictions on who can be intended parents (both in terms of nationality and sexuality), nor do they impose restrictions on the marital status of the surrogate or the intended parents.[6] The guidelines, while not binding law, remain highly influential in the medical practice.

Previously Proposed Legislation in 2008, 2010, and 2014

Prior to the 2016 bill, three major draft bills have been proposed in the Indian Parliament—the Assisted Reproductive Technology (Regulation) Bill of 2008, the Assisted Reproductive Technology (Regulation) Bill of 2010, and the Assisted Reproductive Technology (Regulation) Bill of 2014. Each bill increasingly narrows who can qualify as a surrogate and as an intended parent. Both the 2008 and the 2010 bills explicitly allowed compensated surrogacy. The 2008 bill stated that "ART shall be available to all persons including single persons, married couples, and unmarried couples" (ch. VII, § 32[1]), and defined a couple as "persons living together and having a sexual relationship that is legal in the country/countries of which they are citizens or they are living in" (ch. I, § 2[a]).

Under the 2008 bill, to qualify as a surrogate, a woman must be between the ages of twenty-one and forty-five, could not have undergone more than three surrogacies (ch. VII, § 34[5]), and was not required to be married (ch. VII, § 34[16]). Foreign couples were explicitly allowed to commission surrogates (ch. VII, § 34[19]). However, the 2010 bill defined a couple as two persons who cohabitate in a legal relationship in India (ch. I, § 2[h]), thus excluding gay Indian couples (ch. I, § 2[v]).

The 2010 bill, however, like the 2008 bill, maintained that surrogacy would be available to "all persons including single persons, married couples and unmarried couples" (ch. VII, § 32[1]). The 2010 bill did not require surrogates to be married (ch. VII, § 34[16]), allowed foreign couples to commission surrogates (ch. VII, § 34[19]), and restricted the age of surrogates to a range of twenty-one to thirty-five years (ch. VII § 34[5]). Finally, the 2010 bill changed the three-surrogacy maximum to a limit of five successful live births in total, including the surrogates' own children (ch. VII § 34[5]).

The 2014 bill signaled a shift in surrogacy regulation toward more restriction, but still allowed commercial surrogacy (ch. VII, § 60[3][a]). First, the definition of a couple changed the word "persons" to "a male person and female person" (ch. I, § 2[p]), and defined commissioning couples as married (ch. I, § 2[h]). Intending couples were required to have been married for at least two years (ch. VII, § 60[21][a]). Single persons were not mentioned in the 2014 bill, excluding them as a possible intending parent (ch. I; ch. VII). Moreover, a woman could become a surrogate only if she was an Indian citizen who was married and who had at least one child that was at least three years of age (ch. 1, § 2[zr]; ch. VII, § 60[5]). In addition, the 2014 bill limited surrogates to one successful birth through surrogacy (ch. VII, § 60[5][a]). Finally, foreigners were explicitly prohibited from commissioning an Indian surrogate (ch. VII, § 60[11][a]).

Ministry of Home Affairs Regulations (2015)

The 2014 bill was the first proposed legislation that sought to permit only Indians and people who qualify for the Overseas Citizenship of India to hire an Indian surrogate (ch. VII, § 60[11][a]). While that bill did not pass in the

Parliament, the executive, through the Ministry of Home Affairs, essentially put a halt to transnational surrogacy in 2015 by denying foreigners medical visas for surrogacy purposes ("Foreign Nationals"). In January 2013, the same ministry had prohibited only foreign gay couples and single people from obtaining visas (Rajadhyakshal).

The Surrogacy Bill of 2016

The Surrogacy (Regulation) Bill of 2016 was introduced on November 21, 2016 and was passed by the lower house, the Lok Sabha, but lapsed without vote in the upper house, the Rajya Sabha. A similar bill called the Surrogacy (Regulation) Bill of 2019 was passed by the Lok Sabha, but has not been voted on by the Rajya Sabha. The 2016 bill was the first proposed legislation to prohibit compensated surrogacy completely. Under the bill, any person who undertakes a surrogacy for a fee, advertises surrogacy services, or exploits a surrogate would be punished with ten years in prison and a fine (ch. VII, § 35). On the other hand, uncompensated surrogacy (commonly referred to as "altruistic surrogacy"), in which the intended parents pay only for costs such as medical expenses and insurance coverage but do not compensate the surrogate for her gestational care, would be allowed (ch. III, § 4[ii][b]; ch. III, § 4[iii][b]).

Additionally, only heterosexual Indian couples, who have been married for at least five years and who are incapable of conceiving their own child, would be able to engage a surrogate (ch. III, § 4[iii][c][II]). Even then, the surrogate would need to be a "close relative" of the intended parents, be a mother herself, be married (or have been married in the past), and have never been a surrogate before (ch. III, § 4[iii][b]). The term "close relative" is not defined in the 2016 bill, so it is unclear exactly how restrictive this limitation would be or whether it could be defined so broadly that compensation would be paid illegally to women who are not even relatives.

The 2016 bill calls for the creation of a regulatory structure whereby state-level authorities would be responsible for verifying and granting certificates of eligibility for anyone seeking to use surrogacy to have children (ch. III, §§ 4[iii][a]–[c]). Thus, the 2016 bill proposes to outlaw commercial surrogacy and to implement a rigid regulatory structure that allows uncompensated surrogacy in only narrowly defined instances. However, the standing committee of the Indian Parliament rejected key pieces of the 2016 bill in August 2017. The standing committee called for legalization of compensated surrogacy, thinks that "live-in" couples should be eligible to become intended parents (not just heterosexual married couples), but believes that foreigners should not be allowed to commission Indian surrogates (102nd Report 58, 35).

The Role of the Surrogacy PIL in the Turn Toward Prohibition

I have demonstrated in the prior section that India's policy toward surrogacy changed dramatically from a permissive approach to a prohibitionist model when transnational surrogacy was prohibited in November 2015 and with the 2016 bill's proposal to prohibit all compensated surrogacy. In this section, I explain how certain judges of the Indian Supreme Court pushed the government to adopt a prohibitionist model. The role of the Supreme Court in shaping India's approach to surrogacy is not widely known, because the Supreme Court did not publish a final written decision and instead demanded that the government prohibit surrogacy in its oral hearings.

In February 2015, Jayashree Wad, an advocate in the Indian Supreme Court, filed a public interest litigation challenging commercial surrogacy generally in India (Kusum). The primary contention of the Surrogacy PIL she filed is that the Indian assisted reproductive technology industry has commercialized women's wombs in a manner that is "violative of [the] right to life, liberty, [and] dignity of women under Article 21 of Indian Constitution" (Kusum 2). Wad also argued that surrogacy has adverse health consequences on women, surrogates do not give informed consent, and that surrogates were exploited in other ways as well (Kusum 2). Under Indian court procedure, even people who are not directly impacted by the concerns they raise can bring cases directly to the Supreme Court on behalf of other people whose fundamental rights under the Indian constitution have been implicated (*S.P. Gupta*; Susman).

Following the submission of the Surrogacy PIL, the Supreme Court contacted numerous government bodies, including the ICMR and the Ministry of Home Affairs, to obtain the perspectives of those institutions on the practice of commercial surrogacy (Kusum 4). The Supreme Court Justice hearing the Surrogacy PIL told officials from the central government on October 14, 2015, that surrogacy should be banned and noted that he believed that the process commoditized human life (Choudhary). Furthermore, he asked the central government to explain whether surrogacy was against the dignity of women, and whether surrogacy amounted to the economic and psychological exploitation of women (Choudhary). The case is still pending as of this writing without any final decision having been issued (Supreme Court of India, Civil Appeal No. 8714/2010, *Union of India & Anr. v. Jan Balaz & Ors.*).

In PIL cases, the Court exercises what some have called "creeping jurisdiction," which means that it will keep a case open for long periods of time without issuing a final order (Deva 26). Through this creeping jurisdiction, the Court insinuated itself in legislative and executive decision-making in the Surrogacy PIL by making arguments about surrogacy based in the constitution. The Court pushes for policy change to rectify what it views as large-scale violations of fundamental rights. Using the constitution as a threat, the Court foreshadows how it would rule if it were judicially reviewing legislation on surrogacy. However, it pushes for policy change without issuing a written decision explaining its legal reasoning.

After hearing the views of the Supreme Court on surrogacy, the Ministry of Home Affairs issued a notice that effectively banned transnational surrogacy in November 2015. It refused to grant visas to foreigners for purposes of surrogacy ("Foreign Nationals"). While there is no direct evidence linking the two, the timing of the ban by the ministry and the hearings of the Supreme Court suggest that the decision to ban international surrogacy is related to pressure by the Court (Ramasubramanian). In fact, some saw the government's adoption of a total ban on transnational surrogacy as a way to avoid answering the difficult questions the Supreme Court had posed regarding the rights of various parties in surrogacy arrangements (Ramasubramanian; Mahapatral).[7] It is also possible that the government was already considering banning foreigners from engaging in surrogacy in India and the timing of the Supreme Court hearings were just coincidental, or simply expedited the process that was already under way.[8]

The Supreme Court of India clearly found sympathetic ears in the executive. The Hindu nationalist party, the Bhartia Janata Party (BJP), rose to national power in 2014. The prohibition on all foreigners was adopted in November 2015 after the BJP gained power and also after the Surrogacy PIL was filed. Then one year after the Surrogacy PIL, the BJP sought to ban compensated surrogacy even for Indian intended parents in the 2016 bill ("Cabinet Approves Bill"). However, the ban on foreign gay people and single individuals was adopted in 2013 and precedes the BJP and the Surrogacy PIL.

The approach to surrogacy in the 2016 and 2019 bills reflect traditional notions of family in India. The ability of women to carry children using the gametes of others threatens traditional notions of family by transforming the definition of family. Single people, gay people, and unmarried couples have the potential of having children. By prohibiting compensated surrogacy, those people are effectively prevented from having children (unless they adopt), thereby curbing the transformative effect surrogacy can have on the concept of family. Indeed, External Affairs Minister Sushma Swaraj justified the 2016 bill in terms of values—she stated that allowing homosexual couples to avail themselves of surrogacy simply "doesn't go with [the BJP's] ethos" ("Cabinet Approves Bill").

On the other hand, having children is considered critical for a married couple in Indian society generally (Nadimpally et al. 9–11). The 2016 and 2019 bills reaffirm the family's social centrality by only allowing married, heterosexual, and childless couples to have a "close relative" carry a child for them, as long as the surrogate does not receive any money for the gestational care she provides. Allowing only a "close relative" to provide gestational care to another "close relative" also maintains caste purity. Finally, permitting only uncompensated surrogacy (and prohibiting compensated surrogacy) further reinforces the notion that women's work in the private sphere has no economic value. Thus, the 2016 and 2019 bills perpetuates traditional notions of family (a married man and a woman) and traditional societal values (the need for people to have children and the devaluation of women's work) (Nadimpally et al. 10–11). However, the Parliamentary Standing Committee recognized that allowing only uncompensated surrogacy, and particularly when only a "close relative" can provide gestational care, can lead to abusive situations for certain women in families (102nd Report 47–50).

Marginalizing the Marginalized

Public interest litigation was intended to address violations of fundamental rights of marginalized groups. In *S.P. Gupta v. Union of India*, Justice Bhagwati concluded that the goal of developing PIL was to promote "easy accessibility to justice" and ensure that "large masses of people belonging to the deprived and exploited sections of humanity may be able to realise and enjoy the socio-economic rights granted to them" (*S.P. Gupta*). In this section, I argue, however, that the Surrogacy PIL was problematic because it fails to consider and take seriously the views of the very people whose fundamental rights are at question.

First, the Court would have heard the views of surrogates if they were included as petitioners in the case by the lawyer who filed the petition. However, unlike for other cases, there is no requirement that the person who brings the case has been an injured party (*S.P. Gupta*). In the Surrogacy PIL, a senior lawyer, Jayashree Wad, argues that compensated surrogacy violates the Indian constitution (Kusum). Although the Surrogacy PIL was aimed at protecting future surrogates from exploitation and harm, Wad never once indicated that she has spoken to a surrogate. She neither cites nor provides any surrogates' views in her petition (Wad). None of the orders in the Surrogacy PIL mention any surrogates' opinions. Advocate Radhika Thapar, who was present for the hearings, noted that the petitioner presented "very few incidents of exploitation, projected through various media and magazine reports" (Pandey).

While I am not suggesting that the Court should reform PIL procedures to add a standing requirement, I believe it is good practice for lawyers who bring claims on behalf of other people's rights to understand what those people actually want. If Ms. Wad had gone through the process of talking to surrogates, she may have learned that the money they receive from surrogacy helps their families build homes, educate their children, and pay off debt. Many surrogates also feel happy that they were able to help another couple build a family. Nonetheless, even if she met with surrogates, Ms. Wad would likely have found at least one surrogate, or the family of a surrogate who died, who desires that surrogacy be banned, but even going through that process of speaking to surrogates to find those who oppose it, she would have had a much richer understanding of the issues faced by the women who sell gestational care.

Second, when the Court hears a PIL case, particularly those where the petitioner is not one of the parties that will be impacted by their decision, I suggest that the Court take even more care to ask the interested parties to testify and learn about the challenges they face. Instead, when surrogates approached the Supreme Court asking to intervene in the Surrogacy PIL, they were not allowed (Mishra). They argued that the ban denied them a right to livelihood and reproductive autonomy, discriminated against foreigners, and prevented the creation of families (Mishra). If their views had been taken seriously, then the Court might have considered dismissing the Surrogacy PIL completely.

The Surrogacy PIL is not the only PIL where interested parties were marginalized. Bhuwania, points out, for example, that in the *Sheela Barse* case, when Sheela Barse wanted to withdraw the PIL, instead of dismissing the petition, the Court appointed the Supreme Court Legal Aid committee as the petitioner (39–41). Bhuwania also gives numerous examples where the voices of the impacted parties are not heard at all (11). Surrogates were similarly marginalized in the Surrogacy PIL.

This lack of participation by surrogates in the Surrogacy PIL is even more troubling because, unlike other similar groups, surrogates have a collective-action problem. While sex workers have collective organizations that advocate for their interests at the policy and legislative level, surrogates do not have a similar organization (Dey and Roy; Sangram; Durbar). The primary reason sex workers have collective organizations, while surrogates do not, is because surrogates usually engage in surrogacy once or twice over the course of their lives, whereas sex workers are typically engaged in the profession on a more regular basis. In addition, while surrogates can and often do hide the fact that they are carrying a child for someone else while still living with their families, sex workers have often been abandoned by their families and often live in their own communities (Dey and Roy; Sangram; Durbar).

The medical profession played the initial role in organizing sex workers in order to address the spread of HIV and AIDS. However, when it comes to surrogacy, the interests of the medical professionals and surrogates are not always aligned. For example, while medical professionals rely on surrogates to carry the children, medical professionals make less money if surrogates are paid more.

Despite these collective-action problems, surrogates have sometimes come together to intervene at the policy level. In addition to attempting to intervene in the Supreme Court case, fifty surrogates sent a letter to the National Commission for Women and the ICMR in November 2015, urging them to permit foreigners to become intended parents (Perappadan). Given the challenges surrogates face in organizing together, it is even more incumbent on lawyers who bring claims on their behalf, as well as the Supreme Court, to ensure that surrogates' voices are heard loudly and clearly in any court proceedings about the constitutionality of surrogacy.

Surrogates Want the Right to Sell Gestational Care

There is little scholarly work that investigates the opinions of gestational carriers in regard to surrogacy. Most of the scholarly work on Indian surrogates consists of sensitive and illuminating ethnographies by anthropologists (Pande, "At Least" 292; Pande, "Commercial" 989; Saravanan; Deomampo

167). In this section, I point out that when they are asked about it, surrogates want the right to sell gestational care.

Eight Cornell Law students, Professor Bradley Wendel, and I traveled to New Delhi, India, to (among other things) interview surrogates to understand their views on whether compensated surrogacy should be legal. We were working in collaboration with Professors Aparna Chandra and Mrinal Satish and eight students at the National Law University in Delhi ("In 'Global Classroom'").[9] As part of the fieldwork, teams of four students visited medical clinics and interviewed doctors and surrogates, and also visited surrogacy homes. Surrogacy homes are places where gestational carriers live, especially during the late term of their pregnancies. The homes are run by medical professionals or their agents. In total, we conducted nine semi-structured interviews of surrogates in New Delhi and Anand, Gujarat, and each interview lasted approximately one hour. It should be noted that the surrogates we spoke to were referred to us by fertility and surrogacy medical professionals, and some interviews took place in surrogacy homes. Thus, there is likely sample bias. Nor are the interviews representative of all surrogates.

Although in the interviews the surrogates voiced many concerns about their living conditions and legal issues, all the surrogates we interviewed, including surrogates in their second surrogate pregnancy, thought surrogacy should be legal. The surrogates believed that the law should permit them to continue on their chosen path, noting that being a surrogate enabled them to earn money that would both support their families and help others become parents at the same time.

One woman told us, for example: "I want to do it again, not one but even ten times. I do not think there are any issues and I want to get more people to do it. Without money there is no life" (Sharda and Meera). Another surrogate told us: "The thought of giving a child to someone else is incomparable, there is nothing else that makes me so happy. I also wanted to make money for my child's future. . . . I did not consider it to be bad. You get to give someone a child and the government should not ban this. I want there to be children in all houses. . . . [The proposed surrogacy ban] is not good. Some people have so much money but no children. There is nothing better than what we are doing" (Shanta and Kanta). Yet another surrogate we interviewed told us: "Surrogacy should not be banned. The ban will hurt poor people, will take away opportunity from them. Surrogacy is a win-win situation for both the parties. We get blessings and money from them and they get their own child. This is good work. It is preferable to other jobs that would be available to us" (Amita and Sona). One of the surrogates we interviewed noted that although she did not think surrogacy should be banned, she did think the government had a role to play in making sure that the process works (Anonymous).

Our interviews with surrogates clearly demonstrated that surrogates have valuable opinions to add to the debate. Most often, and perhaps expectedly, surrogates are supportive of the practice in general. They cite the economic benefits surrogacy brings to them and their family, but they also value the intangible social contribution of giving a child to a childless family. Moreover, the surrogates we interviewed recognized that government regulation is necessary, to an extent, to give physical and economic safety to the surrogates. Thus, when surrogates are consulted, they uniformly believe that they should have the right to gestational care.

Unlike the Court, the Parliamentary Standing Committee that was asked to review and comment on the 2016 bill, did hear testimony from women who were surrogates. In their report, they rejected the 2016 bill's proposal to ban compensated surrogacy, but stated that it should be permitted for Indians. While no one can be certain about what factors influenced their decision, certainly hearing from the women themselves who were surrogates was important.

In this section, I have shown that the surrogates we spoke to universally felt surrogacy should be legal—they were financially benefiting from it and felt grateful to provide the blessing of a child to other people. In the next section, I argue that the current private contract model that is used to structure surrogacy arrangements results inadequate protection for surrogates.

The Private Contract Model for Surrogacy Leads to Exploitation

The lawyer who brought the Surrogacy PIL and the Supreme Court are concerned that poor Indian women who sell gestational care are exploited. I agree with them that surrogates are exploited to the extent that surrogates do not have adequate rights and protections during the process of surrogacy. The price, obligations, and other terms of the relationship between the surrogate and the intended parents and medical clinic are privately negotiated. However, the private bargaining model places unfair terms and risks upon surrogates.[10]

The medical professionals are from wealthy classes in society; in relation to the surrogates they have both more social power and more knowledge about the medical process. The surrogates are most often women who do not speak English, live in slums, and are squatters ("CSR Report on Conference"). Exploitation is possible when there is such great income, educational, and social inequalities between the bargaining parties (Hill). Intended parents also enter into contracts with surrogates but their relationship, ironically, is more distant from the surrogate than the medical professionals. Another way to analyze the bargaining relationship and contract would be through the lens of duress, unconscionability, consent, or other contract-law doctrines.

Our interviews with surrogates also illustrate some of the problems surrogates face under a private contract model.[11] One surrogate we interviewed told us that she was not sure if she would receive any compensation if the pregnancy had a negative outcome (Sharda and Meera). Her friend, another surrogate, noted that "[surrogates] do not ask such questions" (Sharda and Meera). Another surrogate we interviewed was unsure about the actual amount she was to receive, whether she was receiving any monthly payments, and how she would receive payment (Devi). The women also did not have a say in how they would deliver the babies they were carrying, and they told us that the prevailing method of delivering the babies was through caesarean sections (Sharda and Meera; Shanta and Kanta). Relatedly, one of the women we spoke with had been informed that the commissioning parents would not pay any additional amount to reimburse her for any post-operation expenses, even though she would be unable to return to work to earn an income (Sharda and Meera). Another interview revealed that women were responsible for any postdelivery medical issues and expenses that might arise (Amita and Sona). All this suggests that they do not understand the key terms of their own surrogacy contracts (if they have contracts at all).

Indeed, one of the surrogates we spoke with told us that her contract had been in English, not in Hindi, and that she could not read it, though she signed it after her husband read it (Amita and Sona). The women also noted that the agent physically held all of the contracts and the women did not have their own copies (Sharda and Meera). Indeed, one of the agents we interviewed showed us a contract that stated explicitly that the surrogate would not be allowed to keep a copy of the contract. The surrogates and agents also told us that the contracts signed by the surrogates were not reviewed by anyone providing legal counsel to the surrogates (Sharda and Meera).

Other studies also demonstrate that many surrogates in India are not treated fairly. A survey of one hundred surrogates finds that the majority of surrogates underwent embryo transfer prior to signing a contract and was only promised payment for a successful pregnancy (Center 41, 58–60). The surrogates bear all the financial and health risks associated with the medical procedures (63–66). Surrogates also bear the risk of miscarriages and receive no compensation for the medical procedures they underwent prior to the miscarriage (63). Finally, only about 10 percent of the contracts reviewed by the Center for Social Research discussed compensation at all, and almost none of the contracts addressed whether there would be any provision of medical care after the birth of the child (65).

In many cases the surrogacy process goes as planned—the embryo transfer successfully leads to a pregnancy, surrogates give birth, the surrogates receive their compensation and do not face adverse health consequences. The medical professionals are, in some cases, benevolent. They provide postnatal care even when they are not legally obligated to do so. Some doctors even view their work as a tool to further social justice, and some provide educational classes to surrogates that go beyond what is required by contract. But, even in cases where everything goes as planned, the allocation of risk clearly reveals the failures in the bargaining process.

Instead of allowing the parties to privately bargain all of the terms of the surrogacy arrangements, the government should adopt regulations that require the medical professionals or intended parents to provide certain rights to surrogates. For example, the regulations could specify that a surrogate should be compensated for undergoing the embryo transfer even if she miscarries, that there should be limitations on the number of embryos transferred, and that she should be provided with postnatal care. Along these lines, legal scholar Cyra Akila Choudhury proposes a labor regulatory model for surrogacy in India. She argues that surrogacy should be regulated by the state just as any hazardous profession would be (Choudhury).

Conclusion: Lessons for Public Interest Litigation

One female lawyer's quest to end surrogacy in India, a quest based on various media accounts she had seen that presented surrogacy as exploitative, empowered the Supreme Court to become an active voice in surrogacy policy-making at the executive level. Though we cannot be certain, the actions of the Supreme Court likely had some level of influence in the adoption of the November 2015 policy by the Ministry of Home Affairs denying visas to all foreigners seeking surrogacy as well as the formulation of the prohibitionist approach in the 2016 bill. During the hearings for the Surrogacy PIL, the judge conducting the hearing made it clear that he thought engaging in surrogacy violated the constitutional rights of the surrogates themselves.

The PIL procedure allows people to bring a petition directly to the Supreme Court based on his or her view about an issue. In this case, one lawyer's ideological opposition to surrogacy gave rise to a constitutional challenge to it. There are no procedural requirements that the parties who are impacted be part of the petition, nor is there a requirement that the person bringing the petition consult with the impacted parties.

The filing of the petition gives judges a platform to advance their own personal views about an issue. In the PIL case, the Supreme Court, through numerous hearings, kept pushing the executive to prohibit surrogacy. The PIL procedures do not require the judges to consult with the impacted parties. In the Surrogacy PIL, when surrogates attempted to intervene, their views had no bearing on the position advanced by the Supreme Court.

The Court has made enormous positive change through many PILs. I am not suggesting that PIL should be abolished, but rather the Court should ensure that it gives adequate consideration to all sides of the issues. In particular, the Court should welcome and invite impacted parties to testify when they are considering issuing broad orders that could deny the right to livelihood and work to many women.

Lawyers that bring PILs should also self-regulate. A model of collaborative lawyering calls for lawyers to take the views and needs of the clients seriously in guiding litigation and litigation strategy (Lopez; White). Even if they are not required to consult with the parties whose rights they claim have been violated, lawyers bringing PILs should do so as a matter of good practice. Public interest organizations like Human Rights Law Network that bring numerous PILs typically always include the impacted parties as petitioners.

The Court and others who care about the well-being of women who engage in surrogacy do have cause to be concerned about the practice of surrogacy. The private contract model that prevails in India leads to unfair terms and risk allocation. If the government were to treat surrogates as laborers, then they could provide for minimum fees and other protections through regulation. A strong regulatory body, possibly funded by the medical clinics, could enforce the regulations. If Parliament adopts legislation on surrogacy, it will likely be judicially reviewed by the Court. Regardless of what the Supreme Court's ultimate decision is, the Court should give former and current surrogates their day in court.

~

I want to thank Debra Castillo and Anindita Banerjee, who invited me to be a commentator at the Cornell 2016 symposium, Gujarat/Guatemala: Marketing Care and Speculating Life. That conference inspired my interest in this topic. I am grateful to Maithili Pradhan, Nathalie Greenfield, and Douglas Wagner for editorial and research assistance.

Notes

1. The first Indian child to be born as a result of IVF treatments was born in 1978; by 2005, there were about 250 IVF clinics in India (ICMR Guidelines 4–5). Commercially, surrogacy was legalized in India in 2002 (Shetty 1633). Driven by the fact that India is one of only a handful of nations that has allowed commercial surrogacy, that number ballooned to an estimated three thousand IVF clinics by 2012 (Bhalla and Thapliyal).

2. In some cases, there may be a sperm donor and/or egg donor.

3. Previously, in January 2013, the Ministry of Home Affairs had prohibited foreign gay people and single people from availing themselves of medical and gestational care. However, Indian single individuals and gay couples continue to be able to hire a surrogate (Rajadhyakshal). Gay Bollywood film producer Karan Jorar recently made headlines for having twins from a surrogate ("Parenthood through Surrogacy").

4. The public interest litigation was created through common law. The Judges' Transfer Case of 1981 is the first comprehensive discussion of the relaxed standing and other procedures that relate to PIL cases (*S.P. Gupta v. Union of India*).

5. For an early assessment of Public Interest Litigation, see Upendra Baxi's "Taking Suffering Seriously: Social Action Litigation in the Supreme Court of India."

6. Foreign nationals and homosexual couples are not discussed whatsoever within the ICMR Guidelines. The guidelines clearly contemplate that married couples would be the intending parents, but they explicitly allow a single woman to undergo ART treatment to have a child of her own. Moreover, the guidelines do not address the marital status of the surrogate (ch. 1–3). Thus, India was known to be a viable option for basically anyone; the tightening of regulations in the surrogacy industry since 2012 has led to a smaller surrogacy market in India and an expanding market elsewhere, such as Nepal (Preiss and Shahi).

7. In a recent article, Amrita Pande also suggests that the turn toward banning surrogacy was because of the Supreme Court and several high-profile cases ("Transnational Commercial Surrogacy").

8. The case filed by Wad was eventually combined with another, the *Jan Balaz* case, which involved the nationality of twins born to an Indian surrogate and German intended parents. While the nationality of the twins has since been resolved, the Court still continues to hold jurisdiction in the combined cases, likely so that the Court can continue to prod the executive to push for policy changes (*Jan Balaz*; Ramasubramanian).

9. My Indian colleagues, Professors Chandra and Satish, submitted a memo of the students' preliminary research findings to the Standing Committee in Parliament that is currently reviewing the Surrogacy Bill of 2016, and we are currently working to produce a report synthesizing our desk research and fieldwork with the goal of providing relevant information to the Indian Parliament as it deliberates the bill. Clinical students also interviewed compensated surrogacy stakeholders in the United States and will produce a legislative policy report on the Child-Parent Security Act, a bill legalizing compensated surrogacy, which is in a committee in the New York legislature (Child-Parent Security). The interviews cited here were conducted by students supervised by an instructor, other students took notes at the interview, and all interviewees reviewed and revised the notes after the interview.

10. Professors Chandra, Satish, and I submitted a memo to the Indian Parliamentary Standing Committee that reviewed the 2016 bill, in which we argued that much of the exploitation we see of surrogates today is due to the private contract model (Chandra, Kalantry, and Satish). The committee adopted many of our recommendations (102nd Report).

11. With the exception of one surrogate who had attended college and had a diploma, most of the women we interviewed had low levels of education and were not confident about the exact details of the contracts they had signed. Instead, the women seemed to trust that the agency and doctors would take care of making sure the process went smoothly. Interestingly, the surrogate who had received a college education had already been a surrogate once and was being paid approximately twice the amount that the lesser-educated surrogates were receiving (Kinjal Jignesh Kumar).

Works Cited

Amita and Sona. Personal interview.

Anand, Utkarsh. "Supreme Court Confirms: Alcohol Ban on Highways Will Include Bars and Restaurants." *Indian Express*, 1 Apr. 2017, www.indianexpress.com/article/india/sc-confirms-alcohol-ban-on-highways-will-include-bars-and-restaurants-4594238/. Accessed 2 May 2020.

Anonymous. Personal interview. Gupta Clinic, New Delhi, 5 Apr. 2017.

Article 21. Constitution of India, 1950.

Assisted Reproductive Technology (Regulation) Bill, 2008. Parliament of India, 2008, prsindia.org/uploads/media/vikas_doc/docs/1241500084--DraftARTBill.pdf. Accessed 2 May 2020.

Assisted Reproductive Technology (Regulation) Bill, 2010. Parliament of India, 2010, www.icmr.nic.in/guide/ART%20REGULATION%20Draft%20Bill1.pdf. Accessed 2 May 2018.

Assisted Reproductive Technology (Regulation) Bill, 2014. Parliament of India, 2014, www.prsindia.org/uploads/media/draft/Draft%20Assisted%20Reproductive%20Technology%20(Regulation)%20Bill,%202014.pdf. Accessed 2 May 2020.

Baxi, Upendra. "Taking Suffering Seriously: Social Action Litigation in the Supreme Court of India." *Third World Legal Studies*, vol. 4, 1985, p. 107.

Bhalla, Nita, and Mansi Thapliyal. "Foreigners Are Flocking to India to Rent Wombs and Grow Surrogate Babies." *Business Insider*, 30 Sept. 2013, www.businessinsider.com/india-surrogate-mother-industry-2013-9. Accessed 2 May 2020.

Bhuwania, Anuj. *Courting the People: Public Interest Litigation in Post-Emergency India*. Cambridge UP, 2017.

"Cabinet Approves Bill to Prohibit Commercial Surrogacy, Sushma Swaraj Slams Celebrities for Misusing Practice." *Indian Express*, 25 Aug. 2016, www.indianexpress.com/article/india/india-news-india/surrogacy-bill-2016-sushma-swaraj-slams-celebrities-for-misusing-practice/. Accessed 2 May 2020.

Center for Social Research: Surrogate Motherhood. 2017, www.csrindia.org/surrogate-motherhood. Accessed 2 May 2020.

Chandra, Aparna, Sital Kalantry, and Mrinal Satish. Memorandum on the Surrogacy (Regulation) Bill, 2016, to the Department-Related Standing Committee on Health and Family Welfare. Cornell University Law School, 13 Apr. 2017, kalantry.lawschool.cornell.edu/files/2017/08/CLPG-NLU-Delhi-Cornell-Memorandum-on-Surrogacy-Bill-2016-1s985d1.pdf. Accessed 2 May 2020.

Child-Parent Security Act Bill of 2016. Assembly Bill A4319, New York State Senate, Regular Session, 2016.

Choudhary, Amit Anand. "SC Seeks Commercial Surrogacy Ban." *Times of India*, 15 Oct. 2015, timesofindia.indiatimes.com/india/SC-suggests-ban-on-commercial-surrogacy/articleshow/49365734.cms. Accessed 2 May 2020.

Choudhury, Cyra Akila. "The Political Economy and Legal Regulation of Transnational Commercial Surrogacy." *Vanderbilt Journal of Transnational Law*, vol. 48, no. 1, 2015, pp. 1–59.

Deomampo, Daisy. "Transnational Surrogacy in India: Interrogating Power and Women's Agency." *Frontiers: A Journal of Women's Studies*, vol. 34, no. 3, *Special Issue: Reproductive Technology and Reproductive Justice*, 2013, pp. 167–88.

Deva, Surya. "Public Interest Litigation in India: A Critical Review." *Civic Justice Quarterly*, vol. 1, no. 19, 2009, pp. 19–40.

Devi, Maithili. Personal interview. 5 Apr. 2017.

Dey, Bharati, and Rita Roy. "Strength in Numbers: Sex Worker Collectives in India." *Amnesty International News*, 27 May 2016, www.amnesty.org/en/latest/news/2016/05/rita-roy-and-bharati-dey-sex-worker-testimony-india/. Accessed 2 May 2020.

Dr. Nayana H. Patel. Akanksha Hospital and Research Center, ivf-surrogate.com/DrNayanaPatel. Accessed 2 May 2020.

Durbar: Durbar Mahila Samanwaya Committee. 2017, durbar.org. Accessed 2 May 2020.

"Foreign Nationals (Including Overseas Citizen of India [OCI] Cardholders) Intending to Visit India for Commissioning Surrogacy." Circular No. 462, Ministry of Home Affairs, Government of India, 3 Nov. 2015, https://www.mha.gov.in/PDF_Other/surrogacy03112015.pdf. Accessed 2 May 2020.

"In 'Global Classroom,' Students Study Surrogacy Law and Policy in India and the United States." *Spotlights*, Cornell Law School, 1 May 2017, www.lawschool.cornell.edu/spotlights/In-Global-Classroom-Students-Study-Surrogacy-Law-and-Policy-in-India-and-the-United-States.cfm. Accessed 2 May 2020.

Indian Council of Medical Research National Guidelines for Accreditation, Supervision and Regulation of ART Clinics in India. Indian Council of Medical Research National Academy of Medical Sciences, India, 2005, pp. 4–5, icmr.nic.in/art/art_clinics.htm. Accessed 2 May 2018.

Jan Balaz v. Anand Municipality. Gujarat High Court of India, 11 Nov. 2009.

Kinjal Jignesh Kumar, Akanksha Hospital, Anand, Gujarat. Personal interview. 3 Apr. 2017.

Kusum, Sonali. *Public Interest Litigation PIL Challenging Commercial, Overseas, Same Sex, Single Surrogacy in India—Contemporary Legal Judicial Developments*. National Law School of India, Bangalore, www.familiesthrusurrogacy.com/wp-content/uploads/2016/05/Indian-Surrogacy-Bill-Background-latest-developments.pdf. Accessed 2 May 2020.

Lopez, Gerald P. *Rebellious Lawyering: One Chicano's Vision of Progressive Law Practice*. Westview Press, 1992.

Mahapatral, Dhananjay. "SC Notice to Govt on PIL Seeking Ban on Commercial Surrogacy." *Times of India*, 26 Feb. 2015, timesofindia.indiatimes.com/india/SC-notice-to-govt-on-PIL-seeking-ban-on-commercial-surrogacy/articleshow/46376012.cms. Accessed 2 May 2020.

Mishra, Prabhati Nayak. "Surrogate Mothers Seek Supreme Court's Intervention." *Daily News and Analysis*, 26 Nov. 2015, www.dnaindia.com/india/report-surrogate-mothers-seek-supreme-court-s-intervention-2149015.

Nadimpally, Sarojini, et al. *Commercial Surrogacy: A Contested Terrain in the Realm of Rights and Justice*. Asian-Pacific Resource and Research Centre for Women (Arrow) Thematic Papers, 2016.

"One Lakh Fresh Auto Permits Get Approval from Supreme Court." *Indian Express*, 12 Nov. 2011, archive.indianexpress.com/news/one-lakh-fresh-auto-permits-get-approval-from-supreme-court/874719/. Accessed 2 May 2020.

Pande, Amrita. "'At Least I Am Not Sleeping with Anyone': Resisting the Stigma of Commercial Surrogacy in India." *Feminist Studies*, vol. 36, no. 2, 2010, pp. 292–312, claradoc.gpa.free.fr/doc/420.pdf. Accessed 2 May 2020.

———. "Commercial Surrogacy in India: Manufacturing a Perfect Mother-Worker." *Signs*, vol. 35, no. 4, Summer 2010, pp. 969–92.

———. "Transnational Commercial Surrogacy in India: To Ban or Not to Ban." *Babies for Sale? Transnational Surrogacy, Human Rights and the Politics of Reproduction*, edited by Miranda Davies, U of Chicago P, 2017, pp. 328–43.

Pandey, Rajni. "Restriction on Surrogacy May Have Far-Reaching Impact." *India Medical Times*, 20 Oct. 2015, www.indiamedicaltimes.com/2015/10/20/restriction-on-surrogacy-may-have-far-reaching-impact/. Accessed 2 May 2020.

"Parenthood through Surrogacy: Karan Johar Confirms Birth of Twins—Roohi and Yash." *Indian Express*, 6 Mar. 2017, http://indianexpress.com/article/india/parenthood-through-surrogacy-karan-johar-confirms-birth-of-twins-roohi-and-yash-4556163/. Accessed 2 May 2020.

Patel, Tara. "India's Rickshaws Clean Up Their Act." *New Scientist*, 15 Feb. 1997, www.newscientist.com/article/mg15320690-900-indias-rickshaws-clean-up-their-act/. Accessed 2 May 2020.

Perappadan, Bindu Shajan. "Surrogate Mothers Appeal to ICMR, Seek 'Dignity.'" *Hindu*, 6 Nov. 2015, www.thehindu.com/news/national/other-states/surrogate-mothers-appeal-to-icmr-seek-dignity/article7848219.ece. Accessed 2 May 2020.

Personal interview with agent. Surrogacy home, Gurgaon, India, 5 Apr. 2017.

Preiss, Danielle, and Pragati Shahi. "The Dwindling Options for Surrogacy Abroad." *The Atlantic*, 31 May 2016, www.theatlantic.com/health/archive/2016/05/dwindling-options-for-surrogacy-abroad/484688/. Accessed 2 May 2020.

Rajadhyakshal, Madhavi. "No Surrogacy Visa for Gay Foreigners." *Times of India*, 18 Jan. 2013, timesofindia.indiatimes.com/india/No-surrogacy-visa-for-gay-foreigners/articleshow/18066771.cms. Accessed 2 May 2020.

Ramasubramanian, Hari G. "Indian Government Hurriedly Notifies Stopping of Surrogacy for Foreign Nationals." Indian Surrogacy Law Centre, 28 Oct. 2015, blog.indiansurrogacylaw.com/indian-government-hurriedly-notifies-stopping-of-surrogacy-for-foreign-national/. Accessed 2 May 2020.

Sangram: Sampada Gramin Mahila Sanstha. 2009, sangram.org. Accessed 2 May 2020.

Saravanan, Sheela. "Transnational Surrogacy and Objectification of Gestational Mothers," *Economic and Political Weekly*, vol. 45, no. 16, 17 Apr. 2010.

Shankar, Shylashri. *Scaling Justice: India's Supreme Court, Anti-Terror Laws, and Social Rights*, Oxford Scholarship Online, 2009, doi:10.1093/acprof:oso/978019569 3201.001.0001.

Shanta and Kanta. Interview, April 7, 2017 (Anand, Gujarat).

Sharda and Meera. Personal interview, April 7, 2017 (Anand, Gujarat).

Shetty, Priya. "India's Unregulated Surrogacy Industry." *The Lancet*, vol. 380, no. 9854, 10 Nov. 2012, pp. 1633–34, dx.doi.org/10.1016/S0140-6736(12)61933-3.

S.P. Gupta v. Union of India. Supreme Court of India, Case no. AIR 1982 SC 149, 30 Dec. 1981.

"Supreme Court Asks Centre to Bring Commercial Surrogacy within Ambit of Law." *Indian Express*, 15 Oct. 2015, indianexpress.com/article/india/india-news-india/

supreme-court-asks-centre-to-bring-commercial-surrogacy-within-ambit-of-law/. Accessed 2 May 2020.

Surrogacy (Regulation) Bill. No. 257, India, 2016, 164.100.47.4/BillsTexts/LSBill Texts/Asintroduced/257_LS_2016_Eng.pdf. Accessed 2 May 2020.

Surrogacy (Regulation) Bill. No. 156, India, 2019, https://www.prsindia.org/sites/default/files/bill_files/Surrogacy%20%28Regulation%29%20Bill%2C%20 2019.pdf. Accessed 2 May 2020.

Susman, Susan D. "Distant Voices in the Courts of India: Transformation of Standing in Public Interest Litigation." *Wisconsin International Law Journal*, vol. 13, The Regents of the University of Wisconsin, 1994, pp. 57–58.

Union of India and Anr. v. Jan Balaz and Ors. Supreme Court of India, item no. 301, court no. 4, section IX/PILW/X, civil appeal no. 8714/2010, 3 July 2017.

Wad, Jayashree. "Petition of Jayashree Wad to Supreme Court of India." 29 Nov. 2016, on file with author.

White, Lucie E. "Collaborative Lawyering in the Field? On Mapping the Paths from Rhetoric to Practice." *Clinical Law Review*, vol. 1, 1994, pp. 157–71.

Witzleb, Normann, and Anurag Chawla. "Surrogacy in India: Strong Demand, Weak Laws." *Surrogacy, Law and Human Rights*, edited by Paula Gerber and Katie O'Byrne, Routledge, 2015.

102nd Report on the Surrogacy (Regulation) Bill, 2016. Presented to Rajya Sabha, Department-Related Parliamentary Standing Committee on Health and Family Welfare, Parliament of India, 10 Aug. 2017, https://cpb-us-e1.wpmucdn.com/blogs.cornell.edu/dist/2/7529/files/2017/08/Indian-Parliament-Report-102-1qs7ole.pdf. Accessed 2 May 2020.

5

Wet Nurses and Migrant Nanas in Mexico's Imaginary Landscape

Emily C. Vázquez Enríquez

My cruel, divisive temperament: my cross to bear.
We all bear it because of our
shared ancestry of milk and filth.

—Carmen Giménez Smith, from "Trigger Warning"

In Mexico, the presence of wet nurses and *nanas*, women who have performed maternal roles for children to whom they are not related, has been accounted for in a large array of narratives from the colonial period up until today. While the main occupation of wet nurses was to breastfeed the children of Spanish and Creole families, at least since the second half of the twentieth century, nanas have been hired by wealthy and middle-class families to move into their house to do housekeeping work and, especially, to take care of the children. Through historical exposition and cultural analysis of narrative accounts for both figures, I discuss some of the main aspects that situate them as crucial figures in the Mexican cultural and national landscape, although they have not yet been recognized as such. At the same time, I examine how their representations in literature, television, and film underscore the long-standing racial and gender-based inequalities that have shaped the conditions of domestic labor, specifically of care work in the context of Mexico.

Depictions of both wet nurses and nanas in the Mexican imaginary construct have remained largely underexamined. On the one hand, while wet nurses are depicted in several literary works that date from the nineteenth century to the end of the second half of the twentieth, I did not find studies dedicated to the analysis of their presence in literature, although historical analyses were fairly easy to locate. On the other hand, nanas, who have been often portrayed in popular culture, lack in both cultural analysis and historical accounts.

The wet nurse's participation in the sociocultural life of Mexico can be traced back from the colonial era to the first decades of the twentieth century. Because they were either indigenous or black women breastfeeding upper-class children, their breast milk became of public interest and gave rise to racial discourses based on the maternal fluid. Usual discourses surrounding breast milk revolved around the idea of its capacity to infiltrate in the upper classes through the bodies of their offspring. Advocates of the anti–wet nursing rhetoric saw such an infiltration as a process by which women of color could contaminate both the body and behavior of the infants. Because of this, during centuries of the habitual use of wet nurses in Mexico, there prevailed an anti–wet nursing discourse centered on prejudices against the female body. It was not until the beginning of the twentieth century that contestatory narratives challenged the long-standing rhetoric.

With the arrival of the bottle-feeding practice, the biological function of wet nurses started to fade away. However, their affective and nurturing role was prolonged by the figure of the nana. If narratives surrounding wet nurses' labor lingered on the argument of the quality of their milk and its alleged capacity to transmit good or bad character, those revolving around the nanas' figure have not engaged in debates of such a vein: apart from a few exceptions, almost every nana depicted in the Mexican imaginary landscape is a synonym of selflessness. Because they enact maternal roles, the notion of motherhood interweaves with discourses addressing them. As I contend, nanas are often constructed as the embodiment of the "perfect mother." This representation revolves around racial and gender-based complexities that expose the unequal relations and affective crises they endure.

In what follows, I trace the ways by which the wet-nursing practice was introduced in New Spain—particularly in the conquered territory of what today is known as Mexico—as well as the main challenges faced by the women who had to assume that role. After this, taking as examples the painting *My Nurse and I* (1937) by Frida Kahlo and the dramatic poem *Salomé* (1959) by Rosario Castellanos, I study the significance of wet nurses for the social reproduction of Mexico. In addition, I examine the portrayal of the affective crises surrounding this form of labor. Finally, considering telenovelas from the second half of the twentieth century and films such as *Under the Same Moon* (2007) by Patricia Riggen and *Babel* (2006) by Alejandro González Iñárritu, I analyze the representation of nanas in television and film. This last section underscores the conflicts associated with the idealization of these maternal figures and examines the depiction of the challenges faced by migrant domestic workers in Mexico and the United States.

Mapping the Wet Nursing Practice from Spain to Mexico

The cultural significance of wet nurses can be traced back to medieval Christian narratives from Spain, where depictions of the Virgin Mary present her as a surrogate mother who uses her milk to save devotees in need.[1] By the beginning of the thirteenth century, in the *Cantigas de Santa Maria*, Alfonso X describes cases in which, with her milk, the Virgin saves the lives and souls of converted sinners. Christian imagery has often portrayed the curative power conferred to the Virgin's maternal milk. For instance, the painting *San Bernardo y la Virgen* (1645–1652) by Alonso Cano depicts the medieval legend that narrates Bernardo's mystic encounter with the Virgin. According to one version of this legend, the Virgin feeds him her milk to transfer sacred wisdom, and to generate a filial bond.

The belief in the far-reaching power of maternal milk was not restricted to the realm of religious accounts. Wet nursing was a popular labor in the medieval European domestic setting. Women from the lower classes used to be wet nurses for wealthy families. This custom was so common that, in *Las Siete Partidas*, Alfonso X enlisted a series of characteristics that wet nurses had to comply with when caring for the offspring of kings. Because maternal milk was perceived to be able to transmit the characteristics of the women producing it, according to Alfonso X, they needed to be healthy, beautiful, and well behaved (45). These views were propagated to the colonized Mexican territory of the sixteenth century.

Because wet nursing, as a form of labor, was introduced by the Spaniards, the milk of the non-Christian natives of the zone was highly problematized. A diverse display of discourses framed the milk of indigenous women as capable of transmitting negative characteristics to the child. However, even though during this period many indigenous women had to act as wet nurses, this was not a usual practice in the indigenous societies, where wet nurses were called upon only when the mother was sick or dead.[2] Nonetheless, following the conquest, "the use of indigenous and enslaved women to nurse creole children was widespread" (Earle 50). Working either as cheap labor or slaves, indigenous women from Mexico, and black women brought either from Spain or Africa, were the main breastfeeding groups in the colonized Mexican territory.

Not long after the conquest of America, Fray Luis de León wrote *La perfecta casada* (1583), in which the author enlists a series of guidelines that women had to follow to become perfect spouses. In addition to focusing on the relationship between wife and husband, the book also underscores the importance of the connection between mother and child. For instance, chapter 18 focuses on the importance of the biological mother breastfeeding her children. Claiming that "milk equals blood," de León maintains that the use of wet nurses could break the genetic bond between mothers and children. Furthermore, the author asserts that by resorting to wet nurses, mothers were putting their children in danger of acquiring the vices and immoralities of the women who were nurturing them.

To the belief that indigenous women were able to transmit depravities through their breast milk, during the seventeenth century was added the belief that, since the diet of the indigenous population was different from the Spaniards' diet, "too close a familiarity with new-world foodstuff, whether indigenous breast milk or cassava, was dangerously transformative for the European body" (Earle 52). Moreover, in the late eighteenth century, Charles IV delivers a ruling advising against having women from other races breastfeeding infants due to the possibility that the children would lose their Iberian heritage (Premo 240). This perception was not only due to questions of class and race, religion also played out an essential role. Whereas the Virgin's breast milk was supposed to have the power to transfer sacred virtues, the milk of women lacking a Christian heritage was thought to have the power to separate infants from the Catholic Spanish state.

Despite official warnings against wet nurses, for centuries they were allowed in the houses of creole families. According to Stephen Webre, the most common reason privileged women wanted the service of wet nurses was "to escape the incommodity of raising their own children" (2). For Kathryn Sloan, another reason consisted in the fact that, "if a mother nursed, it likely acted as a form of contraception, since nursing could delay the recommencement of ovulation" (24); by not breastfeeding, wealthy women could become pregnant more often.

For a woman to work as a wet nurse, first she had to become a mother. In the iconography of the Virgin nursing, Mary is regularly portrayed holding her biological son while feeding someone else's. However, the acknowledgment of the biological children of wet nurses cannot be found in the anti–wet nursing rhetoric. Webre asserts that very often wet nurses had to resort to other women to breastfeed their children. Yet, even if they were able to find another lactating woman, she would have to feed her own child too, and sometimes the milk was not enough. Often, the wet nurse's baby would end up dying.[3]

While some women willingly worked as wet nurses and received a small salary for their labor, many of them did it without any kind of compensation. By the middle of the eighteenth century, in some orphanages controlled by the state, such as the *Casa de Expósitos* in Mexico City, wet nurses were often told that "como mujeres no deb[ían] esperar ningún tipo de retribución por este 'trabajo de amor,' el cuidado de la ciudad y sus habitantes" (Herrera Feria 259). Given these arguments, wet nurses were frequently forced to nurse orphans without compensation. Meanwhile, those who did receive a small salary for their service could nurture up to three children and "se les demandaba que tuvieran buena leche y mejores costumbres, y que se abstuvieran de tener relaciones sexuales con sus esposos" (Carrillo 248). Because of this, wet nurses were commonly put under surveillance, either in the houses of rich families or in orphanages, and deprived of their freedom.[4] In addition, their bodies were also scrutinized. If during the early colonial period and until the first half of the eighteenth century the physical scrutiny was limited to observing the health, color, and weight of the wet nurse, by the late eighteenth and early nineteenth centuries, with the arrival of pediatrics, doctors implemented harsh physical exams. According to Carrillo, by sight and touch, the male inspectors used to examine the breasts and urogenital organs of the lactating women. Some of the qualities the examiners used to look for were "que fueran robustas [. . .] de entre 18 y 30 años de edad [. . .] que tuvieran el pezón bien formado, la areola bien coloreada, y mamas voluminosas" (251). Furthermore, doctors tended to taste the milk to make sure that it was "suficientemente dulce" (253). Despite these conditions, factors such as poverty and slavery forced women to engage in this form of labor.

Similar to what happened in preconquest societies, where the practice of wet nursing other people's children was rare, in many African cultures women tended to do so only when the biological mother was incapacitated (Velázquez 185). Nonetheless, during the colonial era in Mexico, African women were also immersed in this practice. *Diario de México* (1806) collects the testimony of a Spanish woman, Señora Amar y Borbón, who affirms that black women's milk could protect children from rare, life-threatening diseases (473). In addition, there was also the belief in their heavy inclination to sorcery and sexuality, by reason of which, either slave or free, as Velázquez contends, they were constantly accused of crimes they never committed (215).

If the African population in colonial Mexico was at its highest numbers by the end of the seventeenth century, during the beginning of the eighteenth the populace suffered a dramatic decrease. Beatriz Palomo attributes this loss to three causes. First, the government feared that protests against slavery could incite indigenous rebellions (197), so they opted to cut population growth by prohibiting further importation of African slaves. Second, the constant emergence of smallpox outbreaks was deadly to the African-descended population. Finally, rewarding exogamy, the government offered black women the opportunity to gain their freedom by having children with Spaniards (198). Because by the end of the eighteenth century the preference was "comprar esclavos cada vez más blancos [lo que] se manifestaba también en el precio" (199), the number of black wet nurses in Mexico started to decline, and by the beginning of the nineteenth this figure was almost completely gone. Over time, the rejection to recognize the participation of people from African descent in the development of Mexico overshadowed their legacy. The presence of the black wet nurse has been practically disregarded in the Mexican imaginary landscape.

Additionally, neither has the relevance of the indigenous wet nurse in Mexico been fully recognized. Unlike their male counterparts, indigenous women have been eradicated from the traditional historiography and their participation as agents for the cultural, economic, and social expansion of Mexico has been continuously overlooked. However, diverse fictional works have challenged this omission.

Wet Nurses in Literature and Art

Literature's deliberation surrounding the figure of the wet nurse has been the source of diverse debates and representations. *El periquillo Sarniento* (1816), written by Mexican author José Joaquín Fernández de Lizardi and considered the first Latin American novel, offers a negative representation of indigenous wet nurses, blaming their milk for the impertinence of the child they nurtured. Other literary accounts, such as Justo Sierra O'Reilly's *Un año en el hospital de San Lázaro* (1849), also reinforce the anti–wet nurse rhetoric. In O'Reilly's text, at the beginning, wet nurses are seen as capable of saving the life of a baby who had been poisoned through the milk of his sick mother. However, shortly after the appearance of a strange wet nurse, both the baby and the mother die. On the contrary, in Manuel Payno's *Los bandidos del Río Frío* (1892–1893), indigenous wet nurses are seen as the reason by which one of the characters survives and grows strong even after having been taken away from his mother.

In *Pedro Páramo* (1955), Juan Rulfo portrays two wet nurses: Justina Díaz and Damiana Cisneros; each character problematizes how women who perform as mothers are treated as servants by the same individuals they breastfed and raised. In *Como agua para chocolate* (1989), Laura Esquivel exposes a society that sees wet nurses as mere commodities, devices children often use to satisfy their hunger. In the painting *My Nurse and I* (1937), Frida Kahlo also recuperates the figure of the wet nurse while addressing the affective predicament that arises in the person that was nurtured by her. Conversely, Rosario Castellanos's dramatic poem *Salomé* (1959) focuses on the social and cultural displacement undergone by wet nurses. Because Castellanos's and Kahlo's works encompass some of the most complex characteristics regarding the relationship between wet nurses and children, I discuss them further.

In the painting *My Nurse and I*, Frida Kahlo portrays herself as a baby in the arms of her wet nurse. At a first glance, the resemblance to the Christian iconography of Mary breastfeeding is evident. Just as the Virgin was a surrogate for her devotees, the wet nurse is a surrogate for Frida. In this way, two absences are notorious, on the one hand, Frida's mother, on the other, the wet nurse's child. These absences produce a complex social dynamic between woman and child. One of the most prominent elements that produce an affective disjuncture between them is the mask worn by the woman. Through the erasure of her face, the wet nurse is deprived of individuality and portrayed only through the features of her race and the biologic functions of her body. This depiction underscores the commodification of wet nurses and their removal from domestic and national memories.

Whereas, as Kathryn Sloan states, "affective bonds formed between wet nurse and charge, and some surrogates were mothers who had lost their own babies" (7), and as Margo Glantz asserts, wet nurses were "truly maternal," *My Nurse and I* presents a nuanced version of this connection. In the painting, the woman carries the infant but does not embrace her.

Since the mask covers her eyes, she cannot look at the child who is receiving her milk. An infant Frida with an adult face also seems to be distanced from the woman who is nourishing her. Both characters maintain a passive attitude: while the milk is so abundant that it falls out of the female body, all the infant needs to do is to keep her mouth slightly open. Woman and child are portrayed as unengaged participants in an imbalanced circuit of nourishment.

However, although tarnished by an image that evokes a transaction, the painting is far from excluding deep connections; it only complicates them. The wet nurse's face might be hidden, but she instinctively protects her from the rain and feeds her. The adult face of the artist in an infant's corporeality speaks to the continuum bonding that not only through racial heritage but also through biological nourishment exists between her and her nurse. By incorporating an adult face into an infant body, the painting references how the care received during babyhood continues to enrich the psyche and body of the artist. Hence, this amalgamation turns into a recognition of the foundational character of the indigenous wet nurse, and while in the painting this recognition starts in the individual sphere, it goes far beyond it.

Decades before the painting was created, in the 1900–1904 governance report, the president of Mexico, Porfirio Díaz, mentions that wet nurses were trusted with the upbringing of the majority of children in the countryside (57); yet, their cultural and political importance remains largely overlooked. Through the depiction of a woman with a foundational significance, the artist challenges this omission.

In *Salomé*, one of the less-studied works of Rosario Castellanos, the author focuses on three characters: Salomé, Madre, and Nodriza (wet nurse). At the beginning of the poem, Salomé and Madre talk about an indigenous uprising happening in their city, San Cristóbal. The leader of the *chamula* movement was recently captured and sent to jail. Far from engaging in a conversation regarding the social convolution, the dialogue between mother and daughter takes a turn and the former starts to discuss the terrible shape of her relationship with her husband, who despises her. The thought of this rejection makes her evoke the distant figure of her mother, who according to her, "en vez de leche [le] dio el sometimiento." Such a declaration hints at the presence of the wet nurse in the plot while also showing one fundamental element involving the wet nurses' labor. As in *My Nurse and I*, the emotional gap left by the biological mother and never fully fulfilled by the *nodriza* is also addressed. However, whereas in Frida's painting the focus is more directed toward the affective complications for the child, *Salomé* grants farther attention to those of the wet nurse.

The first time Nodriza appears in the poem is through a description: “Entra la nodriza. Es india.” The first feature the reader learns about the new character is her race. Following this introduction, Nodriza joins the conversation of Salomé and her mother, and worriedly talks about the uprising. Looking at her with disdain, Madre responds: “es tu raza, nodriza.” Yet, Nodriza replies: “niña, olvidé su lengua, no aprendí sus costumbres y nunca usé su ropa. No digas que es mi raza. No tengo más familia que esta casa.” This declaration emphasizes the dilemma of the wet nurse, whose sense of belonging is destabilized. At the same time, it recalls Rosario de Swanson’s assertion regarding how “la mujer indígena no solamente careció de derechos sobre su cuerpo, sino también sobre el usufructo de su labor reproductiva, dado que no tuvo hijos pero amamantó hijos ajenos” (442). Even though Nodriza nurtured and cared for both Madre and Salomé, her race and social role prevent her from being considered a member of the family circle.

The tension regarding Nodriza’s identity intensifies when, after she communicates to Salomé and her mother the news about the escape of the indigenous leader, she declares that since the chamulas will see her as a traitor, she will probably be killed, dying “una muerte ajena, puesto que amamanté hijos que no eran míos y me crié en el patio de las huérfanas.” Having lacked kinship and racial bonds, Nodriza fears that she will die in the state of dispossession in which she has always lived. Disregarding the fear of Nodriza, Madre tells her: “basta de fantasear,” and proceeds to admonish her for having failed at her job. The anger of Madre comes from an earlier conversation she had with Salomé, where the latter talked about her desire to fall in love. Following some of the main arguments of the anti–wet nursing rhetoric, Madre blames Nodriza for the bad behavior of her daughter: “te entregué [. . .] este copo de lana para que de él hilaras un dechado perfecto. ¿Y qué me das? Potranca de porfiada cerviz y de ijares inquietos.” This reproach underscores the centrality of Nodriza in the domestic setting, where she is deemed responsible for the character of the daughter. Within this frame, Salomé’s desire produces two effects, it exposes the importance of the wet nurse in the family life, and it creates a scenario that pushes Nodriza to face an indigenous leader.

Against the wishes of her mother, Salomé finds the opportunity to fulfill her desires when the fugitive, called Hombre, breaks into her house: “Señor, ¿cómo acertaste llegar hasta aquí? Te ha guiado mi anhelo.”

Confused by the reaction of Salomé, who instead of fearing him wants to help him, Hombre lashes out at Nodriza, accusing her of pandering the conduct of the young woman. When she explains how Salomé "fue criada en [sus] pechos y no ha conocido más que la esperanza," Hombre lashes out at her again, this time implying that she is a traitor of her race. Nodriza kneels and tells him: "señor, no me castigues. Yo no menosprecié a los de mi raza. Pero entre ellos y entre todos soy la despreciada." Changing his tone, Hombre assures her that he will not cause her any harm, and that all he is looking for is mercy. This brief exchange resolves the tension between both characters, who seem to finally understand and accept each other.

Nonetheless, when Madre finds Hombre, she delivers him to the authorities who kill him. For Rosario de Swanson, "es possible leer el deseo de Salomé como metáfora del deseo de integración de la cultura indígena a la cultura nacional" (441). In this way, when Madre turns him in, she exposes the rejection of this cultural integration. The death of Hombre also destroys the already fragmented relationship between Salomé and Madre. At the end of the dramatic poem, Nodriza takes the grieving young woman into her arms and comforts her with a song, once again embracing her maternal role.

Whereas *My Nurse and I* depicts the complex relationship between an anonymous wet nurse and the person she nurtured, thus underscoring the problematic and long-standing bond between them, *Salomé* speaks to the social and internal conflicts faced by women who not only nurtured other people's children, but who did so in a context of racial and gender-based disparity. Both narratives expose the significance of wet nurses in the emerging Mexican society while also revealing some of the deepest emotional and psychological complexities of their labor.

Nanas in Popular Culture

Ana Carrillo maintains that a few years after the Mexican Revolution, wet nurses disappeared, although "hoy sigue existiendo la leche materna en botella e incluso algunas mujeres lactantes llegan a amamantar niños ajenos [aunque no] como mercancía sino [como] un raro regalo" (258). Moreover, by the second half of the twentieth century, their role as caregivers was assumed by nanas, who also performed as maternal figures in the sociocultural Mexican life. Just as happened with wet nurses, nanas became a very popular figure in Mexico's landscape. The centrality of nanas for the social reproduction of Mexico has been directly and indirectly acknowledged by the film and television industry.

Several expressions of Mexican popular culture have worked as a vehicle to propagate models of behavior. For instance, *Mujer, casos de la vida real*, a highly successful television program that was broadcasted for twenty-two years, from 1986 to 2007, used to be a channel to transmit traditional values targeting women. The format of the show was somewhat simple. Silvia Pinal, the host, would present one or two stories based on letters that, presumably, had been sent by female viewers. The episodes were supposed to be the dramatization of real-life stories sent by women sharing their experiences so the audience could learn from them.

Swinging between the two extremes of the selfless and the selfish, mothers lay at the core of most stories. In one episode, against the wishes of her husband, a mom decides to put her baby in day care because she wants to keep her job. Due to the negligence of the caretakers, the child dies. The transgression of traditional values usually comes with tragic consequences. On the contrary, selfless women tend to be rewarded. In 2003, to commemorate Mother's Day, *Mujer* aired the episode "Amor incondicional," in which the devotion to the child leads to a happy ending after many adversities. While this dichotomy is fairly familiar and has been broadly explored, this episode presents a female figure that for decades has haunted the Mexican popular imaginary. In "Amor incondicional" the devoted woman is not the mother of the child, but the nana.

The fact that a television anthology series that lasted over two decades dedicated one of the most celebrated Mexican holidays to a figure as seemingly marginal as the nana speaks to the centrality of this presence in popular culture. Furthermore, this centrality runs parallel to the persistence of such a figure in telenovelas, which are recognized as cultural products of huge national impact and international circulation (Orozco Gómez 12). The inclusion of nanas in telenovelas goes back to at least the beginning of the 1960s, with productions such as *El enemigo* (1961). In fact, by the second half of the twentieth century, in Mexican telenovelas the young, white-skinned, and wealthy protagonists were commonly accompanied by the maternal figure of their nanas. Usually child-free, single, and Catholics, these women had the sole purpose of comforting the beloved children under their care. With no exception, nanas lived in the houses of the rich families that hired them, appearing mostly in religious and domestic settings. While the mothers of the protagonists tended to be either dead, busy, or gone, the nanas were the loving figures that raised and looked after the youth.

In the telenovela *Marimar* (1994), when the protagonist (Thalía) has her first child, the black nana Corazón (Julia Marichal) is the one who takes care of and feeds the newborn, acting as his main nurturing figure.

While Corazón is an Afro-Mexican nana, apart from a few exceptions, most telenovela nanas tend to be portrayed as indigenous women. However, whereas their race can vary, a steady characteristic is their religion. Nanas are usually depicted as devoted Catholics. Examples of this can be found in the characterization of nanas such as Candelaria (Alicia Montoya) from *Retrato de familia* (1995) and Jovita (Aurora Molina) from *Cadenas de amargura* (1991), who are constantly seen attending church and praying. An exception to such representations is Nana Ramona (Yolanda Mérida) from *Los ricos también lloran* (1979), who practices sorcery for the benefit of Esther (Rocío Banquells), the woman she has always taken care of. However, Ramona turns out to be the biological mother of Esther, and thus the pure nature often attributed to nanas in television is not corrupted.

While in telenovelas, most biological mothers tend to be portrayed as women committed to their children, when nanas are involved in the family life, that depiction changes and mothers are instead pictured as selfish, greedy, shallow, and sometimes as evil beings. However, this destabilization in the portrayal of mothers is not a direct effect of the nanas' presence, but a consequence of the mothers' lifestyle. Nanas are present in the domestic setting because they are commodities that wealthy mothers can afford. In this way, according to telenovelas' narratives, money and free time corrupt and degrade them, while the poverty and full abnegation of nanas turn them into the embodiment of flawless caring figures. In telenovelas, women who resort to nanas are deemed faulty and often meet a tragic ending, which can range from suffering a violent death to being despised by their children. On the contrary, nanas operate as models of motherhood.

Indigenous heritage, Catholicism, and selflesness are the characteristics that tend to prevail in the nanas' imaginary portrayal in television. In addition, they are often depicted as poor or humble, never attracted to anything outside the domestic setting, and always focused on their affective role. Thus, telenovelas tend to offer a simplified version of women that assume maternal roles as their only mode of livelihood. Ignoring the psychological complexities created by an intense affective relationship entangled with a form of labor, through the depiction of nanas, telenovelas present an idealized version of Mexican women. This version portrays maternal figures who are completely devoted to the children under their care, who have strong bonds with God, and who have no sexual or material desires. These characteristics resonate with the Lady of Guadalupe, who is the most important Catholic symbol in Mexico. Given the parallelisms between both figures, nanas can be considered the secular version of *La Guadalupana*.[5]

While the majority of discourses addressing wet nurses tended to disparage them, the process of transculturation and *mestizaje* that allowed for the emergence and national embracement of the Lady of Guadalupe can also explain the acceptance and constant articulation of nanas in the Mexican broadcast networks. In an interview, Emilio Azcárraga Milmo, the billionaire who turned Televisa into a multimedia empire not just in Mexico but in the Spanish-speaking world at large, declared that Mexico can be easily described with only two words: "Guadalupano y Futbolero" (Zapata 366). In this way, through the portrayal of women that have striking similarities with the articulation of the Lady of Guadalupe, television content exploits and profits from the national attachment to this figure, at the same time propagating "value-laden message[s]" (Quiñones 57) focused on modeling women's behavior. In addition, since the nanas portrayed in television are the fictional remnants of wet nurses, because they tend to be portrayed either as indigenous or light-skinned women, these articulations further contribute to the erasure of the legacy, participation, and significance of black wet nurses.

Nanas have also been a recurrent character in Mexican film. For instance, in *Veneno para las hadas* (1984), Carlos Enrique Taboada introduces Verónica (Ana Patricia Rojo), an orphan girl who is under the care of her elderly grandmother and her nana. Verónica inherits the fairy tale books from her deceased mother, however, she is more interested in learning about witches. When she asks her nana about them, the woman talks about witches as if they were real, an incident that produces the death of the child. In *Nosotros los Nobles* (2013), Gary Alazraki's portrays Margarita (Mary Paz Mata), the nana of the wealthy Noble siblings. When they encounter legal problems and are forced to go into hiding, Margarita wants to join them because she sees them as her own. However, they remind her that she is not part of the family and do not let her go with them. In Luis Estrada's political satire *La dictadura perfecta* (2014), when the young nana of two upper-class girls gets distracted by her boyfriend, they get kidnapped.

In the critically acclaimed film *Roma* (2018) by Alfonso Cuarón, the protagonist is Cleo (Yalitza Aparicio), an indigenous woman who is one of two domestic workers living with a wealthy family in Mexico City. In numerous interviews, Cuarón has stated that Cleo is inspired by Libo, the woman who was his nana when he was growing up. One of the most memorable scenes of the film takes place when the family goes to the beach. There, two of the children are dragged by the turbulent currents of the ocean. Cleo, who does not know how to swim, defies the dangerous waters and rescues the kids. Once they are safe, the family embraces Cleo and tells her how much they love her. However, when they are back home, they continue treating her as a mere servant. Whereas some of Cleo's actions conform with the model of the devoted nana, her depiction is much more complex. For example, she has an active sex life, is worried about her appearance, and when she gets pregnant, she does not want to have the child. Through the aforementioned examples, it is possible to attest how Mexican film offers multifaceted, nuanced, and even contradictory characterizations of nanas.

Besides the nature of their labor, a similarity between the nanas portrayed in telenovelas and the ones depicted in film is that both tend to be natives of the countryside living in the city. Because of this, nanas are also migrants, which is why they are commonly portrayed living with the people who hired them. This characteristic, particularly popular in telenovelas from the second half of the twentieth century, reflects the massive migrations from the countryside to the cities between 1950 and 1970. As Hubert Carton de Garammont maintains, these migrations were caused by several factors, one of the most significant of which was "la crisis de la rentabilidad de la economía campesina que se inicia en 1957 con el control del precio del maíz." Men and women tried to escape poverty by abandoning their communities to look for job opportunities in urban areas. This phenomenon led women to follow different paths, from those who worked as seamstress in Mexico City in the 1950s, as shown in Cristina Pacheco's autobiographical narrative, "La voz de la tierra" (2005), to those who left their communities to join the maquiladora industry workforce in the 1990s, as Sergio González Rodríguez depicts in *Huesos en el desierto* (2006), and those who became nanas.

Although the aforementioned examples focus on internal migration of nanas, they also participate in transnational processes, which in the context of Mexico revolve around both its southern and northern borders. Coming from Central America to Mexico, sometimes on their way to the United States, women often seek work as domestic laborers for upper- and middle-class Mexican families. For example, in the 2016 report on the different types of work that women from Central America undertake, El Colegio de México found that just in Tapachula, which is the busiest border city in southern Mexico, "alrededor del 90% de las trabajadoras del servicio doméstico eran de Guatemala" (Güezmes et al. 14). According to the report, most of them are minors, and more than half have reported abuses. In *La fila india* (2013) Antonio Ortuño tells the story of a Guatemalan woman who, after crossing the border, starts knocking on doors, offering to do any housekeeping job. An eccentric man hires her, only to end up enslaving her. While Ortuño's character does not become a nana, the scenario faced by the protagonist speaks to the precarious working conditions that nanas and other domestic workers endure in the context of nonregulated transnational labor markets.

Working as much as eighty hours a week for extremely low salaries, Central American women working in domestic spaces in Mexico are often trapped in what human rights centers such as Fray Matías de Córdova in southern Chiapas have called a modern form of slavery. These conditions extend to the United States, where in many cases immigrant women, often mothers, work taking care of other people's children, many times spending years without seeing their own and "facing wage theft, abuse, and exploitation" (Holder). Notwithstanding this precariousness, domestic workers are central for the economic and social development of the families who hire them. Regarding this centrality, Bryan Caplan contends that, in many cases, American moms are able to pursue their careers and succeed because they hire Mexican women to care for their kids (39). While cultural representations of Central American nanas working in Mexico are scarce or nonexistent, Mexican cinema has accounted for the figure of the migrant nana working in the United States.

In the film *Under the Same Moon* (2007) by Patricia Riggen, Rosario (Kate del Castillo) is an undocumented domestic worker living in the United States. She works for two white American families, as a housekeeper for one, and as a babysitter for the other. Echoing the lack of labor protections for unauthorized workers, Rosario gets fired from her first job without any justification. When she asks to be paid for the days that she had worked that week, knowing that she is undocumented, her boss dares her to call the police. Although she is a babysitter for the second family, and not a nana, one of the scenes underscores the intricacies of this domestic labor. While she is taking care of someone else's kid, back in Mexico her son is under the care of his grandmother. She takes care of a boy that is not hers to make money and be able to sustain her own kid, who in turn is under the care of another person. This circuit is comparable to when wet nurses had to find other women to breastfeed and look after their children, and thus it emphasizes the racialized and gendered historic inequalities related to domestic labor.

Whereas *Under the Same Moon* addresses the economic and legal disparities faced by migrant women, the film *Babel* (2006), by Alejandro González Iñárritu pays a great deal of attention to the affective complexities linked to reproductive forms of labor. This is possible because while Rosario is a babysitter, Amelia (Adriana Barraza), one of the protagonists of *Babel*, works as a nana for an American family. Because of this, her emotional ties to the children who are under her care are more evident. Amelia's story starts when both parents go on a trip, leaving her as the sole responsible figure for the siblings. Because the mother of the children gets injured, the parents stay abroad longer than expected. Their absence coincides with the wedding day of one of Amelia's sons. Going against the wishes of the father, who tells her she cannot go because she has to stay with the children, Amelia asks a friend to look after them while she is gone. However, her friend does not make it on time and, to avoid missing her son's wedding, Amelia takes the siblings from San Diego to Tijuana.

On their way back from the wedding, Amelia accepts a ride from Santiago, her nephew (Gael García Bernal). When they are about to cross to the United States, a border patrol officer sees the children and asks for their passports and the parents' permit. Santiago confronts the officer, gets nervous, and decides to flee. During the persecution, he stops and asks Amelia to take the children and get out of the car, leaving them stranded in the desert. Once they are found, Amelia is detained and questioned. Trying to explain her actions, she declares: "I raised these kids since they were born. I take care of them day and night. I feed them breakfast, and lunch, and dinner. I play with them. [They are] like my own children." Her interlocutor, an unconcerned border patrol officer who is about to deport her, responds: "but they are not your children, ma'am." This dialogue illustrates the incompatibility of Amelia's love for the children with the fact that she is a houseworker, a disposable figure according to the logic of the current global economy that exploits the reproductive labor of migrant women.

As their nana, Amelia provides caretaking services for two children with whom she has created so strong a bond that she has come to see them as her own. However, her migratory status and the nature of her labor, which is commonly seen as "unskilled," make her expendable. Although she has a visa, she does not have a permit to work in the United States. Because of this, after her detention she is immediately deported. The last time Amelia appears in the film is right after she exits US territory. Completely heartbroken, Amelia cannot stop crying while her son holds her in his arms. Regarding Amelia's conflict, Laura Podalski points out that "*Babel* depicts Amelia as a loving caretaker who does not carelessly disregard her charges' well-being and characterizes the motivation behind her decision as a rather understandable desire to attend her own son's wedding (i.e., by her sacred duties as mother)" (141). This representation resonates with the nanas' religious background found in television.

In Amelia's scenes, it is common to see her surrounded by Catholic objects. In her room she has a rosary and at least one crucifix. In a close-up of the contents of her purse, it is possible to see a stamp of Jesus and another rosary. Amelia is depicted as a fervent Catholic and a devoted mother and caretaker. Her devotion to the American children makes her choose to take them with her, rather than abandoning them with a stranger, as was suggested by Santiago. As Podalski indicates, Amelia's story incites us to feel compassion for her: "although Mike and his sister Debbie are situated as the ultimate innocents in the scenes set in the US/Mexico borderlands, *Babel* also insists upon the disproportionate nature of Amelia's suffering" (138). When she asks the officer about the children, he tells her that that information is none of her business. Amelia is forced to leave the United States not knowing if the kids she raised were going to get better and with the certainty that she was not going to see them again.

Precarious Labor: Wet Nurses and Nanas

Grounded on racial and gender prejudices, the majority of discourses addressing wet nurses in the colonial era tended to vilify them, and the magnitude and complexity of their role did not begin to be recognized until the beginning of the twentieth century through literature and art. However, their significance for the social reproduction of the emerging Mexican society has remained largely ignored by dominant historical accounts. Furthermore, whereas the social impact of indigenous wet nurses can be found not just in past but also in contemporary cultural articulations, black wet nurses have been practically erased from the national memory.

As care workers, wet nurses were subjected to social and physical scrutiny. Their bodies became the object of gendered and racial violence, which was enacted through discursive and material methods. In addition, they were often enslaved, and in the rare cases in which they were free and received payment, their wages were extremely low. Because they were often forced to cut their ties with their communities, and even with their families, their sense of belonging was destabilized, thus generating a continual state of dispossession, as is portrayed in *Salomé*. Moreover, as conveyed by Frida Kahlo's painting, the connection between wet nurse and charge was full of complicated affective layers. Whereas Kahlo recognizes her wet nurse as a nurturing figure, she is unable to remember her face. Although the artist is addressing her personal experience, *My Nurse and I* exemplifies how the foundational character of wet nurses has been rendered nonvisible.

In the case of nanas, apart from a few exceptions, their portrayal in Mexican telenovelas tends to follow the model of the idealized mother. Because the televised notions of maternity tend to fluctuate between the dichotomy of good and evil, the nana's idealization is founded over the hyperbolization of characteristics traditionally associated with the image of the "selfless mother." This hyperbolization consolidates them as the embodiment of not merely a good mother, but of a seemingly perfect one. Furthermore, because these figures are often portrayed as Catholic women of indigenous heritage, their proximity to the Lady of Guadalupe becomes noticeable. While the latter represents the sacred motherly image generally recognized as the unifier of the *mestiza* nation, the former can be approached as the earthly materialization of such a nation-building conception. This fictionalization operates as both a scheme to promote behavior models and a way to profit from the widespread national devotion to the religious symbol.

In film, Mexican nanas tend to be portrayed in a more multilayered way. For instance, while nanas' affection for the children who are under their care remains one of their most essential characteristics, films such as *Under the Same Moon* and *Babel* engage in the portrayal of transnational workers facing complex labor scenarios. Because of this, from different perspectives both narratives expose the affective crises and precarious working conditions faced by migrant women working in US domestic settings.

For instance, although Rosario is a babysitter and not a nana, *Under the Same Moon* underscores the lack of labor protections for migrant domestic workers. Additionally, the film addresses the unequal circuit of care produced by the economic disparities that force mothers to leave their children behind and make a living by taking care of someone else's kids. Meanwhile, *Babel* exposes the complicated amalgamation of intense maternal feelings and the form of labor that gives rise to those feelings. When Amelia is deported, her suffering comes from the realization that by losing her job she was also losing the kids she loved. Her deportation also emphasizes the expendability of migrant domestic workers, who can be easily banished from both family life and the national territory. These productions underscore the role of Mexican care workers in the United States, but the specific challenges faced by Central American women working in the Mexican domestic setting, either as nanas or doing housekeeping work, have been scarcely addressed by cultural referents. However, they have become a central point of interest for human rights organizations, which often highlight the invisibility of their labor.

Historical accounts and cultural representations attest to how wet nurses' labor was, and nanas' work continues to be, a site for the enactment of different types of exploitation, which can range from the physical to the economic and the affective. As it is presented in the creative works I examined, this characteristic has led to the reinforcement of long-standing racial and gender-based inequities. In the imaginary landscape of Mexico, either by ignoring the social complexities and economic challenges endured by care workers or by addressing them directly, a diverse array of cultural articulations expose the unbalanced dynamics that continue to reject reproductive justice in the frame of domestic and care labor.

Notes

1. Laura Rodríguez Peinado maintains that the first representation where the Virgin Mary uses her milk portrays her nursing her infant son, Jesus. From such representations, portraying Mary nursing Jesus became a popular iconographic motif in Europe.

2. Anne-Emmanuelle Birn affirms that in the pre-Columbian and colonial periods, when a wet nurse was required, she had to adhere to strict hygienic precepts (679).

3. Julia Tuñón includes some testimonies about this topic in her book, *Enjaular los cuerpos*.

4. Only wet nurses living in the countryside and raising children there escaped this possibility (Carrillo 249–50).

5. While biological mothers such as those played by Sara García could also be compared to the Mexican Virgin, they lack some characteristics associated with a vast majority of the nanas as depicted by television, one of them being their virginity. Furthermore, biological mothers tend to be white and sometimes wealthy, while nanas are overwhelmingly of indigenous features and always of humble origin.

Works Cited

Alfonso X, Rey de Castilla, 1221–1284. *Cantigas de Santa María*. Biblioteca Virtual Miguel de Cervantes, 2009. www.cervantesvirtual.com/obra/cantigas-de-santa-maria/. Accessed 1 May 2020.

———. *Las Siete Partidas*. Biblioteca Virtual Miguel de Cervantes, 2008. www.cervantesvirtual.com/obra-visor/las-siete-partidas-del-rey-don-alfonso-el-sabio-cotejadas-con-varios-codices-antiguos-por-la-real-academia-de-la-historia-tomo-

2-partida-segunda-y-tercera—0/html/01f12004-82b2-11df-acc7-002185ce6064_58.htm. Accessed 1 May 2020.

"Amor incondicional." *Mujer, casos de la vida real.* Televisa, México, 2003.

Ankori, Gannit. *Critical Lives: Frida Kahlo.* Reaktion Books, 2013.

Babel. Directed by Alejandro González Iñárritu. Paramount Vantage, 2006.

Birn, Anne-Emmanuelle. "Child Health in Latin America: Historiographic Perspectives and Challenges." *História, Ciências, Saúde*—Manguinhos, Rio de Janeiro, vol. 14, no. 3, 2007, pp. 677–708.

Blum, Ann Shelby. *Domestic Economies: Family, Work, and Welfare in Mexico City, 1884–1943.* U of Nebraska P, 2009.

Bravo Adams, Caridad, creator. *El enemigo.* Televisa, México, 1961.

Calzada, Jesús, creator. *Retrato de familia.* Televisa, México, 1995.

Cano, Alonso. *San Bernardo y la Virgen.* 1645–1652, Museo del Prado, Madrid.

Caplan, Bryan. *The Myth of the Rational Voter.* Princeton UP, 2011.

Carrillo, Ana María. "La alimentación 'racional' de los infantes: maternidad 'científica,' control de las nodrizas y lactancia artificial." *Enjaular los cuerpos. Normativas decimonónicas y feminidad en México,* edited by Julia Tuñón. Colegio de México, 2008, pp. 227–80.

Carton de Grammont, Hubert. "La desagrarización del campo mexicano." *Convergencia,* vol. 60, no. 50, 2009, www.scielo.org.mx/scielo.php?script=sci_arttext&pid=S1405-14352009000200002. Accessed 1 May 2017.

Castellanos, Rosario. *Salomé y Judith.* E-book, Fondo de Cultura Económica, 2017.

De la Maza, Francisco. *El guadalupanismo mexicano.* Porrúa y Obregón, 1953.

De León, Luis. *La perfecta casada.* Biblioteca Virtual Miguel de Cervantes, 2003. www.cervantesvirtual.com/obra-visor/la-perfecta-casada—1/html/ffbbf57a-82b1-11df-acc7-002185ce6064_3.html. Accessed 13 May 2020.

De Swanson, Rosario M. "Utopía y Distopía en *Salomé,* una pieza poco conocida de Rosario Castellanos." *Hispania,* vol. 95, no. 3, Sept. 2012, pp. 437–47.

Diario de México Tomo IV. 17 vols., 1805–1812, pp. 467–98. books.google.com/books?id=JNVCAAAAYAAJ&pg=PA473&lpg=PA473&dq=Señora+Amar+y+Borbon+diario+de+mexico&source=bl&ots=0UzJI5vMpL&sig=ACfU3U1qmbocfPsh8UsM6C7qqbBF-v2f6g&hl=en&sa=X&ved=2ahUKEwj70LPEvo_pAhWCK80KHdBkDqsQ6AEwAHoECAoQAQ#v=onepage&q=Señora%20Amar%20y%20Borbon%20diario%20de%20mexico&f=false. Accessed 1 May 2020.

Díaz, Porfirio. *Informe del ciudadano general Porfirio Díaz a sus compatriotas.* E-book. Imprenta del Gobierno Federal, 1904.

Earle, Rebecca. *The Body of the Conquistador.* Cambridge UP, 2012.

Esquivel, Laura. *Como agua para chocolate.* Suma de Letras, 2015.

Fernández de Lizardi, José Joaquín. *El periquillo Sarniento.* Catedra, 2007.

Glantz, Margo. *Obras reunidas IV: ensayos sobre literatura mexicana del siglo XX.* Fondo de Cultura Económica, 2013.

González Álvarez, Baldomero. *Higiene de la alimentación en los niños desde el nacimiento hasta la segunda infancia.* Universidad Complutense, 1905.

González Rodríguez, Sergio. *Huesos en el desierto.* Anagrama, 2002.

Güezmes García, Ana, et al. Las trabajadoras migrantes en la frontera sur de México, 2015. www.acnur.org/fileadmin/Documentos/Publicaciones/2015/9852.pdf?-file=fileadmin/Documentos/Publicaciones/2015/9852. Accessed 15 April 2020.

Herrera Feria, María de Lourdes. "Huérfanas, nodrizas y profesoras poblanas a finales del siglo XIX." *Estudios históricos sobre las mujeres en México,* edited by María Herrera. Benemérita Universidad Autónoma de Puebla, 2006, pp. 251–68.

Holder, Sarah. "The Price of Domestic Workers' Invisible Labor in U.S. Border Towns." CityLab June 25, 2018. www.citylab.com/equity/2018/06/the-price-of-domestic-workers-invisible-labor-in-us-border-towns/563087/. Accessed 15 July 2019.

Kahlo, Frida. *My Nurse and I.* 1937, Museo Dolores Olmedo, Mexico City.

Krögel, Alison. "Mercenary Milk, Pernicious Nursemaids, Heedless Mothers: Anti–Wet Nurse Rhetoric in the Satirical Ordenanzas Del Baratillo De Mexico (1734)." *DIECIOCHO,* vol. 37, no. 2, 2014, pp. 233–48.

La dictadura perfecta. Directed by Luis Estrada. Bandidos Films, 2014.

Law, Jules. *Social Life of Fluids: Blood, Milk, and Water in the Victorian Novel.* Cornell UP, 2010.

Mariscal, Ángeles. "Mujeres migrantes atrapadas en una frontera imaginaria." *En el camino,* 3 June 2014, enelcamino.piedepagina.mx/ruta/mujeres-frontera/. Accessed 1 May 2020.

Mora, Carl J. *Mexican Cinema: Reflections of a Society 1896–1988.* U of California P, 1989.

Nosotros los nobles. Directed by Gary Alazraki. Warner Bros., 2013.

O'Reilly, Justo Sierra. *Un año en el hospital de San Lázaro.* Universidad Veracruzana, 2014.

Orozco Gómez, Guillermo. "La telenovela en México: ¿de una expresión cultural a un simple producto para la mercadotecnia?" *Comunicación y sociedad.* Departamento de Estudios de la Comunicación Social. Universidad de Guadalajara, 2006, www.publicaciones.cucsh.udg.mx/pperiod/comsoc/pdf/2006_6/11-35.pdf. Accessed 20 Apr. 2017.

Ortuño, Antonio. *La fila india.* Océano, 2013.

Pacheco, Cristina. *La voz de la tierra.* Sarh, 1986.

Palomo, Beatriz. "Perfil de la población Africana en el reino de Guatemala 1723–1773." *Rutas de la esclavitud en África y América Latina,* edited by Rina Cáceres. Editorial Universidad de Costa Rica and Asociación Pro-historia Centroamericana, 2001, pp. 195–209.

Payno, Manuel. *Los bandidos del Río Frío.* Editorial Porrúa, 2006.

Peña, María del Carmen, creator. *Cadenas de amargura.* Televisa, México, 1991.

Pinal, Silvia, creator. *Mujer, casos de la vida real.* Televisa, México, 1986–2007.

Podalski, Laura. *The Politics of Affect and Emotion in Contemporary Latin American Cinema.* Palgrave Macmillan, 2011.

Premo, Bianca. "Misunderstood Love." *Colonial Latin American Review*, vol. 14, no. 2, 2005, pp. 231–61.

Puga, Ana Elena. "Migrant Melodrama, Human Rights." *Imagining Human Rights in Twenty-First-Century Theater: Global Perspectives*, edited by Brenda Werth, Florian Nikolas, and Paola Hernández. Palgrave Macmillan, 2013, pp. 155–76.

Quiñones, Sam. *True Tales from Another Mexico. The Lynch Mob, the Popsicle Kings, Chalino, and the Bronx.* U of New Mexico P, 2001.

Rodena, Inés, creator. *Marimar.* Televisa, México, 1994.

Rodríguez Peinado, Laura. "La virgen de la leche." *Revista digital de iconografía medieval*, vol. 5, no. 9, 2013, pp. 1–11.

Roma. Directed by Alfonso Cuarón. Espectáculos Fílmicos El Coyúl and Netflix, 2018.

Rulfo, Juan. *Pedro Páramo.* Giron Books, 2013.

Sloan, Kathryn A. *Women's Roles in Latin America and the Caribbean.* Greenwood, 2011.

Tuñón, Julia. *Enjaular los cuerpos: normativas decimonónicas y feminidad en México.* El Colegio de México, 2008.

Under the Same Moon. Directed by Patricia Riggen. Fox Searchlight Pictures and the Weinstein Company, 2008.

Velázquez, María Elisa. *Mujeres de origen africano en la capital novohispana, siglos XVII y XVIII.* Instituto Nacional de Antropología e Historia and Universidad Autónoma de México, 2006.

Velázquez, María Elisa, and Ethel Correa, eds. *Poblaciones y culturas de origen africano en México.* INAH, 2005.

Veneno para las hadas. Directed by Carlos Enrique Taboada. IMICINE, 1984.

Webre, Stephen. "Las nodrizas de Jocotenango: un capítulo de la historia política del género y la ciencia." V Congreso Centroamericano de Historia. El Salvador, 18 July 2000. www.yumpu.com/es/document/view/14266183/las-nodrizas-de-jocotenango-portal-historia-centroamericana. Accessed 1 May 2020.

Zapata, Cesar Fernando. *Desde Las Entrañas Del Monstruo. Anécdotas De Un Inmigrante Mexicano En Estados Unidos.* Create Space, 2008.

Zarattini, María, creator. *Los ricos también lloran.* Televisa, México, 1979.

6

Structures of Affect in Transactions of Care

From Surrogacy Discourses of the Womb to Mahasweta Devi's "Breast-Giver"

Kavita Panjabi

Then, looking down and stroking the table between us she added softly, "In the end a mother is a mother, isn't that true? In the birthing rooms there is the surrogate, the doctor, the nurse, the nurse's aide, and often the genetic mother. Sometimes we all cry."

—Bhadarka, embryologist at Akanksha Clinic for IVF and Surrogacy, Anand, Gujarat, in Arlie Hochschild's *The Outsourced Self: Intimate Life in Market Times*

It's difficult for me mentally to get used to the idea of two simultaneous pregnancies. But I see . . . people's reactions. . . . I made three phone calls and all of them reacted like it was a great idea. So I need to understand why it doesn't sound like a great idea to me. Something instinctively sounds a bit weird. Maybe because it's so different from what I experienced . . . that one overwhelming pregnancy. I was very very involved in *my* pregnancy.

—Doron Mamet-Meged, gay parent of a surrogate baby, Israeli entrepreneur, and pioneer of the transnational baby production business, *Google Baby*, emphasis added

Why are the subjective transitions that commercial surrogacy necessitates and catalyzes so arduous and conflicted? Candid reflective admissions of professionals and entrepreneurs in the trade as in the case of the scientist and the entrepreneur just quoted are indeed exceptional, for to dwell upon and articulate such deep unease is to jeopardize professional and commercial investment in the trade. The point however is that if even prominent professionals and successful pioneering entrepreneurs involved in commercial surrogacy do express—however rarely—such sadness or disquiet about the human implications of its processes, then clearly there are concerns about the social transformations and human adjustments implicated in these processes that call for reflection. Further, if professionals and entrepreneurs experience such affective disturbances, then what is the nature of the conflicting forces that shape the subjectivities of the surrogate mothers[1]—including forces that they may or may not even experience consciously, and far less articulate—in the context of dominant neoliberal discourses of commercial surrogacy that marginalize if not elide altogether their standpoints?

The challenge to the ontological valence of motherhood that confronts the scientist Bhadarka involved in the splitting up of motherhood into genetic donor, biological surrogate, and intended parent throws up critical questions; and these relate not only to what defines motherhood—genes, blood, or capital investment—or to the rights of the surrogate mother over the child she carries versus the right of the intended mother to have a child, but also to how the maps of affect are to be drawn. For the field of affect of commercial surrogacy is compounded by the contrary demands on the one hand of the affective alienation the surrogate mother has to labor at to prepare herself for permanent estrangement from the child she nurtures biologically and the attentive care with which she has to nurture it within her to produce a healthy baby, and on the other of the contrary affects of the alienation of the surrogate mother and the longing of an intended mother for the child she can have only through a surrogacy such as this.

In the second instance, the disquiet articulated by Doron, who is in fact a pioneer in the trade of commercial surrogacy, is an affective representation of further complexities in the field, in relation to eugenics and the exploitation of one population—of the surrogates—in the interest of perfecting another—of the intended parents. For, as evident in *Google Baby*, commercial surrogacy has also led to the practice of organizing multiple pregnancies, either within one surrogate or more, to enable the "choice" of the genetically strongest child at the cost of aborting the rest, and that too without any compensation to one or more surrogates for the "rejected" embryos.[2]

Such suppressed sadness, unease, and disquiet on the part of professionals and entrepreneurs, the discord between deep alienation, sorrow, even shame and the desire for a better life experienced by the surrogates, and the contradictions between the guilt, longing, and anticipated joy of the intended parents, all comprise a dynamics of affect situated at the intersection of commercial interests, economic need, and emotional desires. This complex dynamics of affect that underlies processes of commercial surrogacy serves as a prism of subjective conflicts and suppressed resistances that are in turn reflective of psychosocial ruptures and ethical violations. This affective prism—perceptual, visceral, and emotional—is thus significant because it is expressive of the cultural, social, and philosophical effects of changing relationships between body and capital; it comprises expressions that inhabit a shadowy realm of silence in the material battlegrounds of the transnational biotech industry—for to give rein to them would be to stymie the efficiency of capitalist processes.

This chapter begins by engaging with the discursive structuring of affect in fields of commercial surrogacy in India to trace the modes by which motherhood is "both shaped and conscripted" for "a culture of biotechnological innovation to take root" in the interests of profit in the laboratories of the female body (Sunder Rajan 78). It situates the discussion in the context of the contemporary debates following the Surrogacy (Regulation) Bill of 2016, the ban on commercial surrogacy, and the future prospects of "altruistic" surrogacy in India. The second section, on the problems of ethical practice in commercial surrogacy, begins with a discussion of some recent historical aspects of the markets of care and markets of biotechnology in India, at the intersection of which the industry of commercial surrogacy is located; it then focuses on the problems of ethical practice, beginning with Lyotard, on the negotiations (or the impossibility of them) between personal (including embodied) experience and abstract argument resulting from the asymmetry of different positions of the surrogate mother and a neoliberal transnational industry that privileges economic efficiency over workers' rights. It discusses the modes of asymmetry perpetuated through "modalities and apparatuses of affect" operative in the interests of profit, the lack of access to the standpoint of the mothers, and it ends with a discussion of the unacknowledged "excess" appropriated in the creation of the "commodity" and in the fixing of its exchange value in commercial surrogacy

(Grossberg 315). In the third section this study locates the ruptures in the construction and deployment of the disciplining discourses of surrogacy—the silences, the ambiguities, and the contradictions—showing how these discursive ruptures constitute an ethical lens that reveals suppressed ethical concerns in the realms of commercial surrogacy. In the concluding section I return, via the privileging of sacrificial love in the discourse of commercial surrogacy, to the ethical concerns that now raise other disturbing questions at the prospect of official "altruistic" surrogacy by law in India.

Outlines of the Surrogacy Debate in India

On August 24, 2016, the Union Cabinet introduced and approved the controversial Draft Bill on Assisted Reproductive Technologies (ART) in India, known popularly as the Surrogacy (Regulation) Bill of 2016, banning commercial surrogacy in India. Faced with a backlash from not just the opposition and the surrogacy industry but also feminists, as well as women who are currently involved in commercial surrogacy, it was nevertheless introduced in the Parliament—the Lok Sabha—on November 21, 2016, and is awaiting passage to become an act by law.

Legalized in India in 2002, commercial surrogacy had given rise to what was popularly known as "fertility tourism" and become a booming international business, of over four million dollars and more than three thousand fertility clinics across the country (Verma); by 2016 it had crossed the one billion mark (Pande, "Surrogacy"). Regulatory guidelines for clinics offering ART had been laid out in 2005 by the Indian Council of Medical Research, an institution under the Ministry of Health and Family Welfare, but they lacked legislative backing, resulting in a flourishing surrogacy industry that had lax regulations and no enforcements. Drafts of an ART (Regulation) Bill that had been presented in 2008 and 2010 had focused on the formulation of laws to regulate commercial gestational surrogacy. The turning point came in 2015 with the virtual ban on *cross border* commercial surrogacy, limiting it to married couples of Indian origin only. This was a complete reversal of the Regulatory Guidelines of 2005 and was followed by the Surrogacy (Regulation) Bill of 2016 banning all commercial surrogacy (Pande, "Surrogacy").

While the proposal to set up national and state surrogacy boards as regulating authorities has been welcomed across all constituencies, the provisions of the 2016 bill that have given rise to heated debate include the fact that it prohibits direct payment to the surrogate mother; allows only "ethical altruistic surrogacy" by a "close relative of the intending couple" who must have already have borne a child herself, is not a nonresident Indian (NRI) or foreigner, and can be a surrogate mother just once in a lifetime; disallows foreigners, single parents, homosexuals, and live-in couples from becoming commissioning parents; and bans all sale or import of human embryos and gametes as well as making it illegal for childless or unmarried women to become surrogate mothers. Violation of these laws will be punishable by a jail term of at least ten years and a fine of up to Rs 10 lakhs.[3] Effectively then, it makes only legally wedded, heterosexual, childless Indian couples married for a minimum of five years eligible for surrogacy.

Justifying the provisions of the bill, External Affairs Minister Sushma Swaraj, in addition to drawing much media attention by taking pot shots at Bollywood celebrities such as Aamir Khan and Shah Rukh Khan, who had opted for babies through surrogacy, and exploiting poor surrogates,[4] reinforced the ban on homosexuals and live-in couples through regressive stands on sexuality and marriage that are characteristic of the current right-wing government: "Each country has to make laws that are *aligned with our values*, as per a legal framework. Homosexual couples are not recognised by law in India" ("Surrogacy Bill Gets"). And, in *Indian Express*, she has been cited saying: "We do not recognise homosexual or live-in relationships that is why they are not allowed to commission babies through surrogacy. It is *against our ethos*." As Pande emphasizes, "One cannot but wonder, who are these 'we' who can lay down the norms, and against whose ethos?" ("Surrogacy"). The bill has been criticized widely as a violation of the fundamental right of people to choose modes of parenthood and as a clear reinforcement of the conservative heteronormative ethics of the current government (Malhotra; Bhattacharya; Pande, "Surrogacy"; Rao, "Banning Commercial Surrogacy"). Even Mohan Rao, who holds that "banning commercial surrogacy is the only way forward," advocates the opening up of the option of altruistic surrogacy to all and is categorically critical of this homophobic stance: "Here is where the so-called morality comes in, with Sushma Swaraj talking about 'our ethos.' Our ethos actually accepted alternative sexualities; it was Victorian England that imposed the ridiculous section 377. We need to get rid of this law."

Other critiques of this bill extend to its failure to address the complicated processes of adoption and problems with infertility, both of which are cited as reasons for opting for surrogacy. As Pande points out: "Adoption and other aspects of assisted reproduction are entirely left outside the ambit of the Bill, leaving little scope for critical discussions on gamete donation, the politics of labelling infertility a 'disease' and the current obsession with mandatory parenthood and genetic essentialism" ("Surrogacy"). Rao further extends the argument about genetic essentialism and the need for easier adoption processes and prevention of infertility; he also draws attention to their social implications:

> It's not just discouraging adoption, it is encouraging the worst kinds of patriarchal ideas, like the child is my blood, my line, etc. . . . All women who go in for IVF talk of enormous social pressures to have a baby, from the family, and from society at large. Another aspect to ponder upon is that what is the government doing to prevent infertility? Surrogacy is only one curative option that lies at the end of the road. What must be done much earlier is to prevent infertility and promote adoption. There is a need to encourage adoption by making the process easier. ("Banning Commercial Surrogacy")

Pande extends her critique of the 2016 bill further to the cross-border context, observing that "imposing a ban on surrogacy in India will as likely just shift it to another country in the global south" ("Surrogacy"). Citing the ban on "gay surrogacy" in 2013 that pushed all such cases to Nepal, she holds that the Indian government effectively made surrogates even more vulnerable by forcing them to migrate and make their living para-legally in a foreign land. In fact, Pande asserts that matters like surrogacy cannot be resolved through restrictive policies within national borders, and she argues instead for international cooperation, regulatory bodies that ensure that all signatory countries follow basic minimum standards, and a "fair trade surrogacy" that could bring with it not just fair pay but also dignity to the surrogate mothers in what is perceived to be a tainted profession:

> For many surrogate mothers, a critical move towards fair and equitable surrogacy would not just be an increase in the payments they receive for their labour, but as critically, an affirmation of their dignity as labourers. Almost all the women emphasised the desire that their efforts at forging relationships with the fetus or baby be acknowledged and reciprocated, and not just during the contract period. ("Surrogacy")

The strongest argument in favor of the ban though is Rao's, and it has to do with the reification of choice in an unequal world. He builds his argument for reproductive justice on the grounds that more often than not coercive familial pressures and economic deprivation drive poor women to surrogacy, and he asserts: "We can have reproductive justice only when we have socio-economic equality. In the face of rampant inequalities, what poor women have is reproductive unfreedoms, as they take recourse to commercial surrogacy" ("Banning Commercial Surrogacy"). Rao's radical stand on the exploitation of surrogates draws attention to the deeper contexts of their lives, thus forestalling the question of the surrogate mother's "consent" that other scholars like Pande have raised ("Surrogacy"). His argument actually points to the near impossibility of any law protecting the rights of commercial surrogates in a socioeconomic context that forestalls the very possibility of "reproductive justice"; hence, he insists on a complete ban on commercial surrogacy.

Whether "justice" will be available to surrogate mothers by driving surrogacy into the familial sphere, as the Surrogacy (Regulation) Bill of 2017 does, is also deeply questionable. The ostensible aim of the bill is "to prohibit the potential exploitation of surrogate mothers and to protect the rights of children born through surrogacy"; but there are no provisions that actually work toward preventing such exploitation in the private sphere or the shadow markets of neoliberalism. In abolishing payments, the bill also reflects a failure to take into account the loss of other forms of livelihood during the period of surrogacy, and it maintains a telling silence on issues of maternity leave and compensation for loss of income—the government's proposal of "altruistic surrogacy" not only pushes surrogacy into the realm of unpaid domestic "labor," it also creates conditions for women to be deprived of their existing income. The high probability of coercive surrogacy in the "privacy" that shrouds the politics of class and gender oppression in the domestic sphere has also been highlighted by many. Bhattacharya observes that maids and poor relatives would become ready victims in the confines of the home, and Pande foregrounds the possibility of additional forms of oppression within the family in cases of refusal of "altruism": "It is likely that the coercion of patriarchal family ties and the penalty for refusing to be altruistic towards a close family member is as acute as a contract or the inducement of money" ("Surrogacy" 15). Malhotra too asserts: "The yardsticks governing domestic altruistic surrogacy will offer an opportunity for corruption and exploitation, pushing surrogacy into unethical hands. It could foster an underground abusive trade in surrogacy. Relatives will be generated and surrogates will be impregnated in India and shifted to permissible jurisdictions." On the other hand, Bhattacharya also points to the prevalence of a pervasive network of trafficking for the purposes of surrogacy and procurement of physical organs: "Young and adolescent tribal girls from remote parts of India (such as North East India, Jharkhand, Chhattisgarh, etc.) are either kidnapped or trafficked and are coerced into the practices of surrogacy . . ." (14). The bill thus fails to address both the private practices and the already existing underground networks of exploitation of women in nonformal surrogacy.

It is also important to address the current ground reality of one and a half decades of legally established networks, infrastructure, and personnel in place in the functioning of a now billion dollar industry. The most likely outcome of the ban then is that a flourishing surrogacy industry will be driven underground, endangering the lives of surrogate mothers and unwanted children in ways that may not even be grasped. With the surrogacy industry pushed underground and thriving in the black market zones of the country there will be even fewer safeguards for the surrogates and a complete abrogation of their rights as workers; the absence of protective laws will render both them and the children born of surrogacy more vulnerable to the sharks in the industry as well as to exploitative clients (Bhattacharya; Pande, "Surrogacy"; Malhotra).

Given this matrix of vested interests, Pande's suggestion that we accept the presence of this labor market and work toward the protection of the workers seems more viable ("Surrogacy"). She recommends: "Once we accept that this is, indeed, a labour market, albeit stigmatised, exploitative, and discomforting to many of us, we can start working towards laws that protect the rights of the labourers involved" ("Surrogacy").

The passage from the 2005 guidelines, and the 2008 and 2010 drafts, to the 2016 Surrogacy (Regulation) Bill is marked by a complete turnaround from proposed legislation to a proposed ban on commercial surrogacy. Now it is right-wing patriarchal protectionism that holds sway in the state discourses of surrogacy. What has not been discussed adequately is how this volte-face is also indicative of the Indian government's turn from a neoliberal promotion of a flourishing, international, surrogacy industry to an advancement of a patriarchal right-wing cultural agenda in the guise of progressive gender-sensitive and child-sensitive arguments. This should come as no surprise however, for the current government that came to power on the promise of neoliberal "development" could do so only on the back of the Rashtriya Swayamsevak Sangh (RSS), a massive nationwide organization—with more than thirty thousand branches—of conservative culturalist forces, and the support of militant Hindu right-wing groups like the Bajrang Dal. That these organizations have systematically been gaining ground is evident in their association with casteist violence, and more recently the majoritarian violence ravaging the nation since September 2015 when Mohammad Akhlaq was lynched to death in Dadri, Uttar Pradesh, on suspicion that he had eaten and stored beef. Since then, the spate of lynchings of "people" suspected of cow theft, of transporting beef, or even for just being a "beef eater," that is, Muslim, right up to the cold-blooded murder of sixteen-year-old Junaid Khan of Ballabhgarh, Haryana, in broad daylight in a fully crowded train while returning from Eid shopping in June 2017 have left no doubt whatsoever of the ascendancy of the RSS.

In her insightful work *Economies of Abandonment: Social Belonging and Endurance in Late Liberalism*, Elizabeth Povinelli draws attention to the complex of what she calls late liberalism, relating it to the governance of difference as well as the governance of markets, which are neither fully aligned with each other nor with market fundamentalism. Discussing her work further in *Symphony of Late Liberalism*, she explains in an interview with Khalidi:

> [L]ate liberalism happened and is happening. It happened because, under the unrelenting pressure of anti-colonial movements, new social movements including Black Power movements, Red Power movements, Radical Feminism, the Queer movements, etc. the way liberalism governed difference underwent a serious legitimacy crisis. . . . Running parallel to this crisis was another—the failure of Keynesian economics. Thus the *Symphony* shows the unfolding movement of late liberalism across the two axes of crisis in the governance of difference and the governance of markets. . . . But, again, I do not see the governance of difference and markets composed of the same logic or in a base-superstructure relationship. . . . They do not fully align themselves with each other, nor do they fully align themselves with market fundamentalism.

The Indian government's turnaround from proposed legislation to a proposed ban on commercial surrogacy seems to be located at the intersection of such a governance of markets and governance of difference. For on the one hand is the crisis of the current government's neoliberal agenda signaled by low investment, the drop in agricultural growth, crashing national growth rates, failed promises of employment generation, as well as the more recent fiasco of demonetization; on the other hand is the crisis of difference, of gender, caste, and religion represented by the regressively patriarchal, upper-caste, majoritarian impositions of the RSS, Bajrang Dal, and other such mass organizations (in contrast to the progressive US movements of the late 1960s and early 1970s).

Women's bodies have again become the ground for the waging of yet another patriarchal socioeconomic battle, this time between the economic forces of "progressive" neoliberalism and the cultural hegemony of "regressive" right-wing ideologies. These recent developments thus complicate in no uncertain terms the claims about the role of the nation-state in safeguarding the interests of its citizens in the face of neoliberal exploitations. Sangari's claim to hold the nation thus responsible had indeed carried a powerful valence in 2015, when she had asserted: "Though increasingly tense and fraught as a space for initiating a politics of solidarity, the nation cannot cease to be a space for the critique of neo-liberal policies and the corollary hardening of internal exclusion, surveillance and repression" (13). In 2017 such claims on the nation ricocheted back on us in grim irony—the nation *has* become a space for the critique of neoliberal policies, in the hardening of its own majoritarian and patriarchal forms of exclusion, surveillance, and repression.

The Problem of Ethical Practice in Surrogacy

When societies change rapidly, prevailing ethical norms are challenged by new knowledges and the conflicts arising from transformed practices. Ethical thinking is not a linear process, but a zigzag of contested ideas and interests, in which social responsibility, dignity, and well-being must all find a place (Qadeer and John 12).

Commercial surrogacy stands at the intersection of markets of care and markets of biotechnology, and India is no newcomer to either. While it is well known as an established "exporter" of childcare and domestic workers to the Western hemisphere and now to Far Eastern countries, too, it is less known as a laboratory of both contraceptive and reproduction aiding technologies. This is not only because trials are significantly cheaper to perform here. In fact, the "tactical emergence of ethico-political terrains"[5] of commercial surrogacy can actually be traced back to the debates on informed consent and bodily rights that gathered force around the resistance to hazardous contraceptive technologies in the eighties and nineties of the last century.

A number of clinically controlled contraceptive technologies, then banned in the Western world, as they were yet untested to be proven safe, were deployed rampantly in the state-sponsored family planning program in India. Norplant, Depo-Provera and Net-en distributed by none less than National Health Centres, under pressure from population control lobbies and funding agencies of the north, led to a movement against hazardous contraceptives. Rajashri Dasgupta reports that in 1986 three women's groups filed a public interest litigation (PIL) in the Supreme Court about "the safety of the Net-en injections, the unethical nature of the trials as the experimental nature of the contraceptive was hidden from the women 'volunteers' and the potential for abuse in family planning programmes" ("Women"). And in 1998 another PIL led to the Supreme Court directing the drug controller of India (DCI) to ban QS or quinacrine sterilization "because of the illegal and unethical nature of the human trials, and the lack of safety testing." Dasgupta observes that the experience of this movement seems to have been mixed, for activists have been unable to either convince scientific bodies to stop conducting or monitoring such trials, or prevent the sale of these contraceptives in the open market. On the other hand, she asserts that "they have been successful in preventing the entry of contraceptives like Depo Provera and Norplant into the Family Planning Programme. The two litigations led to the formation of a set of rules and regulations in drug testing and to the QS Ban" ("Quick-Fix" 304).

The movement against the unethical—and even illegal—trials with contraceptive technologies was also, as Dasgupta reminds us, "instrumental in politically educating an entire generation of feminists and health activists in India on informed consent and patients' rights in clinical trials" ("Quick-Fix" 304). The point then is not regarding a lack of awareness about the need for informed consent and rights in the field of ART; the point is that the huge numbers of women who offer themselves for surrogacy in the open market are often not aware of them, or not in a position to demand both information and their rights.

That the search for a humane arrangement of surrogacy is confounded by the tightrope trajectory of a discourse that "manages" the realities of the biological and affective labor(s) of mothering and the economic drives of capital is not new. In their discussion of the 2008 draft of the surrogacy bill, Qadeer and John had argued that there had been next to no public debate on the ethical, social, and medical questions around infertility and surrogacy in India. Since then there has been discussion on the social and some medical questions too, as the debate following the 2016 bill demonstrates; the ethical dimension however has received short shrift. One reason for this may relate to the fact that ethical concern in surrogacy centers primarily around justice for the surrogate mother (and the child she bears), and ethical practice, as Qadeer and John too emphasize, "must take its cue from the experiences of surrogate mothers" (11). On the other hand, conservative right-wing oppression of women perpetuated through the "moral celebration of women's altruism" that "reinforces the stereotype of women as 'naturally' nurturing and selfless" also creates an idiom in which the living woman's suffering can find no expression; and the elision of coercive conditions within the patriarchal family itself constitutes an idiom of silence that cannot be broken (Pande, "Surrogacy").

It is not surprising that the wrong suffered by the surrogate mother is not signified in either the discourses of neoliberalism or those of right-wing conservatism; the tragedy however is the lack of understanding of the wrong suffered by her even by the critics of both the market and the state, who do have the ability to hear the surrogate mother and at least inflect the dominant idioms, if not transform them. The problem, however, lies not so much with them as with the very location and conditioning of the surrogates in the industry. Mukherjee observes that "the asymmetric power relationship within surrogacy gives hardly any decision-making power to the gestational mothers as compared to the intended parents and medical practitioners." Saravanan's findings in Gujarat suggest further reason for the silence of the surrogate mother in the very principles of their selection for the workforces of commercial surrogacy: "Inertness and submissiveness are the traits sought by IVF clinics in a surrogate mother. Failure to display submissiveness results in replacement with another surrogate and there is polite rejection on medical grounds when they are observed to have aggressive characteristics" (27). The conditioning of the worker in the surrogacy industry is such that submissiveness to the demands of the medical practitioners and intended parents is a basic requirement and surrogates have "very little say in any of the decisions, including those pertaining to their own bodies" (Saravanan 26). An assertive sense of agency is a disqualification and leads to rejection; the result is a carefully selected, compliant, submissive workforce of surrogate mothers, and the writing out of their standpoint from the discourses of surrogacy.

The central problem that forestalls the question of ethical practice in surrogacy relates to the lack of access to the surrogate mothers' standpoint, for these "laborers" in the marketplace—and domestic laboratories—of surrogacy are barely audible in the crossfire between the discourses of market and state. The surrogate mothers' experiences are buried in a palimpsest of ambiguities and silences, and this poses a central problem for issues of reproductive justice. For it is not merely a question of their ability to give voice to their perspectives but of the asymmetry of positions wherein the personal experience of the surrogate mothers is challenged by abstract arguments of neoliberalism on one hand and right-wing conservatism on the other. It is clearly a case of the *differend* elaborated by Lyotard: "where the plaintiff is *divested* of the means to argue, and becomes for that reason a victim . . . the 'regulation' of the conflict . . . is done in the idiom of one of the parties, while the wrong suffered by the other is not signified in that idiom" (12). The morality of neoliberalism is a morality of profit, for neoliberal policies sideline not only workers' rights but virtually every public good that is not typically monetized. Birch and Siemiatycki have shown how neoliberalism also puts in place a discourse that privileges monetary over social objectives, and makes it difficult to justify practices of equity, social justice, and environmental concerns. As Povinelli too has argued, "In neoliberalism to care for others is to refuse to preserve life if it lies outside a market value" (159). The investments in the industry have to pay off, for: "Within a neoliberal state, any social investment that does not have a clear end—a projected moment when input value (money, services, care) can be replaced by output value—is not merely economically suspect but morally suspect, no matter the life-enhancing nature of the investment" (160). The surrogate mother, in signing a contract of which she is given no copy, agrees to participate "voluntarily" in a system in which her well-being has no value, her life is secondary, and her exploitation is elided.

In *Economies of Abandonment*, Povinelli raises a set of extremely thought-provoking questions about the forms of discourse instrumental in erasing out of all consideration the social harm upon which rests the transformed meaning of "care" not just in commercial surrogacy but also in wider realms of the care industry today: "What discourses of social belonging and abandonment [allow the creation of] a narrative form that conjure[s] away the social harms of the durative present? What does care consist of such that when a form of creating harm for others is thought of and experienced as a form of caring for others?" (58). A range of ethical approaches, from those of Marxist-feminist accounts of labor and alienation and critiques of neoliberal practices to those of reproductive justice, reveal different dimensions of the exploitative nature of commercial surrogacy work. Emphasizing questions of gendered labor and alienation, Kalindi Vora highlights, through the lens of reproductive labor, "the types of *value-transmitting activities* that subjects undergo for the benefit of those who consume them. . . . Through counselling and conversation, medical personnel encourage surrogates to see themselves as gestation providers whose only link to the fetus is the renting of a womb imagined as an empty and otherwise unproductive space. This formulation of surrogacy and pregnancy makes possible the commodification of the womb and the disaggregation of the work of mothering into distinct biological and affective components—necessary conditions for the transnational distribution of this work" (Vora, "Disaggregation" 12; emphasis added). This disaggregation is the basis for the international division of reproductive labor wherein "the work of producing vital energy through biological and affective labor is distributed unequally at the level of international exchange, as are opportunities for its consumption" (Vora, "Limits" 682).

The critical point in Vora's argument about the unequal power relations governing the internationally disaggregated labors of motherhood is about the unacknowledged *excess* involved in the creation of the "commodity" and in the fixing of its exchange value: "What is produced by these activities *exceeds* what is recognizable in the commodity's exchange value. It makes plain the connection between the exhaustion of biological bodies and labors in India to extend 'life' in the First World and a longer history of power relations underpinning what may seem like an emerging form of biopower in sites like commercial surrogacy" (684; emphasis added). I wish to focus on this excess, on that which exceeds what is *recognizable* in the exchange value of the surrogate's labor and is yet involved in the exhaustion of biological bodies and labors. For even if central to the surrogate mother's experience, that which is not "recognizable" in this economy clearly cannot not find a place in its discourse, thus resulting in an erasure of the surrogate's experience of exhaustion and exploitation. Several dimensions of unacknowledged "excess" have entered the debates on surrogacy, especially in relation to the potentializing of bodies that "entails risks for participants and particularly surrogates, who risk their health, the stability of their families, and their reputations" (Vora, "Potential" S105). The "unrecognized" excess thus involves not only the psychological work of distancing oneself from the child one nurtures within the womb, it also involves the risky "labors" of a surrogate mother undergoing multiple simultaneous pregnancies—and abortions—in the interest of producing the "perfect" baby for the First World family, with the "excess" unpaid for; the health hazards the surrogate mother risks that may be in "excess" of the payments for the normal pregnancy and delivery;

the psychosocial work of overcoming the social stigma associated with surrogacy in countries such as India; and the emotional labor of keeping the family stable through the psychological and social upheavals that surrogacy catalyzes (Pande, "Mother-Worker").

That which exceeds the commodity's exchange value however is rendered as excess in the first place with the surrogate's work being defined as mere biological "renting" of the space of the womb. As Vora points out, "Assisted reproduction, tissue engineering, and stem cell research all share in the process of using technologies to reorganize or reconceptualize the body as a site of potential productivity. This creation of productivity is reproductive, speculative, and as such valuable to the market . . . [and relates to the equation] Cell: Factory: Body: Industrial society" ("Potential" S100–01). Such reconceptualization of the body in commercial surrogacy is marked by the exclusion of both the affective as well as the biological nurturing by the surrogate mother, as well as of the risks to her body and being that surrogacy may involve—for the womb is not, as is made out to be, a lifeless space in no place; it is a live organ wired into the biological, physiological, and psychosomatic processes of the body that are all affected by any medical intervention such as the planting of one or more embryos into it. The dehumanization of the womb as rented space erases out of the picture all the physical and psychological processes associated with it.

The most basic form of excess in all this of course is to be found—or is *not* found actually—in the way in which the body is affected by intensity, for affect is the impact of emotion that cannot be fully realized in language, and this is something I shall turn to in the next two sections of this chapter on commercial surrogacy and "altruistic" surrogacy, the mandate for times to come in India.

The Affective Potentializing of the Mother-Worker: Discursive Ruptures as Ethical Lens

That commerce has a way of negotiating affects in the interests of profit is a well-established fact now. Hochschild's *The Managed Heart: Commercialization of Human Feeling* established, as far back as 1979, that the modes of governance of emotions and affectional action in the workplace constitute emotional labor that actually goes beyond "surface acting" to "deep acting," where actors are trained to go beyond pretending to feel to actually feeling (40–42). The adjustment of workers' emotions involved in such labor is geared toward transforming a sense of being exploited, or even trapped, into a sense of voluntary participation (45–46). Hochschild's observation of workers in commercial enterprises such as Delta holds valid for a commercial surrogate too, in that "the worker must give up control over how the work is to be done" as work policies are determined by the industry from above: "The whole system of emotional exchange in private life . . . is thrust into a commercial setting, it is transmuted. A profit motive is slipped in under acts of emotion management, under the rules that govern them now, under the gift exchange" (*Managed* 119).

The ways in which companies draw upon public perceptions of women as motherly or sexually attractive to "attach profit to these qualities" often result in women's estrangement from these aspects of their being, and Hochschild's research also reveals that many female flight attendants have to turn to therapists to deal with the loss of sexual interest (182–83). The complexity of affective transmutations in commercial surrogacy, however, could make even such intense forms of emotion management in realms of commerce seem like child's play.[6] For commercial surrogacy is not only limited to systems of emotional exchange, it also "disciplines" modes of actual embodiment too. Instead of a trajectory of transmutations of emotion, feeling, and social exchange from private to commercial settings, what marks commercial surrogacy is a constant trapeze act in the intertwined realms of psyche *and* embodiment, wherein the body experiences the affects of the contrary emotional pull and push of nurturing and alienation not only as an aspect of psychological response or social interaction but also in deeply embodied form, *within* the very womb. What is the affective experience of simultaneously loving and rejecting a person; of being *made* to simultaneously love and reject a person; and of being made to simultaneously love and reject not an Other, but one who is a vulnerable part of oneself, physically carried (and wired) within the womb, biologically fed by one's bloodstream, affectively nurtured by one's care? Further, since a surrogate "has to be a good mother to her own child before she can be a mother-worker for someone else's baby," what are the transmutations that have to be affected from the emotional realm of motherhood of one's own child to the economic realm of motherhood and the sale of the child in the near future (Pande, "Mother-Worker" 980)?

Direct access to the standpoint of surrogate mothers then has been scarce; however, important recent research by feminist scholars who have reached out to engage with surrogate mothers has begun to make some access possible (Vora, "Sociality," "Limits," "Risk," and "Disaggregation"; Hochschild,

Outsourced; Pande, "Mother-Worker "). It is usually available to us in the form of affective expressions of experiences of sadness, alienation, shame, or the desire for a better life, especially for their children—and sometimes of indignation, and anger too (Pande, Mother-Worker"; Hochschild, *Outsourced* 87–103). Yet there are arrangements and histories that figure and prefigure surrogacy in ways too complex for the surrogates conditioned by the strategic discourses of commerce and the manipulations of the patriarchal discourses of history to grasp fully the impact of these processes on their lives. Kumkum Sangari points out perceptively that such arrangements of "familial, state and market led patriarchal regimes . . . [to] produce subjects and agents of self-directed violence who absorb rather than externalize the social costs and contradictions of contemporary capitalism" (2; emphasis added). And, equally perceptively, Kalindi Vora draws our attention to the fact that women who enter into surrogacy work simultaneously also "enter into layers of other historical contexts that prefigure them in important ways" ("Limits" 697). What is common to both, these contemporary arrangements as well as these gendered histories, is the reconstitution of structures of affect across a history of reconstitutions of motherhood that underlies the interpellation and conditioning of women into becoming agents of "self-directed violence" to serve patriarchal, social, and economic interests. These arrangements and histories of affect that prefigure and figure surrogate mothers, sometimes in ways that they may not even have any knowledge of, constitute the area of exploration in this section.

Transnational commercial surrogacy in India, as Vora has discussed, is located within a much older history of the colonial division of labor as "indices of new forms of exploitation and accumulation within neoliberal globalization," but "they also rearticulate a historical colonial division of labor" (Vora, "Limits" 683). I would emphasize that this history also constitutes a transnational and hierarchical field of affect within which the experience of commercial surrogacy has to be understood. In relation to the buyers of surrogacy, Vora herself observes elsewhere: "One of the potentializing features of gestational surrogacy that is represented in the notion of wombs for rent is a spatialization reminiscent of colonial figurations and fantasies of newly encountered land as empty and unpopulated" ("Potential" S100). Further, as it involves both affective and biological labor, transnational surrogacy reinforces unequal relations of affect, for it "can serve . . . to make the consumer feel 'more human,' and to continue to disenfranchise the humanity of those whose unrecognized productivity allows for this investment" ("Limits" 697). This further feeds into a history of the "import" of childcare and domestic workers from South and Southeast Asian countries to the West in which "the devaluing of racialized and gendered service work has perpetuated a discourse of white middle- and upper-middle-class families as needing more care than working-class families and families of color . . ." ("Limits" 697).

New in transnational commercial surrogacy is the "relationship between physical bodies and social meaning" and the ways in which surrogate mothers are trained into "being simultaneously biological things and human persons" (Vora, "Potential" S97). Vora has shown, very perceptively, how "the bodies of women are potentialized to become both surrogates and a locus for new social meaning" ("Potential" S97). This process of potentializing actually works as much at the affective level as at the bodily, and an examination of the structuring of affect yields some insight into the ethical dimensions of this fraught transition to the social imaginary of commercial surrogacy.

All new social and political meanings have to be narrativized into being. Even the modern nation had to be narrated into being in the social imaginary. Ben Anderson's *Imagined Communities* is an elaboration of how the nation is imagined into being and then sustained by continuing narratives of nation—in daily newspaper, in sports, in literature, culture, and cinema. Ernest Gellner too had highlighted the role of invention in the structuring of "modernity" and especially of modern nation-states: "Nationalism is not the awakening of nations to self-consciousness: it invents nations where they do not exist" (168). What is even more interesting in the context of the discourse of commercial surrogacy is what follows this famous articulation in the second half of the sentence: "but it does need some pre-existing differentiating marks to work on, even if . . . these are purely negative" (Gellner 168). What we have then is a coming together of contradictions—the new nation-states are structured as modern, but on the strength of preexisting marks, even if "these are purely negative"—the discourse of surrogacy too is structured on "modern" medical, usually Western notions of motherhood, but it works on older marks of motherhood in ways that range from negative to contradictory, to at best ambiguous.

Extremely telling then in the narratives of transnational commercial surrogacy are the silences as well as the contradictions and ambiguities of the neoliberal discourse that is instrumental in the affective potentializing of women for surrogate motherhood, for these are ruptures that reveal a lack of fit between social values and economic imperatives; and analyses of these ruptures, I argue, reveal the machinations of capital as well as a battlefield of suppressed ethical concerns in the realms of commercial surrogacy.

One of the chief ambiguities surrounding commercial surrogacy in the production of the dual mother-worker subject, as Pande terms it, is that it is positioned "somewhere between contractual labor and motherly altruism" ("Mother-Worker" 978). Surrogates in turn use the "continuous shift between economic and interpersonal registers in the clinic to imagine a long-term beneficial connection to commissioning parents" (Vora, "Potential" S97). While such altruism enables surrogate mothers to transcend objectification as a biological machine and relate to the work of surrogacy in more human terms, the basic underlying ambiguity can be played both ways—in facilitating the "adjustment" of the surrogate mother to the surrogacy industry, and in the interests of the buyers of surrogacy too. Pande quotes Raveena, a surrogate counselor, and hostel matron, as saying, "I teach my surrogates one crucial thing: don't treat it like a business. Instead, treat it like God's gift to you. Don't be greedy." When such ambiguous play on contractual labor and motherly altruism is swung in the direction of the clients, then the underlying thrust of the emphasis on surrogacy as God's gift is an "instruction . . . not to negotiate the wages" ("Mother-Worker" 978–79).

Two more sets of affectively unresolved and related constructions in the production of the mother-worker are built on absolutely contradictory requirements of the nurturing yet detached mother and the perfect yet disposable mother—one who has to be detached because she is to work toward the ideal end of ensuring her own disposability. That women workers of the Global South are made to feel disposable under the workings of global capital is a well-established fact of the scholarship on globalization, but it needs to be brought into more focused ethical scrutiny, and one of the ways of doing this is in terms of what Sangari refers to as the production of "subjects and agents of self-directed violence who absorb rather than externalize the social costs and contradictions of contemporary capitalism" (Pande, "Mother-Worker" 977; Sangari 2). What makes the experience of this violence of commercial surrogacy even more complex is the push and pull of contrary affective requirements. For the counseling sessions not only reiterate the notion of the womb as a machine to be let out, they simultaneously insist on a "loving" relationship with the child in the womb. Pande quotes a doctor training potential surrogates at a clinic in Anand: "If some child comes to stay with you for just nine months, what will you do? You will take care of it even more, love it even more than you love your own, because it is someone else's" ("Mother-Worker" 978). The "disciplining" of the surrogate is thus premised on an internally contradictory affective premise in which she is "constantly aware of her disposability and the transience of her identity as a worker and yet loves the product of her transient labor (the fetus) as her own" ("Mother-Worker" 978). It is also such that she "has to be a good mother to her own child before she can be a mother-worker for someone else's baby" ("Mother-Worker" 978). So she has to be a perfect mother, yet disposable. What is noteworthy here is that the sense of disposability as a worker, and the demand of the qualities of a perfect mother, both actually inhibit the women from developing identities as workers, thus preventing them from negotiating for higher wages ("Mother-Worker" 980).

There is of course evidence of the surrogates' resistance to the medical narratives that render them disposable, and such resistance usually takes the form of a search for self-worth in relationships with both intended parents and the child; but the structuring of the mother-worker subject is such that all attempts to resist their own indisposability and claim motherhood undermine their identities and sometimes even rights as workers, opening up possibilities of further economic exploitation. One set of such narratives relates to the surrogates resisting the commercial and contractual nature of their work of mothering by establishing personal relationships with the intended parents. While this may be read as a form of resistance to disciplining discourses that underline their disposability, Pande has shown how "these ties also make the remuneration structure more informal, often to the detriment of the surrogates" ("Mother-Worker" 987). Another challenge comes in the form of the surrogate claiming relationship with the baby/babies she carries. Pande cites surrogate Parvati asserting her claim through her intimate association and blood tie with the baby: "After all, it's my blood even if it's their genes" ("Mother-Worker" 987). This is a doubly powerful claim as it challenges the medical hierarchization of genetic ties over blood ties as the basis for kinship as well as "ownership" of the child. While such resistance to one's own disposability may be affective expression of a profound ontological experience of deprivation, yet, when claims to motherhood are articulated in the discursive fields of commercial surrogacy they actually undercut the surrogate mothers' claims to rights as workers and put them at a disadvantage in negotiating better terms of contract because, as Pande elaborates: "Ironically, these resistances at the discursive level often reinforce the primary identity of these women as *selfless mothers* rather than as wage-earning workers, which further undermines their ability to negotiate the payment received" ("Mother-Worker" 970; emphasis added). Thus it becomes clear that attempts by surrogate mothers to challenge the constructions of their own disposability push them into realms of "informality"—realms that are by definition excluded from the formal valuations and negotiations of capital—such that claims to motherhood may ironically warrant further economic sacrifice rather than greater compensation for deprivation.

The other critical question we need to ask is that, given the ethical unease that continues to mark commercial surrogacy despite it having become a billion dollar industry just in India alone, how do the discourses of this industry "manage" this unease? Povinelli's insightful analysis in *Economies of Abandonment* offers us some insight in this respect in relation through the positing of a critical question about the logic of discursive modes harnessed in the perpetuation of inequality: "How do specific arrangements of tense, eventfulness, and ethical substance *make affectively and cognitively sensible* and practical, [the] late liberal distributions of life and death, of hope and harm, and of endurance and exhaustion across social difference?" (Povinelli 13; emphasis added). Her account engages critically with the affective attachments and practical relationship of subjects to such unequal distributions; and her analysis of the temporality of such discourses shows how the ethical concerns of a process are "deferred to some future anterior perspective" in which "the future anterior is what will have been the ultimate truth, good, and justice of this existing action, event and experience" (3). The justification of a future end, she explains, "erases the durative present out of focus. . . . In late liberalism . . . the ethical nature of present action is interpreted from the point of view of a reflexive future horizon and its cognate discourses, such as that of sacrificial love. The . . . suffering disappears when seen from the perspective of what it will have been—or been for . . ." (3).

Seen in this light, the dimensions of the surrogacy discourses that relate to the category of sacrificial love, such as altruism and the construction of selfless mothers discussed earlier, serve as the future anterior justification of the present suffering the surrogate mother undergoes. What society and industry construct as sacrifice is actually the surrogate's experience of her body being consumed, being exhausted, for as Sunder Rajan too asserts, when surrogates get incorporated into the logics and circuits of global capitalism this population "shifts from being sacrificed to being *consumed*; the worker's body becomes available to systems of capital . . . as a source of value generation" (99). So for ethical concerns to become at all operative, the consideration of the surrogate's mother's suffering has to be restored from the perspective of the future anterior, where it is assessed through gendered, classist, and neoliberal ideological lenses such as those of the selflessness or altruism of poor women in the Global South, to the durative present in which it is experienced by impoverished and marginalized women in both affective and *embodied* forms.

The ethical concerns that call for attention in commercial surrogacy then relate not only to the realities of "unrecognized" and unpaid for excess (in the creation and valuation of the "commodity") that involve both the affective labor of the surrogate mother as well as the biological and psychological risks she hazards; they also relate to the discursive modes of disciplining surrogate mothers that result in the production of subjects and agents of self-directed violence, whose possibilities of resistance are always already co-opted and consideration of whose suffering is always already deferred.

Conclusion

Given that one of the strongest ethical critiques of commercial surrogacy hinges on the critique of its privileging the discourse of "altruism," it is indeed ironic that the Surrogacy (Regulation) Bill of 2016 that bans all commercial surrogacy and prohibits "payment to the surrogate mother" allows only "ethical altruistic surrogacy." Further, the fact that only surrogacy by a "close relative" is permitted drives surrogacy not only into the realm of altruism but also into the informality of private domestic space shielded from any public scrutiny or ethical accountability. Pande too asserts in her recent critique of the 2016 bill: "In effect, altruistic surrogacy obliges women to be reproductive gift-givers. By doing away with contracts and payments, a policy mandating altruism in surrogacy formally reifies the age-old belief that women need not be compensated for their reproductive labour" ("Surrogacy").

The critically acclaimed Bengali writer Mahasweta Devi's story "Breast-Giver" ("Stanadayini"), first published in 1978, is a penetrating fictionalized account of the impoverished wet nurse Jashoda as *dudh ma* or "milk mother." It is not about the production of babies; yet it is about the wet nurse's substituting for biological mothers so that they may preserve their figures, as "progressive suckling will ruin their shape" (1075). Their husbands can thus find a way to "*combine* multiple pregnancies and beauty" (1075). In this sense of substitution of reproductive labor, Jashoda is also a surrogate mother. I draw here upon just a few instances of Mahasweta Devi's "Breast-

Giver" and Spivak's 1997 analysis of it because they highlight certain modes of appropriation of "labor" and structures of affect associated with surrogacy within the confines of "domestic" space that foreshadow uncannily the future consequences of the 2016 bill.

In her analysis of Mahasweta Devi's story Spivak focuses on the subaltern Jashoda, who serves as a "professional mother" in the role of a wet nurse for the children of all the sons of the upper-class Haldar household, and observes that "Jashoda's body produces a surplus that is fully consumed by the owners of her labour-power and leads to no *capital* accumulation . . . although rearing children is indirectly an 'investment in the future' " (87). Instead, what there is in such surrogacy is "pre-capitalist surplus–appropriation" (87). How do we account ethically for such surrogacy, that inhabits the shadowy realms of capital in a neoliberal economy, in which there is extraction of surplus but no accumulation—and no exchange either?

Literature also serves as a significant source in the attempt to grasp the standpoint of the surrogate mother in India because it may articulate, from vantage points outside of both the confines and the circuits of surrogacy, her affective experiences that are subject to layers of silencing as much within domestic confines as within the industry. Second, it may also tap into deeper "structures of feeling" that constitute the field of force within which the surrogate mother is situated and operates, but may not consciously recognize.

In regard to Jashoda's surplus labor of producing milk for the master's household, Spivak observes that "as soon as the (exchange) value of Jashoda's milk emerges, it is immediately appropriated" (86). The 2016 bill prohibits "payment to the surrogate mother"; wherein then is the exchange value for the surrogate mother's "labor" and what is the nature of the exchange? The bill may be premised on assumptions of the existence of pure altruism, but it is an assumption that has called for the most heated of debates and its validity may be further called into question by what Charis Thomson refers to as "procreative intent." In the context of Jashoda, Spivak holds that "if you consider her in a subject-position, it is a situation of exchange, with the child, for immediate and future psycho-social affect" (91). In fact, even in the context of commercial surrogacy where the exchange value is fixed in monetary terms, expectation of psychosocial affect premised on procreative intent is not unknown:

> ARTs have made it possible to disaggregate the work of motherhood into (1) the provision of an ovum and gestation a fetus,

> and (2) the work and care of child-rearing and what Charis Thomson calls "procreative intent," and then to differentially-value these kinds of labor and distribute them across class and national lines. . . . At the same time, however, a number of surrogates describe expectations of future responsibility on the part of the client to the surrogate and her family that lie outside the surrogate's fees and correspond to local notions of familial duty. (Vora, "Disaggregation" 12)

It is through the consideration of embodiment and affect, and engagement with modes of sex-affective production, that Spivak brings us back to the subjectivity of the surrogate mother. She cites Ferguson to highlight that "women as mothers are placed in a structural bind by mother centred infant and small child care, a bind that ensures that mothers will give more than they get in the sex-affective parenting triangle . . ." (91–92). The formulation "mothers will give more than they get" may mark a situation of affective inequality between mother and child, yet it underscores the nature of the relationship with the child as being one of affective exchange. The basic nature of surrogacy *is* exchange, and in contexts where there is no monetary value put to this exchange, as in the case of altruism, the imperative of exchange would come to rest even more intensely on the exchange of psychosocial affect, especially when the surrogate mother is no professional stranger but a "close relative." Referring to the way in which the story draws to a close, with Jashoda dying "friendless, with no one left to put a bit of water in the mouth. . . . forsaken by all and. . . . alone" (1088), Spivak quotes further from the story and draws attention to the failure of exchange that is, in effect, a failure of affect:

> It is the failure of this exchange that is the substance of the story. It is the failure, the absence of the child as such that is marked by the enigmatic answer-question-parataxis toward the conclusion . . . : "Yet someone was supposed to be there at the end. Who was it? It was who? Who was it? Jashoda died at 11 pm."

The ontological vacuum created by the denial of affective exchange that the surrogate mother finds herself in, and that Spivak signals as the grim thrust of "Breast-Giver," a "narrative that recounts the failure of affect" (122), may well portend the consequences of "altruistic" surrogacy of the future in India.

Notes

1. I choose to use the term surrogate mother to keep in focus the complex nature of the surrogate mother as both worker and mother rather than just surrogate, the functional term prevalent in the industry that deflects attention from the nurturing care that the surrogate extends to the baby in her womb *as a mother*.

2. In relation to India, Bhattacharya cites: "some fertility clinics of India implant up to five/six embryos in a surrogate's body, which is life-threatening, bearing long-term biological implications on the surrogates' bodies leading not only to preeclampsia or gestational diabetes but also could damage organs like liver, kidneys and thyroid. Importantly, surrogates are paid only for one baby; often denied payment for delivering twins or triplets, or down syndrome [*sic*] babies; there are even incidences of delay in payments (Bhattacharjee; Rudrappa). Most importantly, these women receive no financial help should any complications arise in their post-pregnancy period following surrogacy" (13).

3. Approximately $1,600 in US dollars, roughly equivalent to the current annual salary of an associate professor at a state university in India.

4. "[R]ich people outsource pregnancies to poorer women because their wives cannot go through labour pain. We have put a complete stop to celebrities who are commissioning surrogate children like a hobby, despite having biological ones" ("Surrogacy Bill Gets").

5. This is Sunder Rajan's term (3).

6. One can only hope that the deep irony of this sentence will not be read as condescension.

Works Cited

Anderson, Benedict. *Imagined Communities: Reflections on the Origin and Spread of Nationalism*. Verso, 1991.

Bhattacharya, Rituparna. "Draft Surrogacy (Regulation) Bill 2016: Rhetoric or Surrogate-centric?" *Space and Culture*, vol. 4, no. 2, 2016, pp. 9–21.

Birch, Kean, and Matti Siemiatycki. "Neoliberalism and the Geographies of Marketization: The Entangling of State and Markets." *Progress in Human Geography*, vol. 40, no. 2, 2015, pp. 177–198.

Dasgupta, Rajashri. "Quick-Fix Medical Ethics: Quinacrine Sterilization and the Ethics of Contraceptive Trials." *The Unheard Scream: Reproductive Health and Women's Lives in India*, edited by Mohan Rao, Zubaan, 2004, pp. 279–309.

———. "Women Are Not a Disease." *Missing Half the Story: Journalism as if Gender Matters*, edited by Kalpana Sharma, Zubaan, 2010, pp. 188–213.

Devi, Mahasweta. "Breast-Giver." *Breast Stories*, translated by Gayatri Chakravorty Spivack. Seagull, 1997, pp. 39–75.

———. "Stanadayini." *Bachai Galpa*, 3rd ed., edited by Soma Mukhopadhyay, Mandal Book House, 2009, pp. 1–21.

Gellner, Ernest. *Thought and Change*. Weidenfeld and Nicolson, 1964, pp. 147–78.

Goffman, E. *The Presentation of Self in Everyday Life*. Anchor Books, 1959.

Google Baby. Directed by Zippi Brand Frank. Films Transit International, 2009.

Grossberg, Lawrence. "Affect's Future: Rediscovering the Virtual in the Actual." *The Affect Theory Reader*, edited by Melissa Gregg and Gregory J. Seigworth, Duke UP, 2010, pp. 309–38.

Hochschild, Arlie. *The Managed Heart: Commercialization of Human Feeling*. U of California P, 2003.

———. *The Outsourced Self: Intimate Life in Market Times*. Metropolitan Books / Henry Holt & Company, 2012.

Khalidi, Raja. "Elizabeth A. Povinelli's Symphony of Late Liberalism in Palestine." *E-flux conversations*, conversations.e-flux.com/t/elizabeth-a-povinellis-symphony-of-late-liberalism-in-palestine/6004. Accessed 30 July 2017.

Lyotard, Jean-François. *The Differend: Phrases in Dispute*. Translated by Georges Van Den Abeele. U of Minnesota P, 1992.

Malhotra, Anil. "Draft Surrogacy Bill Violates Fundamental Right of People to Choose Modes of Parenthood." *Indian Express*, 6 Mar. 2017, indianexpress.com/article/opinion/columns/surrogacy-bill-ban-commercial-2998128/. Accessed 20 May 2017.

Mukherjee, Ritika. "The Baby Business: A Study on Indian Market of Commercial Surrogacy and Its Implications." Session 157: New Perspectives on Women's Reproductive Choices. Population Association of America 2015 Annual Meeting, 30 Apr.–2 May 2015, San Diego, paa2015.princeton.edu/abstracts/152404. Accessed 20 May 2017.

"New Surrogacy Bill Bars Married Couples with Kids, NRIs, Gays, Live-Ins, Foreigners." *Indian Express*, 25 Aug. 2016, indianexpress.com/article/india/india-news-india/surrogacy-bill-sushma-swaraj-married-couples-can-now-opt-homosexuals. Accessed 24 June 2017.

Pande, Amrita. "Commercial Surrogacy in India: Manufacturing a Perfect Mother-Worker." *Signs: Journal of Women in Culture and Society*, vol. 35, no. 4, 2010, pp. 969–92.

———. "Surrogacy Bill's Missteps." *Feminist Law Archives*, Partners for Law in Development, 7 Apr. 2017, feministlawarchives.pldindia.org/surrogacy-bills-missteps-amrita-pande-2016. Accessed 24 June 2017.

———. "Transnational Commercial Surrogacy in India: Gifts for Global Sisters?" *Reproductive BioMedicine Online*, vol. 23, 2011, pp. 618–25.

———. *Wombs in Labor: Transnational Commercial Surrogacy in India*. Columbia UP, 2014.Povinelli, Elizabeth A. *Economies of Abandonment: Social Belonging and Endurance in Late Liberalism*. Duke UP, 2011.

Qadeer, Imrana, and Mary E. John. "The Business and Ethics of Surrogacy." *Economic and Political Weekly*, vol. 44, no. 2, 2009, pp. 10–12.

Rao, Mohan. "Banning Commercial Surrogacy Is the Only Way Forward." *Governance Now*, 16–30 Sept. 2016, www.governancenow.com/views/interview/banning-commercial-surrogacy-only-way-forward-mohan-rao. Accessed 20 June 2016.

———. "Why All Non-Altruistic Surrogacy Should Be Banned." *Economic and Political Weekly*, vol. 47, no. 21, 2012, pp. 15–17.

Sangari, Kumkum. *Solid:Liquid: A (Trans)national Reproductive Formation*. Tulika Books, 2015.

Saravanan, Sheela. "Transnational Surrogacy and Objectification of Gestational Mothers." *Economic and Political Weekly*, vol. 45, no. 16, 2010, pp. 26–29.

Spivak, Gayatri Chakravorty. " 'Breast-Giver': For Author, Reader, Teacher, Subaltern, Historian . . ." *Breast Stories*, by Mahasweta Devi, translated by Gayatri C. Spivak, Seagull, 1997, pp. 76–137.

Sunder Rajan, Kaushik. *Biocapital: The Constitution of Postgenomic Life*. Duke UP, 2006.

"Surrogacy Bill Gets the Cabinet Nod." *The Hindu*, 24 Aug. 2016, www.thehindu.com/news/national/Surrogacy-bill-gets-the-Cabinet-nod/article14591267.ece. Accessed 24 June 2017.

Surrogacy (Regulation) Bill. No. 257, India, 2016, www.prsindia.org/uploads/media/Surrogacy/Surrogacy%20(Regulation)%20Bill,%202016.pdf%202016.pdf. Accessed 24 June 2017.

Verma, Tarishi. "What Are the Surrogacy Laws in India?" *Indian Express*, 6 Mar. 2016, indianexpress.com/article/research/karan-johar-surrogate-children-yash-roohi-what-are-the-surrogacy-in-laws-in-india-here-is-everything-you-need-to-know-4555077/. Accessed 24 June 2017.

Vora, Kalindi. "Indian Transnational Surrogacy and the Disaggregation of Mothering Work." *Anthropology News*, Feb. 2009, pp. 9–121.

———. "Limits of 'Labor': Accounting for Affect and the Biological in Transnational Surrogacy and Service Work." *South Atlantic Quarterly*, vol. 111, no. 4, 2012, pp. 681–700.

———. "Potential, Risk, and Return in Transnational Indian Gestational Surrogacy." *Potentiality and Humanness: Revisiting the Anthropological Object in Contemporary Biomedicine, Current Anthropology*, vol. 54, no. S7, Oct. 2013, pp. S97–S106.

7

Artificial Bodies

The Politics of the Posthuman in Argentine Science Fiction Novels

Silvia G. Kurlat Ares

In 1999, N. Katherine Hayles summarized the third wave in the posthuman turn as the redefinition of autonomy and agency. If the concept of life were to be extended to include artificial systems, it would also become necessary to redefine how such systems could change and adapt. For Hayles, these questions were the scaffolding of posthumanism itself: how to relate identity, individuality, and community when the liberal humanist subject had shrunk to the point of microscopic dimensions with the resultant instability of values assigned to life (222–57). Such concerns were conspicuously absent from the canonical narratives of Argentine science fiction, with some interesting exceptions such as Leopoldo Lugones's short story "Yzur" (1906) and Carlos Gardini's "Primera Línea" (1982). But they have emerged at the forefront of works produced since the turn of the twenty-first century. Since the early 2000s, as neoliberal and populist agendas have disrupted traditional party systems, displaced blue-collar workers from their long-established forms of employment, and generated new forms of consumer and visual cultures, Argentine science fiction has consistently addressed the conundrums of posthumanism. Among the central tropes of this new science fiction is the radical reimagination of the family. Instead of the heterosexual couples and biological offspring that dominated realist and historical novels since the nineteenth century, the emerging body of speculative fiction conspicuously disrupts what Doris Sommer famously described as the "founding romance" of the nation-state: "the object is not just to tease but literally to engender new nations. . . . Fathers of nations couldn't afford to simply lord it over mothers if they hoped to produce legitimate bourgeois children" (18).

I have argued elsewhere that for most of the twentieth century, Argentine novels preserved the role of women as symbols of the motherland; marriage and maternity, consequently, served as metonymic substitutions for allegiance to the project of nation-building. By the same token, male figures were generally portrayed as the standard bearers of rational, liberal projects whose completion could only benefit their countries and bring societies closer to utopia. In stark contrast, the novels we are going to discuss here either contest or ignore such formulations. They provide new political and ideological interpretations and assign new sets of symbolic values to female and male characters. Families are utterly disarticulated: fathers who in the past provided the vocabulary and imagery of law and order are often absent or uninterested in the outcome of their choices; children (all children, whether biological or adopted) rebel and denounce their parents' choices as unethical, arbitrary, or politically illegitimate; and finally, women's bodies are no longer conduits of the nation, but the sites of speculative transactions rooted in an ever-changing reality that is now very far from the idealized, telluric ontologies of previous decades. Family, community, and identity are all reworked to create, as J. Andrew Brown said, "a new mythology and different ways of remembering individual experience" (146). Within this framework, biology ceases to play a teleological role in the ideological buildup of state programs.

Argentine science fiction of the new millennium thus decouples the production of the universal subject from the sustainability of the nation. In doing so, it may provide the mirage of some alternative templates of future communities, but its sharpest critical gaze is turned upon the present. The cyborgs and clones explored in this chapter expose everyday ideological inconsistencies and suggest that other forms of being human are possible; that diversity and difference can and should ground what Rosi Braidotti calls a "multifaceted subject"; and that this subject, always in flux and always becoming, embodies an "expanded relational self, engendered by the cumulative effect of social and planetary factors" ("Posthuman Critical Theory" 22).

Located in dystopian worlds that can clearly be recognized as possible Argentina(s), novels like *El corazón de Doli* (2010, Doli's heart), by Gustavo Nielsen (b. 1962), and *Casa de Ottro* (2009, Ottro's house), by Marcelo

Cohen (b. 1951), rework cultural and economic relationships through new forms of subjectivity and otherness in the bodies of clones and cyborgs. In the next pages, I will explore how these other-bodies and biologies allow for a meditation on the value of agency in the absence of community and how community can be rebuilt without resorting to modernity's ideological constructs. In both novels, individuals who have been left behind, or whose rights have been ignored or trampled, build their subjectivity and citizenship by making their technological differences the core value of a new form of sociability. Hence, I will argue that these novels posit the passage to the posthuman conceptual framework in Latin American countries by turning away from binary ideological worldviews (i.e., civilization-barbarism, city-countryside, lettered intellectual-people, etc.) with their implied and inscribed perspectives of self and identity as exceptional. Breaking away from reification reframes what it means to acquire full consciousness; that is to say, it redefines a multiple subjectivity that is forever changing and adapting to the complexity of the world. By the same token, this passage also implies the unfolding of all that can be possible, both as a positive and a negative future-vision for the country.

As we shall see, this transition has been met with extraordinary resistance by literary and cultural critics. At stake is not simply an issue of resistance to science fiction (even when the point can be easily argued). There are also political and ideological ramifications to such a transformation, which first seemed to emerge as an apparent abandonment of the question of history and its explicative (and teleological) power as understood by the Argentine *intelligentsia* until the mid-nineties. As the political sphere became more radicalized in the late sixties, the Argentine novel developed into the locus of a fierce debate about the social and political role of intellectuals and radicalized the realist attempt to deploy contemporary ideological agendas. By the mid-seventies, this double agenda became manifest in a writing program whose aim was to dispute not only official accounts of history but historiography itself: the novel was to replace history, as official history could not be trusted. The corpus of novels that attempted this operation with varying degrees of success include *De dioses, hombrecitos y policías* (1979), by Humberto Constantini; *Lugar Común La Muerte* (1979), by Tomás Eloy Martínez; *El Beso de la Mujer Araña* (1976), by Manuel Puig; and *Cuerpo a Cuerpo* (1979), by David Viñas. The results were uneven. By the time the Shanghai group emerged in 1989, the question of realism as a political and ideological program and the relationship between narrative and history came to a formal end.[1]

To better understand this debate and how and why the writers discussed here turned away from genres such as realism and historical fiction, the first section of this article will provide a brief background of Argentine literary debates at the start of the twenty-first century. This will allow readers to better appreciate the political and cultural role science fiction narrative plays in Argentine culture. In the second and third sections, I will analyze how *El corazón de Doli* and *Casa de Ottro* situate the bodies of clones and cyborgs in the disenfranchised neighborhoods and shantytowns of Buenos Aires and characterize them as the locus of a changing social and political environment. These altered and artificial biologies offer alternative models of citizenry to those displayed in the politically engaged historic novels that provide the hegemonic political model prior to the early 2000s.[2] They also allow the writers to tackle the question of emerging subjectivities.

In addition, in these sections I will show how both novels embed discourses of medical research and liberal modernist politics into their narratives to convey market commodification (most bodies can be sold or used), dubious ethical choices (all bodies are subject to experiments in social engineering), and social codification (cyborgs and clones are perceived as utterly dominated and devoid of agency). While they undo all expectations and contest all ready-made approaches to ideology, they are not programmatic novels about the future. In *El corazón de Doli*, the scientist father, who operates a hospital that produces clones as repositories of healthy organs, is an absentee figure who cannot or is unwilling to put forward any notion of fairness or equality. In *Casa de Ottro*, the social scientist mother, who was to design the social and political agendas of an imagined rational sense of progress, is unwilling to deal with the crisis around her or acknowledge any form of complexity. In both cases, founding parental figures, whose symbolic places were traditionally associated with discourses of progress and liberty, end up producing a negative system that "perpetuates familiar patterns of exclusion, exploitation, and repression" (Braidotti, *Posthuman* 83). Hence, the novels posit forms of otherness as sites of resistance to economic, social, and cultural control, and prejudice (clones fight for agency; cyborgs propose a better ideological understanding of the real). In his analysis of the rhetorics of monstrosity in the late nineties and early 2000s, Gutiérrez Mouat identifies a gothic strand of Latin American literature, which has often used freaks and monsters to narrate political and social violence by bringing forward extreme forms of alterity that cannot be negotiated. However he fails to see that in their very alterity, the technological(ized) others also articulate a new form of subjectivity that is able to speak about the ever-changing experiences of identity as an aggregate of both individualized and collective experiences. I will explore the meanings of this transformation.

Last, in the conclusion, I will summarize how the novels work out the conflict between self and collective, or individuality and community, and why this opposition becomes manifest in clone and cyborg bodies.

The Argentine Novel at the Turn of the Century: Dystopia as Politics

Argentine science fiction has a long tradition that can be traced back to the nineteenth century, but it was only during the last fifty years that the modality acquired increased visibility and legitimacy. Despite its prestigious lineage, writing science fiction is still understood by many as a lesser literary choice at worst and a curious and rather reckless experiment at best. In interviews, writers are routinely asked about their reasons for choosing this narrative form and frequently offered a variety of substitute terms from speculative to alternative fiction. Even though authors like Nielsen and Cohen (whom many consider Borges's intellectual heir) are unapologetic for their practice of science fiction as a critical method, their answers still tend to be somewhat evasive. Both writers agree on the need for a critical narrative that provides them with a language and imagery that realism (as practiced in Argentina since the mid-sixties) lacks. In an interview, Nielsen said: "La sociedad de la novela no es ésta en la que estamos viviendo, porque no hay todavía clonación de repuesto, pero tampoco es un futuro muy lejano. El futuro te puede llevar al dibujito animado. En mis novelas normalmente hay mucho dibujo animado, mucho cómic, mucho cine clase B, que les da un plus que me divierte" (The society of the novel is not the one in which we are living because there is still no spare cloning, but neither is it a very distant future. The future can lead you to a cartoon. In my novels, there usually are a lot of cartoons, a lot of comics, a lot of class B cinema, which gives them a bonus that amuses me; Friera).[3] Cohen, who has often discussed the issue of science fiction in his writing, also discussed his distrust of realism in an interview: "Me daba pavor el realismo, el ombliguismo, el desdén por una inmensa cantidad de cosas que no son el país, la promiscuidad de la vida. . . . Y sobre todo el realismo, porque en ese momento había numerosos indicios de que la literatura argentina estaba cambiando después de una década bastante opaca, aunque Fogwill y Aira ya estaban escribiendo" (I dreaded realism, the self-centered approach, the disdain for an immense amount of things that are not the country, the promiscuity of life. . . . And above all, I was terrified of realism, because at that time there were numerous indications that Argentine literature was changing after a fairly opaque decade, even though Fogwill and Aira were already writing; "Entrevista"). For these writers, science fiction fosters the critique of social and political issues without disputing their place in history. It thus opens up a discussion about Argentine sociability from a highly critical perspective.

Nielsen and Cohen's belief that realism was unable to narrate the Argentine experience was shared and discussed by a number of writers during the nineties. It was a popular topic in the publications of the Shanghai Group, which included many writers for *Babel* magazine (Daniel Fuebel, Luis Chitarroni, Alan Pauls, Ricardo Ibarlucía, Daniel Samoilovich, Diego Bigorre, Sergio Chejfec, Sergio Bizzio, Jorge Dorio, and Martín Chaparrós, among others) and journalists who contributed to the cultural supplement of *Tiempo Argentino* (such as Rodrigo Fresán, Daniel Guebel, and Juan Forn). Fogwill, Laiseca, and Aira became this group's most important aesthetic and literary referents. They were admired for their avant-garde writing programs, their disdain for engaged realism, and, in particular, their acidic take on the common sense of the cultural field. Although most of these writers did not turn to science fiction, several mentioned the modality as one of their preferred (and formative) readings. In the mid-eighties, many began to talk about and quote science fiction books, which led to the publication of a famous cultural supplement on the subject as early as 1985.[4]

The economic crisis that shook the country in the early 2000s cemented the impression that the old paradigm of the realist novel, so intertwined with the modernization project, was truly over as a political agenda.[5] The new century opened with at least two main literary trends that did not seek to explain or justify the present through some long-forgotten or misunderstood event. This perspective departed radically from the literature that had become hegemonic in the Argentine cultural field since the late sixties and seventies. The rise of the historical novel can thereby be understood as an attempt at explaining the failures of modernization as much as the horrors of the dictatorship (1976–1983). By tracing the origins and causes of different historical turning points, the novel took the mantle of history. By the mid-nineties, these operations were questioned and rejected by writers seeking to narrate the political experience in critical rather than hagiographic terms, on the one hand, and to analyze the contemporary as a lived, present event, on the other. By the early 2000s, Argentine literature was characterized by the predominance of narrative styles that underlined the immediacy of experience with raw vocabulary and imagery. These novels explored low-income neighborhoods and attempted to narrate the daily lives of the rapidly impoverished middle- and low-income classes during the ascent of populism. Marred by economic and social crisis, these narratives also naturalized the vocabularies of dystopia as they explored the national ethos from increasingly critical points of view.

The dystopian turn in Argentine narrative was not out of step with international developments. The 1980s had also been a turning point in utopian and dystopian narratives in the English-speaking world. Narrative dystopian strategies had provided writers in the United States and the United Kingdom with the ability to speak about the new social and political realities of the Reagan era. In Argentina, this type of dystopian text started to appear as early as 1986 with Cohen's *Insomnio*, but its presence would not be felt until much later. It would not be until the early 2000s that writers started to explore science fiction as the narrative form that best allowed them to analyze the country's ideological buildup without resorting to the conceits of the historical novel. By then, all sorts of texts were approaching the issue from a variety of mediums. The works that best—and most cruelly—narrate this transformation are Rafael Pinedo's famed trilogy, *Plop* (2002), *Frío* (2004), and *Subte* (2006). Other notable texts include Fogwill's *Runa* (2003); Oliverio Coelho's *Tierra de vigilia* (2000), *Los invertebrables* (2003), *Borneo* (2004), and *Promesas naturales* (2006); and Pedro Mairal's *El año del desierto* (2005). Writers like Gustavo Nielsen and Marcelo Cohen can be comfortably placed on this long list, as both have consistently worked with critical dystopic worlds that provided new ways to narrate the contemporary cultural, social, and economic Argentine experience.

In addition, comics addressed the way that new political subjectivities faced the transformation of the social sphere and reflected on everyday politics framed by the backdrop of a dystopian Argentina. The award-wining *La burbuja de Bertold* (2005) and *Planeta Extra* (2009), by Diego Agrimbau and Gabriel Ippóliti; *Cieloalto* (2012), by Agrimbau and Pietro; *Reparador de Sueños* (2011), by Matías Santellán and Pablo Serafín; and *El cuervo que sabía: Un melodrama de ciencia ficción* (2011), by Kwaichang Kráneo (pseudonym of Carlos David Lima), are among the many that reflect upon these issues. Finally, movies also followed suit, including *Adios, querida Luna* (2001), *Filmatrón* (2007), and *Los santos sucios* (2009), among others.

All these novels, short stories, comics, and movies discuss the ideology and the failures of the Argentine liberal project, the rise of neoliberal policies and populist agendas, the increase of violence in everyday life, and the emergence of a new kind of subjectivity.[6] All fit Moylan and Baccolini's now-classic definition of a critical dystopia, where "the dystopian text usually begins directly in the terrible new world; and yet, even without a dislocating move to an elsewhere, the element of textual estrangement remains in effect since the focus is frequently on a character who questions the dystopian society . . . the text is built around the construction of a narrative of hegemonic order and counter-narrative resistance" (5). In an earlier text, Moylan analyzed how critical dystopias configured this site of resistance by turning the confrontation with an alter reality into an experience of ideological awareness. Dystopias, said Moylan, offer a way to renegotiate what we know as a negation of a critical utopian moment: "and thus [they] make room for another manifestation of the utopian imagination within the dystopian form . . . [and they] negotiate the necessary pessimism of the generic dystopia with an open, militant utopian stance that not only breaks through the hegemonic enclosure of the text's alternative world but also self reflexively refuses the anti-utopian temptation . . ." (195). According to Moylan, these narratives give voice and space to dispossessed and denied subjects who attempt to create a social reality that allows them not only to survive but also to create a form of opposition based on difference and multiplicity. This is why dystopias offer a new site of resistance or, in other words, a new map for what political opposition might look like in the twenty-first century. From now on, one would need to understand that the oppositional politics at play in the text were not anchored in an agenda or political how-to, and foundational metaphors about family and loving couples no longer functioned. The ethical stance that narrative provided required an updated imagery. Within this framework, motherhood lost its biological determinacy, along with its ontology. Women characters incarnated forms of relational power; they were neither the other of men nor the site of reproduction. Meanwhile, men failed to form families or were absentee fathers; their journeys tended to showcase their inability to hold on to power and to envision the future. There are no foundational romances and no (re)productive couplings, as children are often monsters who seek relational systems outside of the safe spaces of the household.

Yet, this transformation was often either misunderstood or misinterpreted. Argentine critics and readers were used to the idealized revolutionaries and intellectuals of the historical novel that reflected on the dark years of the dictatorship; they were familiar with the easily allegorized families that populated Argentine literature for over sixty years and that inhabited the politically committed novel of the second half of the twentieth century. The new subject that emerged from the corpus described on the previous pages created a radical difference whose ideological engagement was often difficult to perceive, as it had walked away not only from history but also from the party system and state and social institutions, including the traditional couplings and families that hinted that the future was possible. Moreover, the fact that the utopian impulse had ceased to be a concrete program in the novels and had now become a mirage, a faint possibility on a faraway horizon, seemed terribly disturbing. Josefina Ludmer discussed several of these novels early on and raised her concern about what she perceived not only as a loss of literary value but also of political aim. In an article published in 2002, she associates them with the absence of literature because whether they were real or fictional was irrelevant. She explained that science fictional texts in particular were devoid of temporality; they stood in a perpetual present where reality and fiction melded, nullifying the existence of a utopia. In consequence, the future they portrayed is a return to the past. Ludmer further argued that the implosion of the family unit implied the disintegration of subjectivity. However, this kind of criticism seems to ignore what Ruth Levitas defined as the main function of utopia: "Utopia may still express desire, but it does not articulate hope" (qtd. in Moylan and Baccolini 16). The novels we are going to discuss in the pages that follow are about the articulation of the vocabulary needed to express hope as resistance.

Other Bodies: The Bioethics of *El corazón de Doli*

By the time he published *El corazón de Doli* in 2010, Gustavo Nielsen was already an established Argentine writer who had published a number of well-received novels, such as *La flor azteca* (1997) and *Auschwitz* (2004), and coauthored a children's book, *Los monstruos del riachuelo* (2001), with Ana María Shúa.[7] He had also written several collections of short stories and has twice been a finalist for the prestigious Premio Planeta Argentina. He won the Premio Antorchas in 2003 and the Premio Clarín de Novela in 2010. However, his novels are not well known outside of Argentina and have yet to be translated into English.

Nielsen's novels consciously stay away from historic and psychological narratives ("9 temas"). An accomplished architect by trade, his novels stage a carefully scaffolded approach to graphic cruelty and violence. Readers are able to follow evil's banal proliferation into society and witness how it is often backed by indifference and prejudice. Nielsen's wry, dry sense of humor undoes the clichés of Argentine sociability by exposing the consequences of everyday behaviors. For this reason, critics like Fernando Reati have included his novels among Argentine narratives that deal with the social memory of the last dictatorship (1976–1983) and its tainted legacy. Even though his novels do not deal with politics directly and it is not possible to ascribe them to a specific, recognizable statecraft program, they are all a deep meditation on ethical values, social and civil life, and the uniqueness of human experience. Moreover, reading his books is a rather disquieting experience, as realism quickly gives way to dystopic universes that do not read as a future or alternative Argentina but rather as an intensely Argentine ideological experience, a sort of embodiment of poet Osvaldo Lamborguini's dictum: "Argentina no es ninguna raza ni nacionalidad, sino puro estilo y lengua" (Argentina is neither race nor nationality, but pure style and language). Nielsen's novels are rooted in the lived experiences of the national ethos. In an interview granted at the time of *El corazón de Doli*'s publication, Nielsen said: "Desde un punto de vista literario, la política no me interesa, no estoy hablando de una sociedad del futuro. Establecí reglas para definir la humanidad de los personajes. Un clone que tiene un cuerpo para donarlo al hermano cuando éste lo necesite y un hermano que por maldad y capricho hasta es capaz de quitarse un órgano. Me interesa ese momento, qué piensa el ser humano cuando su cuerpo se ve amenazado" (From a literary point of view, politics do not interest me, I'm not talking about a society of the future. I established rules to define the humanity of the characters. A clone that has a body to donate to his brother when he needs it and a brother who by malice and whim is able to remove an organ. I am interested in that moment, in what the human being thinks when his body is threatened; Friera). *El corazón de Doli* is the fictional, biographical account of a pair of twin brothers, Sergio and his clone, Víctor, who have been created by artificial insemination as an original and a spare. In their world, sexual relationships are slowly disappearing; artificial insemination, selective breeding, and cloning have become the preferred methods of reproduction. Narrated by their detached father, *El corazón de Doli* follows the unequal education of the sons and tells how Víctor falls in love with the clone of Sofi, Doli, who will eventually be sacrificed so the former can live. The novel does not explore the scientific know-how or technological apparatuses needed to create these clones. It assumes that the technology is there, the resources are available, and society at large has accepted cloning. As is often the case in Argentine science fiction, the question here is not about the science but about the ethical, moral, and legal questions that such a development could bring forward.

In the novel, families often opt to have their children's clones to provide any spare parts should the originals need them in case of illness or accident. Bodies have been commodified and their market naturalized by social interactions. Clones are literally disposable bodies. The twins' relationship showcases objectification and commodification as inhuman experiences, which are amplified by who and what their parents are. Sergio and Víctor's family is rich; their father is the owner and main researcher in the clinic that creates clones for both their own provincial town and a good portion of the country. He links knowledge and oppression, as well as commodification and death; in his practice, rationality, reason, and order are turned inside out, revealing the denial of agency and a betrayal of the flow between self and other. His indifference to the abuse suffered by all clones (including his son) also betrays the irrationality and lack of ethics of his own profession and belief system.

The twins' mother is a stay-at-home woman who imagines herself to be part of the B list of the Argentine jet set and cannot understand why celebrities do not attend her many soirées. A caricature of the middle- and lower-class obsession with fame and celebrity culture, she represents an old form of womanhood while, at the same time, she is defined by and delinked from biological and social constrictions. She is both caring mother and evil guardian. Obsessed with her "real" son, Sergio, she dotes on him with all of her love while denying Víctor, whom she sees as both a monster and a slave, of any affection. Meanwhile, it turns out that Sergio, her (re)production, is himself a monster of negativity and criminality.

The novel is a parody of Argentina's middle-class obsession with consumerism, marketing, and mass media. In a society that boasts that only authentic things have any value ("sólo tiene valor lo auténtico" [only the authentic has value] is the slogan repeated over and over again by characters and institutions), everyday life is built around copies and simulations of "real" goods created in central countries. Such is the case of the twins' uncle, who has a fast-food chain called McPollen Fritten (a name that distorts both the words for "fried chicken" in Spanish—pollo frito—and the name of McDonald's). The chain's main food ingredient turns out to be monstrous, mistreated, mutated birds that lack bones and beaks; they can no longer be called chicken because they are trademarked goods. Furthermore, the town's main soccer team was put together because the richest man in the country requested that one be formed using his own son, an exceedingly good player, as an original. Ten copies of him were created and trained, resulting in a winning team and giving the father both an investment and a family. In addition, money is counterfeited on a regular basis, as its value is always changing, and economic crime becomes only a misdemeanor. People regularly undergo plastic surgery in order to improve their appearance to the point that employees of McPollen are asked to create permanent, fake smiles to better attract customers. Even though this ploy backfires, some of the characters choose to keep their new, grotesque smiles in order to hide their real emotions from others. More importantly, value is also attributed to people by the state; originals are considered "true" citizens with full rights, while clones (who carry documents with an R that means "repuesto" [replacement], a chilling reference to Germany's Nuremberg Laws of the 1930s) cannot even have bank accounts or carry credit cards.

Paradoxically, clones provide the only kernel of authenticity in a society that operates on the belief that simulacra, as Baudrillard would have expressed, is the only possible understanding of the real. The "authentic" characters have nothing that seems real or truthful. The clones represent what should or may be of ethical value either through their choices (e.g., the clone policeman that lets Víctor go free after an accident kills Sergio because he understands the complexity of his situation) or through their service to others (e.g., when Víctor takes care of his deranged, elderly mother despite her mistreatment and abuse of him). It is not the clones' mere existence that forces a shift in dominant (social, political) paradigms within the narrative. It is rather their choices and the way in which they exercise free will. In an article that discusses clone narratives, Amit Marcus points out that these texts often display an anxiety about encounters with otherness by posing ethical questions about which behaviors are morally ambivalent, reprehensible, amoral, or illegal. In Nielsen's novel, clones are often created with the consent of their families, but not of the individuals to be cloned. Children and babies are not asked if they desire their spare counterparts. Sergio and Víctor are created at the same time and educated as identical twins. In many cases, clones are told what they are and are expected to accept it. There is an insistence on pointing out that they are not people but mere copies and instruments. The "truth" about their destiny is delivered at a young age to ensure obedience to the sacrifices they will make for their counterparts. It is, in this sense, a form of social and cultural indoctrination. In other cases, individuals choose to be cloned to reach some form of immortality; it gives them the sense that they have infinite, vicarious lives. Such is the case of Calda, Sofi and Doli's mother/

original, who clones herself twice, once with all her genetically possible illnesses, and again as a "clean" copy that is able to save the first. In these cases, the characters do not believe that the individual experiences of the clones make them separate personas with their own memories and feelings instead of mere replicas of themselves. Moreover, the fact that many of the clones might die upon the request of their families is not considered a crime. The replication of humans through cloning, with all its unsettling moral consequences, thus becomes, as stated by Marcus, "a symptom of a radical capitalist society whose members have lost all moral inhibitions and treat human beings, even their own families, as commodities rather than autonomous subjects who are worthy of respect" (410).

In Nielsen's novel, questions about human autonomy and human rights become the centerpiece of an exploration of what it means to have personhood. As the novel progresses, Doli, who initially does not know she is a clone, writes poetry and imagines a future with her own biological children delivered naturally, with no medical interventions or cloning. When she is finally told the truth, the first thing she rejects is an instamatic camera given to her by her sister; in her view, the images are simulacra of the real. A photo album with them in it becomes a reminder of her lack of choice and her inability to exercise free will. In the same scene, when she is resisting Sergio, who is about to rape her, Doli says that she is not in his plans; she does not accept them (142). The horror of her rape and the awfulness of her acceptance of her obligations toward Sofi are further underlined by Víctor's despair and rebellion as he realizes what has happened over the next few chapters.

Víctor's reaction to Doli's death and, later, to the acknowledgment of her rape, allows for an exploration of what it means to resist social constraints and to understand what our own behavior exposes. After becoming utterly depressed by his girlfriend's death, Víctor goes fishing with Sergio. While at sea on that stormy night, Sergio reveals to him what he has done. Angry, Víctor decides to kill him, but a freak accident takes his brother's life before he can. It is never clear if Víctor was ever able to actually lower his weapon or hit Sergio. Nonetheless, he focuses on his intent; in his mind's eye, he is an assassin. Before surrendering himself to the police, in the most horrifying scene in the novel, Víctor literally disassembles his dead brother's body in the McPollen's butcher shop and reduces him to mincemeat that he then proceeds to cook and eat. In doing so, Víctor, who up to this point was a commodity himself, turns his brother into the object of consumption par excellence. Though macabre and grotesque, the scene is at the same time liberating; as Sergio's body disappears, Víctor is finally able to acquire the personhood he never had. A scene of true ritual cannibalism, the passage also reverses the signs of power linked to the disappeared body that had marked the narratives of the missing in earlier decades. Sergio's death signifies Víctor's freedom, even if he is incarcerated and eventually kidnapped himself, as he is now the original. But here, the symbolic reversal also carries a moral price. Reati, always attentive to how issues of power emerge in a text, asks: "¿Es que somos de verdad esa masa de fluidos y tejidos musculares que se pueden reducir a un balde de mazacote triturado? El significado de la destrucción del cadáver de Sergio en *El Corazón de Doli* tiene que ver con una pregunta sobre los límites de un poder absoluto sobre el cuerpo de otro" (Are we really that mass of fluid and muscle tissue that can be reduced to a bucket of crushed hodgepodge? The meaning of the destruction of Sergio's corpse in *El corazón de Doli* is an inquiry into the limits of exercising absolute power over the body of another; 275).

In a way, once Víctor is granted his freedom, he vanishes; his body is still his, he is still alive and present, but who he was is now transformed. In the novel, Sergio and Víctor are presented as psychological and intellectual opposites. Some of their differences are rooted in their clearly distinct educations, but their origins are also genetic and moral. Sergio chooses to embrace all social ills as they benefit his status in town. He never feels any pity for his brother or for those unfortunate enough to have been born second-class citizens. Víctor, on the other hand, surrenders to his own destiny until he loses what is most precious to him. His rebellion expresses a form of visceral fury that knows no bounds and breaks all taboos. It is a displaced rage; its aim should have been at society, but instead, it symbolically zeroed in on the body of his dead brother, the recipient of all the benefits of the very social system that enslaved him. As he becomes the monster feared by his mother, Victor not only reveals the true nature of his social environment, as Eco would have said, he also becomes someone who can be redeemed through an apprenticeship of the self that brings forward a desire to be different and to behave differently. When Víctor sees himself in a fellow manufactured "pollen" destined to be killed, processed, and eaten, he understands his role in society and finally chooses autonomy. Empathy becomes a tool for freedom. For the most part, the novel plays with the soap-opera trope of the evil twin or with the literary doppelgänger motif as a way to address the issue of sameness/difference in the original/clone relationship. But at the pivotal moment of Sergio's death, readers become unsure of how to adjudicate positive values as Víctor's identity seems to devolve. Talking about how clones function as doubles, Marcus has pointed out that often "narration demonstrates that there are no exact repetitions or perfect duplications, since each repetition of a series of events creates another interpretation, in fact another *fabulae* or story" (420). Hence, the meaning of Víctor's crime and eventual transformation also alters the narration, for he will have a chance to choose differently. As an original, Víctor will have his own clone, whom he will educate as a son and who will never carry the "R" in his documents. Víctor will seek Sofi, Doli's sister who now has her heart, and eventually marry her. And in the end, he, his clone, and Sofi will choose to form a strange extended family with his father, who will finally give up the clinic and his lovers.

Víctor's rebellion is not his descent into madness and violence, but his willingness to create a future for himself and for his clone despite social and cultural pressure. This new future represents both an expiation for the gruesome act that allows it into being and a form of resistance, as Víctor does not comply with any form of social expectation for clones. His resistance, at times passive, at times violent, eventually will create its own form of sociability by reorganizing how subjects engage with and relate to each other. It is in this way that clones survive in/with their human counterparts or, sometimes, replace them as better, improved versions of their originals. As Nayar points out, "the clones are created from humans, they are brought up and treated as the Other but their organs are harvested and assimilated into humans so that eventually the clone body and the human body become one" (62). What the novel does through those other bodies is to split open the limits of social, legal, and juridical discourses and provide the vocabulary for agency and resistance.

Marcelo Cohen's Cyborg or the Freedom of Self

Marcelo Cohen is probably one of the best living Argentine writers. Although translations of his work are only now starting to appear in English, he has earned several prestigious awards, including the Konex Prize (2004) and the Premio de la Crítica de la Fundación del Libro (2012). He is the author of several collections of short stories and essays, and several novels, including *El país de la dama eléctrica* (1984), *El sitio de Keleny* (1987), *El oído absoluto* (1989), *El testamento de O'Jaral* (1995), *Donde yo no estaba* (2006), and the novel I will discuss here, *Casa de Ottro* (2009).

As with Nielsen, Cohen's novels operate in a tense rejection of mimetic realism, which he has called "insecure realism" in several essays and interviews. The main focuses of his fiction are the relationships between everyday life and our technologized environments and between the utopian impulse and the concrete pragmatics of politics. In an interview, Cohen said, "A veces me dicen que lo que escribo es raro: parte de esa rareza, me imagino, proviene del cruce entre el carácter especulativo tecnológico con las pasiones de la novela realista" (Sometimes they tell me that what I write is weird: part of that rarity, I imagine, comes from the cross between its speculative, technological character and the passions of the realist novel; "El reencatamiento"). Cohen's novels are populated by new religious forms, strange radical groups, and political and economic interests that seem to tear apart the very nature of individual experience. All of these groupings are built on the echoes of Argentine ideological experiences.

Conflict characterizes life in the imaginary island nations of the Panoramic Delta, where most of Cohen's novels are set. Far from utopias, they are recognizable, yet strange; close, yet distant. Sometimes dystopian, sometimes postapocalyptic, the setting serves as the locus for social and political thought experiments that can be recognized as part of the country's nation-state program, or the modernization efforts that took place during the twentieth century in Argentina. In the Panoramic Delta, these efforts are stretched to their limits, exposing their contradictions and exploitations and creating complex exercises in ideological estrangement. Rich in social and political conflict, the islands are also scarred by the use of technologies that, more often than not, impact sociability and the individual's free will. Yet technology (as is often the case in Argentine science fiction) is presented as already old, almost archaic, already used and discarded by more powerful centers, both dangerous and appealing. As such, Cohen's novels are a methodical deconstruction of the political common sense of the cultural field. As with Nielsen, his main concern centers on the immediacy of narrative events and their impact on our ethical system.

Casa de Ottro is a rereading of the populist trend of the late nineties and early 2000s and is set in the highly technologized, regulated Ushoda Island. The main character of the novel is sociologist Fronda Pátegher, the daughter-in-law of Collados Ottro and the executor of his estate. An unusual character, she is an intellectual for whom motherhood was just another social experiment. She was also a libertarian leftist who was instrumental in organizing and winning the governmental campaigns of her late father-in-law, becoming not only his ideologist but also the brain behind his power. Fronda's allegiance to her father-in-law and estrangement from her philosopher husband is not a covert political operation, as the novel is a long meditation on the nature of power and on the ascent of populism in collusion with the left in Latin American countries. Since I have written extensively on this aspect of the novel, here I want to concentrate on the biological transformation of two of the characters, Ottro's faithful servant, Cañada, and Fronda's estranged son, Riscos.[8]

Cañada is a cyborg (cyborgue in the novel) who became Ottro's goddaughter when he decided to stop the women from his blue-collar town from aborting girls, his first political gesture. The abortions were part of a campaign aimed at restoring the demographic imbalance of the island, as there were 30 percent more females than males. Ottro's effort to stop them is both an imposition of state power over the bodies of blue-collar women and a protective measure for their baby girls: power is exercised as a double-edged rationality. His scandalized (and tactical) gesture is a symbolic intervention over the blue-collar female body and foreshadows Ottro's paternalistic relationship with Cañada, who starts working in Ottro's household as a servant when she's a teenager. Little by little, Ottro convinces her to undergo plastic surgeries that slowly transform her body into something alien. Fronda, though ambivalent about Cañada's transformation, often ponders her father-in-law's motives:

> Le pagó vértebras de vanadio ultraligero para reemplazar las que el peso le había desviado; le pagó el mejoramiento de la cara con loza diboxena, el injerto de supervisión hogareña en el bíceps derecho. . . . En los laboratorios sociales, entre los jóvenes de la revuelta, circulaba la idea de que los ciborgues domésticos salían sumisos, cumplidores, algo aprensivos y casi pachorrientos de tan serenos. Ahora pienso que, con la excusa de protegerla de un mundo mal intencionado, Ottro permitió que Cañada creciera recluida y madurase casta. . . . Ciborguizándola, los médicos neutralizaron una minusvalía. Pero también sospecho que Cañada encuentra en la lentitud una inconsciencia útil para pasar por alto sus disminuciones. (30–31)
>
> He paid for the ultralight vanadium vertebrae that replaced the ones that the weight had shifted; he paid for the improvement of her face with diboxena, for the home vigilance graft in her right bicep. . . . In social laboratories, among the youth of the revolt, there existed the idea that domestic cyborgs were submissive,

> compliant, somewhat apprehensive and almost sluggish in their serenity. Now I believe that, with the excuse of protecting her from a malicious world, Ottro allowed Cañada to grow up confined and chaste. . . . By cyborg-ing her, the doctors neutralized a disabled woman. But I also suspect that Cañada finds a useful unconsciousness in her slowness, something that allows her to ignore her weaknesses.

When readers meet Cañada, all they can see is her technologized body and subservient status. Yet, she proves to be more than a servant or machine and becomes the voice of political and ideological ethics in the novel. First, she resists Fronda's attempts at democratizing the household and refuses to eat with her in the same room. Then, she seems to be impervious to Fronda's attempts to analyze her from either a social or a political perspective, rejects Fronda's rationalizations of her feelings about Ottro and his family, and eventually starts contesting not only Fronda's work as a politician but also Ottro's political project. When Cañada speaks, she provides a solid counterargument to all possible ideological excuses for supporting populism. Though built like a low-class worker with minimal education, she not only rejects Fronda's political arguments but also offers an ideological counterpoint to the blind spots of her discourse. As the relationship between Fronda and Cañada reveals itself through their conversations, it becomes clear that Cañada resents Ottro's family for not passing a mandatory education law from which she might have benefited, for imagining political programs that did not contemplate diversity or change, and for believing more in the idea of utopia than in real people.

For Cañada, everyday life and family are the cornerstones of authenticity. Whereas Fronda's career collapses and her family disintegrates (her former husband is in self-imposed internal exile and her estranged son is in a permanent state of at-times criminal rebellion), Cañada's work toward maintaining the household and protecting her family provides a sense of stable reality. Although Fronda will never lose her sarcastic, sometimes condescending view of Cañada, the cyborg provides a sense of community and solidarity that Fronda's memories and political abstractions lack. When Fronda finds Cañada sewing a shirt by hand, she cannot avoid concluding: "No creo que quiera demostrar, pero demuestra, lo delicadamente humano que es el silencio contra la barahúnda ininterrumpida de los pájaros: contra la radio que desgañita desde la pieza de Orilla. *A los ciborgues les gusta mostrar involuntariamente las grandezas humanas*" (I do not think she wants to demonstrate, though she does, how delicately human silence is against the unbroken babble of the birds, the radio that groans from Orilla's room. *Cyborgs like to unintentionally show human greatness*; 252; my italics). Rather than find resistance in grand utopian impulses, objects, or time, Cañada locates it in the everyday. As she states, for her all relationships are family relationships, consensual grouping, or what Donna Haraway described as making kin: "kin is an assemblage" ("Anthropocene" 162). What Cañada brings back to Fronda (the failed mother, unable to birth or to bring forth the nation) is, in this sense, her own blue-collar, impoverished, crime-stricken family. Cañada's brother and niece, Pozos and Orilla, join the women in the house after Orilla is rescued from a sex-slave ring. The family arrives against Fronda's will, but wriggles their way in until they stay. As disruptive as their presence seems to be, they offer Fronda a glimpse of normalcy and solidarity, as each of them help her with the tasks associated with executing Ottro's estate. As Cañada reminds her, nobody is anything by themselves (309). The sense of community built by Cañada and her family, in contrast to Fronda's political (liberal/populist) common sense, restores the materiality of free will, play, and creativity not only to cyborgs but also to a variety of other subjects. The reification of the imaginary of the lower classes is broken thanks to the construction of networks of solidarity and community that these technologized bodies facilitate.

Riscos, Fronda's son, is the second character who reinforces Cañada's role as a biosocial site of resistance to both political discourse and social expectations. Described by his mother as a "monster of transgression," the privileged character, who has enjoyed the benefits of "afluenza," starts to understand the hypocrisy of his society and the roles his parents and grandfather have played in it (129). At first, Riscos believes in nothing, wants nothing, and expects nothing but resents everything. His "transgression" is notable as he leads a rebellion through the island, which he initially thinks will make it possible to recover the most instinctive forms of human nature. At the start, this rebellion takes on neofascist traits; young people attack defenseless animals and passersby for the sheer pleasure of staging cruelty and breaking established forms of social coexistence. Those same youngsters attack the homeless, the dispossessed, and street prostitutes, arrogating to themselves a moral role in which they do not believe but consider necessary for social hygiene. Some get themselves killed by opposing political fractions. They privilege perversion and oppose sociability until discovering that they themselves have become another form of entertainment, another attraction in the island's political system. At this point, they walk away from any form of politics and, eventually, turn to drugs, alcohol, or anything that feeds compulsive behaviors.

As the novel progresses, Riscos begins to intervene in his own body in a way that is both parallel and opposite to Cañada. First, he implants himself with computers to augment his sense of the real and to communicate with others. Later, he pulls out all his teeth in a political gesture that makes him visually equal to the island's Elders. Eventually, Riscos turns to religion both as a way to find some sort of communal life and to further irritate his nonreligious mother. Although his political evolution follows the typical ideological path of the right in twentieth-century Argentina, the unique aspect of his journey manifests in his idea "del vivir juntos" (of living together), which articulates both a lack of confidence in the classic party system (as well as the inability of political programs to bring utopia to fruition) and a desire to create a community anchored in an aesthetics of resistance (179). For him, politics are literally a representation, a staging of militant antihumanism.

Little by little, Riscos's rebellion takes aim at his mother's political and ideological programs. He starts going into her room to yell at her for her choices. By the time Riscos leaves Ottro's house to join a guerrilla movement and live with his friends and lovers, Fronda admits to herself that politics has not allowed her to have the kind of real, meaningful relationships that Riscos has been seeking for his entire life. Riscos reiterates this when he tells Fronda, "Tanto militar contra el mal y perdiste de vista el sufrimiento. El de los demás" (So much fighting against evil and you lost sight of suffering. The suffering of the others; 268). Pain and suffering allow Riscos to relate to others, providing him with a sort of transversal hope and ethics. Although he established more solid ties than Fronda, his contradictions will not allow him to make any sort of permanent connection; he will leave his mother alone and never reconnect with his father.

If Cañada's alter-biology represents a new form of sociability and solidarity built from below, Riscos (who could be read both as her opposite *and* as the failure of humanism to fulfill its own promises) represents the instability and inadequacy of existing systems to present proper, balanced answers to social and cultural changes. The intervened bodies of both Cañada and Riscos provide models of the transformation of the sense of self and community, identity and empowerment.

Some Conclusions

In the opening paragraphs of this chapter, I proposed that novels written in Argentina in the early 2000s showcase the passage from the human to the posthuman. In Nielsen's novel, this passage is articulated by a sense of hopelessness and dejection against which characters are forced to fight. Negative feelings are used as the building blocks of a resilience anchored in the characters' own renewed sense of humanity. In Cohen's novels, the same passage is articulated through a reconstruction of the values of everyday life and meaningful relationships. The transformed bodies at the center of both novels require confrontations with the humanist/antihumanist stances, on the one hand, and, on the other, an evaluation of what is at stake when we talk about basic human values such as solidarity, pity, and love. Since these values do not operate within religious or ideological paradigms, they create complex ethical strands that cannot be easily defined or ascribed to any given political project. The loss of a working agenda to guide our understanding of the novels is only partially due to their location in peripheral countries and production during late capitalism. The phenomenon is global, as noted by Fredric Jameson's analysis in *Archaeologies of the Future*. The imagined futures of the novels we have discussed defamiliarize us from our present experience: "the present—in its society, and in its physical and psychic dissociation of the human subjects who inhabit it—is inaccessible directly, is numb, habituated, empty of affect. Elaborate strategies of indirection are therefore necessary if we are somehow to break through monadic insulation and 'experience' for the first and real time, the 'present' " (287).

This is precisely why writers like Cohen and Nielsen distrust mimesis and choose to write science fiction instead. The losses of meaning and empathy in their novels become forms of consciousness, or ways to grasp the system of relationships in the world. Because Nielsen's subjects are outside of society, they have to create their own aims and ambitions. Because Cohen's have been alienated, they have to recover what has been lost. Understanding the system of relationships that allows their characters to exist and survive is not a given. Riscos, for example, may be a cautionary tale about evil, but neither Víctor nor Cañada offer a parable of good. Rather, they redefine the meanings of autonomy and agency as they change and adapt to their shifting social and cultural environments. By returning to the foundational families of nineteenth-century liberal discourse and undoing not only the symbolic roles of their members but the aims of their master discourses (medicine, law, political planning, social engineering, etc.), the novels are able to rebuild the complex matrix of relationships between subjects and their social, cultural, and economic environments. There is no originary, fatal capture of an allegedly "unmarked" subject by a single matrix of power, be it the phallus, the logos, Eurocentric transcendental reason, or heterosexual normativity. Power is not a cartel operated by a single masterful owner, but rather differential mechanisms of distribution of material and discursive effects, which also impact on subjectivity (Braidotti, *The Posthuman* 22).

It is in this sense that we understand the issue of the posthuman as it appears in the novels we have discussed. The reshuffling of the concepts of identity, individuality, and community exposes the meaning and material conditions of power. In a 1997 conversation with Donna Haraway, just as science fiction production was about to explode in Latin America, Thyrsa Nichols Goodeve reminded her: "SF is about offering us reading protocols, ways to unpack the density of our experience under technoscience, as when you say, 'While some of the turns of the sticky threads in these tissues are helical, others twist less predictably. Which thread is which remains permanently mutable, a question of analytical choice and foregrounding operations. The threads are alive; they transform into each other; they move away from our categorical gaze' " (Haraway, *Modest* xxviii). These threads, the novels show, freed from rigid paradigms, freed from assigned social or cultural expectations, are not a goal but a doing, an exercise in daily, ethical choices.

Notes

1. See Kurlat Ares, *Para una intelectualidad sin episteme.*

2. Some of the first reading hypotheses of these novels can be found in Silvia Saítta's "En torno al 2001 en la narrativa argentina" and Beatriz Sarlo's "La novela después de la historia."

3. All translations are mine unless stated otherwise.

4. "Ciencia ficción en la Argentina," *Suplemento Cultura Diario Tiempo Argentino*, 29 Dec. 1985.

5. The economic and political crisis that hit Argentina in December 2001 caused three presidential turnovers in the course of two weeks. It began when the peso decreased in value, causing a halt in foreign trade, which complicated the country's internal debt and several international relationships. The increase in taxes that resulted as an attempt to resolve the financial woes only increased inflation. As companies started to collapse, the unemployment rate (which had been growing for

over three years at the time) reached between 18 and 20 percent by some estimates. Meanwhile, social and political instability led to riots. Deemed by economists as one of the worst recessions since 1929, it took Argentina almost seven years to come back from the crisis. Although extreme poverty declined, the middle class collapsed and never entirely recovered. Moreover, poverty indicators show that the lower class reached close to 30 percent.

6. See my analysis, "Rafael Pinedo's Trilogy: Dystopian Visions and Populist Thought in Argentina's Turn-of-the-Century Narrative."

7. As noted by Fernando Reati in a long footnote in his analysis of the novel, this is a rare case in which two authors, unbeknownst to each other, published two novels on very similar topics almost simultaneously. By 2005, when Kazuo Ishiguro published *Never Let Me Go*, Nielsen had presented the original manuscript of his novel twice to the Premio Clarín de Novela ("Clonación" 268).

8. The last chapter of my book *La Ilusión persistente* (2018) analyzes the works of Marcelo Cohen at length, including the political and ideological aspects of this novel.

Works Cited

A. A. "Soy un tipo un raro, un *freak*. Entrevista con Gustavo Nielsen." *La Nación—ADN Cultura*, 29 May 2010, lanacion.com.ar/1267474-soy-un-tipo-raro-un-freak. Accessed 2 Aug. 2017.

Braidotti, Rosi. "Posthuman Critical Theory." *Critical Posthumanism and Planetary Futures*, edited by Debashish Banerji and Makarand Paranjape, Springer, 2016, pp. 13–32.

———. *The Posthuman*. Polity, 2012.

Brown, J. Andrew. *Cyborgs in Latin America*. Palgrave Macmillan, 2010.

Cohen, Marcelo. *Casa de Ottro*. Alfaguara, 2009.

———. "Entrevista a Marcelo Cohen." Los Inrockuptibles, 3 Sept. 2014, losinrocks.com/entrevista-a-marcelo-cohen-a082baf2519b. Accessed 10 Aug. 2017.

———. "El reencatamiento del mundo. Entrevista con Marcelo Cohen." Interview with Pedro B. Rey, *La Nación—ADN Cultura*, 16 Jan. 2010, lanacion.com.ar/nota.asp?nota_id=1221141. Accessed 10 Aug. 2017.

Friera, Silvina. "Gustavo Nielsen y su nueva novela, *El Corazón de Doli*." *Página/12*, 19 Apr. 2010, pagina12.com.ar/diario/suplementos/espectaculos/4-17661-2010-04-19.html. Accessed 20 Aug. 2017.

Gutiérrez Mouat, Ricardo. "La retórica de la monstruosidad en la narrativa latinoamericana contemporánea: Un panorama crítico." *Hispamérica*, vol. 34, no. 101, Aug. 2005, pp. 3–13.

Haraway, Donna. "Anthropocene, Capitalocene, Plantationocene, Chthulucene. Making Kin." *Environmental Humanities*, vol. 6, 2015, pp. 159–65.

———. *Modest Witness Second Millennium: Femaleman Meets Oncomouse: Feminism and Technoscience*. Routledge, 1997.

Hayles, N. Katherine. *How We Became Posthuman: Virtual Bodies in Cybernetics, Literature, and Informatics*. U of Chicago P, 1999.

Jameson, Frederic. *Archaeologies of the Future: The Desire Called Utopia and Other Science Fictions*. Verso, 2005.

Kurlat Ares, S. G. *Para una intelectualidad sin episteme: El devenir de la literatura Argentina, 1974–1989*. Corregidor, 2006.

———. *La Ilusión persistente. Diálogos entre la ciencia ficción y el campo cultural*, Instituto Internacional de Literatura Iberoamericana, 2018.

———. "Rafael Pinedo's Trilogy: Dystopian Visions and Populist Thought in Argentina's Turn-of-the-Century Narrative." *Travesía: Journal of Latin American Cultural Studies*, vol. 25, no. 3, 2016, pp. 431–47, doi:10.1080/13569325.2016.1167022.

Ludmer, Josefina. "Temporalidades del presente." *Boletín 10 del Centro de Estudios de Crítica Literaria*, Dec. 2002, pp. 91–112.

Marcus, Amit. "The Ethics of Human Cloning in Narrative Fiction." *Comparative Literature Studies*, vol. 49, no. 3, 2012, pp. 405–33.

Moylan, Tom. *Scraps of the Untainted Sky: Science Fiction, Utopia, Dystopia*. Westview Press, 2000.

Moylan, Tom, and Raffaella Baccolini, eds. *Dark Horizons: Science Fiction and the Dystopian Imagination*. Routledge UP, 2003.

Nayar, Pramod K. *Posthumanism*. Polity, 2017.

Nielsen, Gustavo. *El corazón de Doli*. Editorial El Ateneo, 2010.

———. "9 temas y 62 respuestas." Nuevo Texto Crí*tico*, vol. 21, nos. 41–42, 2008, pp. 170–71.

Page, Joanna. *Creativity and Science in Contemporary Argentine Literature: Between Romanticism and Formalism*. U of Calgary P, 2014.

Reati, Fernando. "De torturas y vejaciones como un arte nacional: *Auschwitz* de Gustavo Nielsen." Revista Escribas III, Escuela de Letras- Facultad de Filosofía y Letras, Nov. 2006, pp. 69–77.

———. "Clonación, distopía posthumana y pérdida de la identidad en *El Corazón de Doli* de Gustavo Nielsen." *Juego de espejos. Otredades y cambios en el sistema literario argentino contemporáneo*, edited by Jorge Bracamonte and María del Carmen Marengo. Alción Editora, 2014, pp. 261–87.

Saítta, Silvia. "En torno al 2001 en la narrativa argentina." *Literatura y Lingüística*, no. 29, 2014, pp. 131–48.

Sarlo, Beatriz. "La novela después de la historia." *Escritos sobre literatura argentina*, Siglo XXI Editores, 2007, pp. 471–82.

Sommer, Doris. *Foundational Fictions: The National Romances of Latin America*. U of California P, 1991.

8

Unbearable Futures

The Science/Fiction of Care Markets in the Global South

Anindita Banerjee and Debra A. Castillo

About halfway through Alex Rivera's near-future science fiction film *Sleep Dealer* (2009), a foreman in a factory located on the south side of the US-Mexico border gives a tour of the premises to a teenager newly arrived as a migrant laborer from the deeper, impoverished agrarian south. "This is the American Dream," he declares. "We give the USA what it has always wanted: all the work without the workers. Jose is working in a slaughterhouse in Iowa and Maria is a nanny for a little girl in Washington. . . . Plug in, boy, your future starts today." In this scenario, the child, the most emotive embodiment of the future, undergoes a curious set of displacements along with the other icon of futurity, the American Dream. Literally about to be disembodied, the young migrant witnesses the hypertechnologized dematerialization of child care, in which dismembering a cow and bathing a little girl involve identical automated gestures mediated through a remote-controlled, computerized system. Refracted through the double vision of child and caregiver, the American Dream itself is reenvisioned in a wasteland neither inside nor outside the politics of recognition. While the female migrant's work of nurturing in this space paradoxically entails a complete lack of care for both giver and recipient, the male child is left gazing upon the contingency and disposability of the body that undertakes the labor of caring.

It is a similar borderland/wasteland in which we must also situate the photograph of the newborn child from Nepal discussed in the introduction to this book. "Embraced by the establishment and the public alike," the heartwarming image that emerged from the 2015 earthquake nevertheless constituted much more than a typical depiction of international humanitarianism and intercultural mutual aid in the aftermath of disaster. Among the many portraits of loss and mourning, and indeed many human-interest stories of hope, it stood out for its powerful aura of futurity. The child nestled in the arms of an Israeli Defense Forces soldier could even be called elementally science fictional: how many times have we witnessed on movie or television screens this very same juxtaposition of the huge yet faceless agent of the state, his allegiance to the good forces in a postapocalyptic world clearly marked and prominently displayed, holding in his arms the spark of new life?

In fact, the science fictionality of what the picture actually depicted instantly transformed it into the epicenter of an international media controversy and the catalyst of legislative debate in several nations. Although the soldier most certainly represented what his uniform and insignia stood for—a functionary in a government-sponsored airlift especially organized for Israeli citizens stranded in Nepal—the baby was not just any baby, Israeli or Nepali or of any other nationality that could be assigned by straightforward criteria of birth or genealogy. This child, along with twenty-five others born under similar arrangements between same-sex couples from Israel and migrant surrogates from south of the border with India, was rescued not on the basis of his or her past or present rights to be cared for by the Israeli state but on the presumption of the *futurity* of his or her status as a citizen-subject. Along with the status of recently born or unborn products of transnational reproductive labor, the earthquake reignited public debate about another undeniable category of the future: the aspirational horizons of same-sex couples and unaccompanied women from India, both of whom were driven to the Nepali clinics to perform radically divergent roles in the market. Barred by Israeli law from domestic commercial surrogacy, the former had constituted a significant part of the booming international baby trade in India until a legislative resolution in 2012 restricted its customers to heterosexual couples in demonstrably stable marriages. The same forces of shrinking demand, in turn, had turned the women into migrant wombs for rent.

In the early days after the airlift, the futures of the approximately 150 fetuses commissioned by Israeli clients still remaining in Indian women's bodies on the territory of Nepal remained unclear. In response to international outrage, the attorney general of Israel issued an order to allow the women to give birth on Israeli soil; but while it was assumed that the babies will obtain citizenship, there was no clear provision as yet for the gestational mothers' legal status in either India or Israel after giving birth (Robertson). These protracted battles have brought into even sharper focus the differential equation of vastly diverse bodies, alive or immanent, stranded, as one news report put it, "without disaster insurance" (Narayanan). The metaphor of insurance, perhaps unconsciously, echoes many contractual aspects of commercial surrogacy, such as the provision of adequate care to carriers in anticipation of an acceptable human product and promises of compensation to the client in the case of unforeseen adverse contingencies affecting the outcome. More significantly, however, the lack of insurance in this particular instance renders visible a paradoxical hierarchy of value, and its attendant commitment of care, in the futures market of life itself.

If media and scholarly attention could be taken as a measure of the reciprocal relationship between value and care, it is clear by now that both the global surrogacy market and its arbitration of futures outpace, as science fiction inevitably does, not only the regulatory mechanisms of nation-states but also the eyes of the journalist and social scientist. Just as the very existence of the Nepali clinics took the international media by surprise despite the amount of literature produced over the last decade on the Indian surrogacy industry, remarkably little seems to be known about the women who populate them. Although both migration and the work of care in this instance could only materialize at the newest frontier of global reproductive labor, neither the past nor the present of the workers themselves seem to matter much. While their immediate futures are determined on a sliding scale, not by the precarity of their own lives but rather by the projected value of the products they are carrying, the latest version of gendered migrant care workers are themselves rendered spectral. Like the factory floor of *Sleep Dealer*, care work in this context paradoxically engenders a complete lack of care. The surrogates' dematerialization matches the fictionality of their tremendous burdens of the future, but the investment in their continued well-being appears to be inversely proportional to that in the newborn proudly displayed in the metonymic arms of the consumer.

This disjuncture is palpable in the lack of recognition of the surrogates themselves as subjects by the various states implicated in the crisis. While India very successfully transformed the national burden of fertility into a competitively priced commercial asset, its regulatory bodies withheld any formal commitments to workers engaged in reproductive labor. The creation of the Nepali centers was the consequence of the only legislative process associated with the reproductive industry in India, which, like a previous set of loose guidelines issued to the clinics about ensuring the emotional detachment of surrogates, targeted the welfare of the child; in contrast, a draft regulation called the ART (Artificial Reproduction Technology) Bill, introducing guidelines for the safety and security of workers, languished in parliament since 2008. Nepal, meanwhile, willingly housed the clinics as long as the workers were not its own citizens (Narayanan).

Despite the visible continuities between the embodied, gendered work of childrearing and childbearing, marked and shaped by migratory geographies of bodies and biomatter in the fictional and nonfictional scenarios previously described, Latin America and the Indian subcontinent have not been considered together as historical and future markets of care. The parallels between Rivera's science fictional scenario and the Nepali surrogacy clinics serve as a rich point of departure for this comparative investigation of the future market of reproductive work, particularly in its relation to the nexus of care and value. Consequently, it is through science fiction from Latin America and the Indian subcontinent—the first a long-standing source of gendered migration for childcare work in North America and the second the primary site of the burgeoning global surrogacy market—that we propose to examine how narratives of emerging care markets, whether discursively science fictional or generically marked as such, grapple with this redoubled failure of care in both its theoretical structure and its implications for the future.

Our bifocal analysis of the future of care from these two locations explores the capacity as well as the limits of science fiction for historicizing and connecting childrearing and childbearing, two forms of etiolated caregiving, and maps the science/fiction of care markets onto two kinds of contemporary displacement: gendered migrant labor and assisted reproduction technologies. Our aim is to put back the gendered, racialized body, routinely dematerialized in futuristic discourses about outsourced child care and surrogacy alike, at the center of a global economy of care.

Fractured Borders, Future Markets, and Bio-Cartographies of Care

The Nepal surrogacy crisis presents a limit case for the radical reconfiguration of bodies and borders that constitute the focus of much recent scholarship on biomarkets in general and reproductive technology in particular. Melinda

Cooper and Catherine Waldby theorize the global bioeconomy of "clinical labor," including the Indian gestational surrogacy market, in terms of the coeval dissolution of boundaries defining living matter and the frontiers of geopolitical nation-states. As developments in biomedicine "bring the production process *inside* the body and puts organs, blood, and cell lines into circulation *outside* the body, scrambling the classical Marxist distinction between the living and the dead," clinical labor subjects the biological to a process of "material abstraction" (12–13). The actualization of this process, however, is far less seamless. As illustrated by the multiple, heterogeneous regulatory regimes involved in the Nepal surrogates' predicament, it seems that mobility in the business of childbearing is indeed determined by "patchworks of permission and prohibition" that function very differentially for different actors across a multitude of borders (63). As Cooper and Waldby point out, while "intending parents may elude national regulatory restrictions and travel to a jurisdiction where surrogacy markets are permitted, . . . [w]omen who work as oocyte vendors or gestational surrogates may need to travel to urban or provincial clinics, and remain there for the duration of the process" (63).

In the futuristic speculative landscape of "reproductive labor arbitrage" (67), both media and scholarship on the subject have primarily focused on the transnational movement of "living technologies" such as frozen eggs, sperm, and embryos (Landecker) on the one hand and the proliferative, increasingly diverse global networks of clients and brokers on the other. The fact that all the workers in the Nepali clinics were women from India, however, brings into sharp relief the importance of secondary, seemingly smaller-scale circuits of gendered migration. Its protagonists, despite appearing relatively "fixed" in "local" infrastructures (Bergmann 284) in comparison with intended parents, internationally networked facilitators, and the global market of surrogacy itself, in fact are deeply enmeshed in circuits of migrancy that are not immediately visible in large-scale structural analyses. Furthermore, the women who had made the journey across the Nepal border not only confound the geopolitical paradigms in which India's future market of gestational surrogacy has been discursively framed so far—within the juridical and regulatory framework of a single nation-state participating in the global exchange of service labor through the World Trade Organization and General Agreement on Trade and Services (Cooper and Waldby 79–80)—but also reveal a fractured contiguity between childcare work, the dynamics of displacement, and the clinical labor of gestational surrogacy mediated by translocal specificities. The continuities between informal care work and reproductive labor in which they were enmeshed by themselves do not appear geographically novel, as they reflect and reproduce well-documented worldwide trends in the feminization of labor markets (Ehrenreich and Hochschild). What distinguishes the spectralization of the Indian surrogates in Nepal in the eyes of multiple nation-states as well as the media, however, is embedded in the peculiarities of gendered migration across the *internal* borders of place and class within the Indian subcontinent.

Ever since a bilateral treaty in 1950 created an open border between India and Nepal, Nepal has been a steady sender of childcare workers for middle- and upper-class Indian households located in the subcontinent as well as in the transnational diasporas of the Gulf states and the USA (O'Neill; Gurung). In addition to challenging the traditional trajectory of migratory labor, traveling north rather than south, the Indian surrogates' work in Nepal is fraught with the gender politics of this particular border. In the largely unregulated flow of labor across the open border, as Sondra Hausner and Jeevan Sharma have recently documented, Nepali women are subjected to an informal but particularly oppressive regime of surveillance and stoppages under the aegis of antitrafficking measures. Another "local" perspective on surrogacy in India, rarely taken into consideration in large-scale studies of global reproductive markets, perversely mirrors the conflation of child care, sex work, and surrogacy in the Nepal-India borderlands. As the anthropologist Amrita Pande demonstrates in her groundbreaking ethnography of surrogates, their families, and communities in the Indian state of Gujarat, even when no transnational migration is involved, a pervasive stigma of sex work not only isolates gestational surrogates from their familial kinship structures and social networks ("Commercial"), but also accounts for a distinctive lack of care in their own relation to reproductive labor. Pande, who makes a case for commercial surrogacy in India as "a new kind of sexualized care work" ("Not an 'Angel' "), and Gina Maranto report that surrogates often disavow their work as legitimate, describing it as a last resort foisted upon them by poverty, indebtedness, and the attrition of stable employment for the male wage-earner in the family.

Anthropological research in the provincial city of Anand, Gujarat, where the Indian international surrogacy market was pioneered in 2002, reveals that "the surrogate-prostitute comparison plays a critical role in the disciplinary project" of the clinics (Pande, "Commercial" 979). Although Pande does not explicitly couch her analysis of the hostels—factory-dormitory-type walled enclosures in which surrogates are housed and closely monitored for the duration of their pregnancies—in terms of migration, the habitus in which women workers are both subjected and trained to reproduce a peculiar deficit of care are almost identical to the factory floor in *Sleep Dealer*. Like Maria and her adolescent observer, economic migrants who have physically gravitated toward the futuristic borderland of Tijuana only to find themselves in a womblike enclosure attached to cables resembling umbilical cords that literally suck out their vitality toward unseen northern destinations, the surrogates often find themselves in a state of double displacement. Recruited by neighborhood brokers from slums and tenements housing labor migrants, the women undertake a second migration to the quasi-carceral space of the clinic, removed from even the tenuous network of care on the margins of cities like Anand that news reports describe as the "Wild West" of India's booming surrogacy market (Kumar). In the complete absence of either social support or local, state, or federal administrative oversight, gestational surrogates become, de facto, wards of the clinic—the sole potential source of care for both the mother-worker and the in vivo product of her clinical labor.

In the nested circuits of spatial and social displacement outlined earlier in this chapter, however, care can neither be sustained nor holistically extended under the very structural logic of assisted reproductive technologies. Cooper and Waldby aptly capture the capacity of surrogacy to foreclose any possibility of mutual recognition—and therefore of care—between the clinic, the mother-worker, her burden of the future, and the consumers awaiting its emergence: by "order[ing] reproductive biology into a set of modular units and processes . . . the uterus is technically and legally isolated as a component that can be contractually ordered, detached from the selfhood of the surrogate and repositioned in a production chain at the behest of the clinic and the commissioning couple" (84). Reports of the "job training" that surrogates undergo at the clinics emphasize the final frontiers of displacement inscribed upon the reproductive laborer's body itself. Whether through the metaphor of a short-term tenant or a motherless child in paid care (Pande, "Commercial" 978), clinics cultivate a new relation with the self in which "the uterus is an empty space [to be] hired out, . . . situat[ing] the surrogate in a previously unimagined relationship (or lack of relationship) to the child" (Vora 271).

The bodily logic of dismemberment here flows seamlessly from the spatial logic of migration, placing the clinics, the surrogates, and the fetuses in a temporary state of purely functional, mutually instrumental care for the duration of the reproductive process, both before and after which the surrogate as a subject ceases to exist per se. Like Rivera's science fictional nanny, providing the embodied labor of child care in the virtualized state of a cyborg—and in the process of nurturing life mimicking the butcher in the slaughterhouse—the denizens of the hostel-clinic are "trained" to "simultaneously be a temporary (yet professional) caretaker . . . while constantly aware of their own disposability" (Pande, "Commercial" 978). The slaughterhouse, not coincidentally, also serves as the figure through which the activist Ranjana Kumari recently characterized the care deficit in the Indian surrogacy industry: "In this business, the baby is the product. The surrogate is the means of production. Even those who care for the surrogate do so until the product is delivered. The surrogate is waste material for them after the delivery" (Kumar).

The intersecting vectors of migration, disposability, and the failure of care constitute what we term in this chapter the "bio-cartographies" of the future market that the Indian Lawmakers' Association identified in 2010 as "a pot of gold." They also coalesce in the first film that examined this market in some depth. The Israeli filmmaker Zippi Brand Frank's *Google Baby*, whose formal designation as a documentary belies its insistent futuristic edge, closes with two interconnected scenes, one unfolding in the iconic Akanksha clinic in Anand, Gujarat, and the other in the living room of an Israeli surrogacy broker. In the first scene, an unidentified surrogate undergoing a caesarian section (earlier in the film, the director of the clinic and its chief obstetrician, Naina Patel, informs the interviewer that all babies are born by c-section "to prevent the wear and tear" of natural birth) calls to the surgeon at a moment of experiencing intense pain, a failure of the basic anesthetic procedure in the operation. After several such appeals to which Dr. Patel responds with a cursory reminder "to take God's name," the patient is injected with an unidentified substance that results, at least in the close-up view of the camera, in the sudden silencing of the body on the table and the transformation of its features into a corpselike state while the baby's lusty cries in the background testify to the successful outcome of the production process.

While the fate of the surrogate remains unknown, the camera cuts to the broker, who is bemoaning the lack of care displayed by his recent clientele. In the past, he exclaims, prospective parents—including himself and his partner who had traveled to the United States for a surrogate before the emergence of the Indian market—attempted to cultivate a close relationship with the gestational mother. These days, in contrast, both biological and communication technology had opened up the possibility of "shopping far and wide," leading to the widespread practice of implanting multiple fetuses from multiple vendors into multiple bodies, enabling the intending parents to pick and choose which ones to terminate. Such moralizing, while ironic in the context of a film that makes no bones about the lack of care at every level of the existing market, nevertheless projects an even bleaker future. The widely publicized Israeli rescue of newborns after the Nepal earthquake, juxtaposed with the nearly complete absence of migrant reproductive workers from media and legislative discourses worldwide, indicates that this future may have already arrived.

Phantom Care, Surrogacy as Parable, and the Science Fiction of Migratory Life

The terrifying scope of this future, in which gendered bodies as well as their future reproductive potentials can be "wasted" at will by the same phantom entities that assume their care in lieu of family or the state, was explored by Manjula Padmanabhan in the critically acclaimed play *Harvest* as early as 1997. Consonant with the author's own prefatory note that "the germ of the idea" for the work was "the flourishing illegal trade in human organs in India" (4), the considerable scholarly literature examining its continuing relevance reads *Harvest* primarily as an extrapolation of "documented research that identifies major cities in India, Egypt, Turkey, and Eastern Europe as centers for a multimillion-dollar international trade in human organs, particularly kidneys and corneas, purchased from living donors among the local poor" (Gilbert 125). The fact that Padmanabhan's science fiction—in which an unemployed man's recruitment by a multinational corporation called InterPlanta draws his entire family into a global trade not just of body parts but "whole body transplants" (86) for distant, phenotypically Caucasian, clients—became so recognizable as reality within a decade of its publication lends considerable force to the diverse interpretations of the play.

Scholars have analyzed Padmanabhan's futuristic depiction of organ trade as a critique of structural inequities engendered by globalization (Gilbert), technoscientific neocolonialism (Mathur), global capitalism (Pravinchandra), and racialized debt (Kim). Although surrogacy, the science fictional ledge on which *Harvest* leaves its spectators, has received only cursory attention, it is through this seemingly minor thematic component of the play that we can begin to tease out a nuanced map of a future economy of care. Surrogacy, in other words, helps us put back the bodies in Padmanabhan's play about bodies without organs, and generates a bio-cartography of displacement and gendered labor whose coordinates are much more concrete than the generalized dichotomy of the Global North and South.

It is striking that the as-yet-unrealized specter of whole-body transplants—which, as scholars have widely noted, serves as an apt metaphor for the totality of a biomarket divided between North and South and a logical culmination of the plot, in which InterPlanta and its putative clients literally consume Om's entire family in a kind of predatory cannibalism—reveals itself at the end of the play through the portal of gestational surrogacy. Om, "in a corpse-like state," has abandoned the stage to recruit himself to InterPlanta again after his brother Jeetu is removed in an act of mistaken identity (80); the two men's mother has disappeared forever in a futuristic "sarcophagus," a plush "videocouch" (79) provided by the corporation. The only characters that confront each other on stage are Jaya, whom Om had disavowed as his wife and declared to be his sister in the belief that the brokers only desired single males, and the virtual image of the receiver/consumer, whose gender has also unexpectedly changed. A projection called Ginni that had diligently enforced the family's nutrition and hygiene through a "contact module" installed in their single-room dwelling (7), expressing her ardent sense of "duty and pleasure" (23) while foisting upon them the disciplinary regimes of food "fuels" (15), a clean toilet, and the videocouch, emerges as a male persona calling itself Virgil. This disembodied entity drops the bombshell that it was neither Om nor Jeetu but Jaya who had been the most desirable commodity all along.

> Jaya. You said you wanted Om!
>
> Virgil. I did not ask for Auwm. He came to us.
>
> Jaya. You said you wanted a healthy body—
>
> Virgil. Yes, Zhaya—yours!
>
> Jaya. Mine? But it was Om who got the job!
>
> Virgil. We're interested in women where I live, Zhaya. Child-bearing women. (85)

The disclosure that Om was a mere surrogate for Jaya in the eyes of the market and its consumers—by the male consumer, moreover, who has been using a female surrogate, Ginni—reaches back to engulf the entire play.

Surrogacy, as both a symptom and the ultimate consequence of an economy of abandonment, becomes the parable through which we can read the nested structures of displacement, detachment, and dismemberment in the complex interplay of racialized, gendered bodies doomed to perpetual migrancy.

As Jaya is revealed to be the real protagonist of the drama, Om, the normative head and breadwinner of the family, metamorphoses into the quintessential surrogate. To be sure, Om's signing himself—and by extension his wife, mother, and brother—away to InterPlanta illustrates a feminization consonant not just with indebtedness as Jodi Kim has noted (220–22), but also, following Cooper and Waldby's analysis, with his transition from wage work to the existential precarity of clinical labor (28–29, 67). The lens of surrogacy, however, allows us to map the broad structural analysis of Om's transformation onto the embodied microcosmos of the "grimy, despairing, poison-fumed" (7) family dwelling that constitutes the entirety of the set of the play. In the physicality of this space, the family is already incarcerated even before InterPlanta agents effectively seal off its inhabitants from the world in a cocoon of care vicariously supervised by Ginni. The environment in which Om, as a wage migrant in the burgeoning metropolis of the rapidly globalizing Indian economy, maintains his dependents has irredeemably frayed the very foundations of the family. Unmoored from any networks of sociality and visibly abandoned by both the state and the employers from whom Om has eked out a meager living before being made redundant, it is but a small step to the symbolic dismemberment of the family whereby Om legally declares himself to be single and unattached. By renouncing his role as provider and anchor of the patriarchal family, he renders both his spouse and his brother into phantoms.

Once the clients, with the corporation as enforcer, step into this void to take over the role of primary caregiver and arbiter of not only the good life but of life itself, the economy of abandonment in which the migrants find themselves becomes doubly visible not just in Om but also through the female characters. In the science fictional regime of care maintained by the discipline of the body market, the figure of "Ma," Om's mother who should by rights assume the matriarch's role in the extended family structure, recedes farther and farther into the luxuries provided in exchange of life until she is literally entombed by them. Jaya, neither the recipient nor the source of any care, is disturbingly unperturbed by both Ma's dematerialization and Om's disavowal of their marital relations.

As the mother is gradually replaced by the surrogate-substitute Ginni, who scolds and cajoles the family into a lifestyle that will both clean up and boost up their bodies and make them fit for world-class clinical consumption, we recognize Om's contractual obligation of casting off kinship as startlingly similar to those of real women in future surrogacy clinics. Illustrated in vivid detail in *Google Baby* and documented widely by scholars, the complete consignment of married women, usually with one or more children at home, to the clinic's care also occurs in the name of protection—not only from the unsanitary physical conditions of urban migrant ghettos and the emotional and physical demands of caregiving but also from sexually transmitted diseases through intercourse with their husbands. And indeed, the surrogate's body in *Harvest* is decontaminated as a prelude to the sterilization and quarantine of the family's room. The first procedure Om undergoes in the play is a lengthy "sanitation process" in "a cage shaped like a tunnel," mounted on an industrial conveyor belt in the InterPlanta facilities. As if undergoing gynecological screening, he must get naked. Then the disinfection begins: "The water is hot, scented. Then cold . . . it stings a little, this second water. Smells like some medicine . . . I don't know what's happening. A man ahead of me screams and cries, but we're in separate little cages now, can't move" (12).

It is not surprising, therefore, that contamination—whether environmental, microbial, or sexual—creates the only potentialities for a poetics and politics of recognition in Padmanabhan's play. Infection constitutes its only site of gendered, racial resistance. The sole mutual relationship of care that emerges among the family members exiled in their own home-turned-clinic is through the illicit sexual relations between Jaya and her brother-in-law Jeetu, a male prostitute who rebelliously proclaims that he would "rather sell his body than sign it away" (33) and periodically threatens to bring his germs home. As indicated earlier, Jeetu ends up serving as Om's surrogate in the actual process of the harvest. More significant, however, is the stigma of prostitution that Jaya shares with him by entering into their extramarital relationship, creating a perverse solidarity between the bodies of male and female surrogates. This shared stigma, which would also subject real-life gestational surrogates to social exile as discussed in the previous section, becomes the conduit through which the abandoned wife stages her final act of resistance. Recognizing her lover's eyes in the spectral Virgil's face—"But then Jeetu was paid in phantoms!" (84)—leads Jaya to insist that she would only carry a child through an actual physical encounter.

> VIRGIL. Zhaya, I'd love to travel to be with you, but I can't.
>
> JAYA. You who are so powerful, you who can travel from body to body—

Virgil. The environment you live in is too polluted for me, Zhaya—

Jaya. Then you are a phantom after all. (88)

. . .

Virgil. I can set it up so that we can be together, go places, anywhere you want—right inside your room.

Jaya. I don't want your make-believe travels! . . . I want real hands touching me. I want to feel a real weight upon me—

Virgil. And it's all possible—

Jaya. No! Not without risking your skin! Never! Do you hear me, whoever you are, whatever you are? Never! There is no closeness without risk! (89)

Pollution, whether incarnated in the nonclinical body or the physical environment, here becomes the prerequisite of care. Jaya refuses to be dislocated, dismembered, and ultimately wasted like Jeetu, Om, or even Ma. Eschewing the mobile geographies of global biotechnology, she struggles instead to overcome her disposability by embracing the intimately local, embodied bio-cartography of risky yet palpable contact.

Annihilated Bodies, Ecologies of Care, and Future Markets of Waste

Latin America in the late twentieth century is unfortunately bursting with histories of authoritarian regimes that engaged in the most violent acts possible against their own populations. The most infamous of these actions involve mass disappearances and, floating up in the jetsam, stories of child laundering. Across the continent, from Argentina, Uruguay, and Chile to Guatemala, censored voices talk about disappeared women who were pregnant when detained, or made pregnant through rape, and of their babies, who were distributed to military families who wanted children or, even more chillingly, were allegedly sold on the organ market. The mothers, of course, were murdered, assigned to mass graves or dumped in the ocean. The legacy of this too-familiar story can be located in the rough continuum found in the contemporary twenty-first-century discussions of feminicide, building on the inherited social presumption that there is impunity to kill women just because they exist, and because women are in surplus, not needed to reproduce citizens for the nation.

These antecedents help ground a continentwide analysis, which we can only point to here, of a tenderness/caring deficit or foreclosure of care from at least two historical perspectives: first, the whispered stories of child laundering in countries across the entire continent, with their trail of disappeared mothers and stolen children, and the continuation of these stories in feminicide; and second, in a different, seemingly less overtly violent history, the stories of the immigrant mothers who leave their children in very dangerous situations in home countries in order to try support them from a distance by caring for children in the Global North, or conversely, the resentments of those children left behind by migrant women, who feel abandoned and suffer from what Cacho has called "social death." In some respect then, the migrant mother is almost equally as disappeared as the political militant or indigenous victim of war—she becomes unavailable to national discourse at the same time as she is lost to her children.

The bodies and imaginaries of these real (and also speculative, specular) lost and abandoned children, these tortured and disappeared women, haunt Latin America as a whole. In the calculus of these abuses and "choices," we are reminded once again that "care" is less an ethical concept than a proxy for other kinds of social determinations, something that can be deployed strategically for advocacy or condemnation, especially when used to reference local political expediency or the status of marginalized others. In Hochschild's perception, inevitably from the perspective of the Global North: "Nannies do emotional labor to cope with grief, depression, anguish they feel apart from their own children; even as they work to positively attach themselves to the First World children they care for. Surrogates do the emotional labor of separating themselves from the baby they carry, and from the part of their body that carries that baby. We could describe both of these as the emotional labor of estrangement" (33). A bit later she adds, "Indeed, these separations of oneself from maternal identity were *part* of the labor she sold" (36). To think about the labor of care, then, is to think from the perspective of the market in which care is, at best, a luxury, a class-based moral concept that is at the same time projected onto poorer classes (those women who are seen as natural caretakers for children in the Global North) and refused them (the poor don't care for/about their children, as evidenced by this abandonment).

More and more, recent Latin American speculative novelists have been focusing on this poisoned legacy of the care deficit, the lose-lose proposition of the murdered mothers and traumatized children left behind by the merciless neoliberal policies of globalized late capitalism. These works represent a new kind of testimonial narrative, responding to what scholars like Hans Fernández have identified as the "impasse" of traditional 1980s to 1990s–style testimonies, in which "witnesses propose to narrate traumatic experiences that, given their extreme emotional complexity, are difficult to codify, often becoming unnarratable" (60). And these stories—or nightmares—become the particular province of contemporary "sur-realistas" (realists from the South). In such stories, there is nothing so mild as emotional labor, or the value of caring, or honorable identities derived from expectations about gender roles and relations between mothers and children. Instead, there is rage and violence at the heart of the maternal relation where caring was presupposed to naturally reside.

A number of recent twenty-first-century Latin American texts come from the perspective of this injured history, the extreme care deficit where children are orphaned at birth and women are seen as disposable breeders or cattle to be culled and butchered. To cite only a sampling from among these texts: Lina Meruane (Chile), *Fruta podrida* (Rotten fruit, 2007), where women are responsible for drenching fruit in the pesticides that make them perfect products for export to the USA, while also serving as organ donors and ongoing sources of fetuses for sale to meet the mysterious research purposes of the local hospital; Rafael Pinedo (Argentina), *Subte* (Subway, 2012), where women are taught that the only way to give birth is by cutting out the baby in a self-inflicted caesarean that inevitably kills them; Susana Sussman (Venezuela), "Khunta" (2005), where alien babies peck their way out of their mothers' wombs, killing them; Rafael Courtoisie (Uruguay), *La novela del cuerpo* (Novel about the body, 2015) with its chilling market of body parts, babies, and pets for wealthy and capricious clients; Paz, Segade, and Tentoni's pitiless story about drugged women who are impregnated and give birth next to the sea only to watch with indifference as their babies are sorted and recycled; Jorge Baradit (Chile)—the first Latin American ever to win the most prestigious science fiction award in Spanish, among many other prizes—whose most famous work includes an interconnected series of novels that follows the stories of adolescent girls plucked from the womb as five-month fetuses to be tortured and inserted into anacondas, or military AIs, or turned into ghosts, in a kind of monstrous surrogacy.

Chile is in some sense the antipode of the United States, metaphorically if not mathematically, something writers like Meruane and Baradit clearly exploit in their work, where the technological detritus of the industrial north conflates with sur-realistically imagined spiritualities. Late-twentieth-century Chile has had a particularly fraught relationship with the United States, first through the US-sponsored coup, which on September 11, 1973, overturned the democratically elected government of Salvador Allende, and later, during Augusto Pinochet's twenty-five-year dictatorship, as the incubator for the model of neoliberal capitalism later exported across the Global South. Thus, these novelists' contestatory narratives are rooted in the push and pull of the so-called Chilean miracle, developed by the delighted Chicago Boys, led by Milton Friedman, who were given a whole country to experiment with and dispense economic advice (the result, as is well documented, has been a superficially promising GDP, environmental degradation, greater impoverishment for many, and immense wealth for a privileged few).

The unnarratable/unnarrated/oversaturated story of these past forty years, says Carvajal, speaking of the Truth Commission in Chile, is the history that should be written, but which is hidden not just in the trauma of the victims but also in deliberate state-sponsored silences—the "whitening" of history effected by acknowledging human rights abuses but ignoring the victims. This process leads to the inevitable overlaying of official history on unofficial narrative, of confusions about what "really happened," and the resultant poisonous "eruptions of memory" in other spaces and at unexpected times (2–3). For example, the response of President Sebastián Piñera in the wake of the 2010 earthquake, committing Chile to the recovery of bodies lost at sea during this natural disaster, inevitably reminded Chileans of the Pinochet regime forty years earlier, involving the dumping of "disappeared" persons into the ocean, bodies that were neither acknowledged nor recovered.

Shamanic Cyberpunk, Womb Politics, and Care Beyond Nostalgia

Jorge Baradit is a former punk rock musician, who in addition to his speculative fiction (*Trinidad*, *Ygdrasil*, *Policía del karma*) has written alternative history (*Lluscuma*, *Kalfukura*, *Synco*), has a significant presence in live cast television, podcasts, a collective blog, and a very elaborate online transmedial project and graphic novel *Policía del karma* (Karma police, 2011). He describes his work variously as realist fiction, afterpunk, postpop, retrofuturist, and cybershamanic. In his collection of occasional essays and creative fragments published under the Amazon imprint with an aggressive English title and more descriptive Spanish subtitle, Baradit writes that he grew up in a confluence of contradictory, superimposed, official, and unofficial histories that made Chile seem less like a functioning democracy than a low-budget theme park, cosponsored by unusually mendacious politicians and slippery technocrats. It is a country overlaid with an accumulated bricolage of decaying and hypermodern technologies that make it a perfect sur-realist cyberpunk site.

Despite the imbrication of the Chilean story in the late twentieth to twenty-first centuries with US international politics and economics, in the final analysis, the result is emphatically not, Baradit says, business as usual of colonial or postcolonial nostalgia: American or European imaginary constructs privileging their projections of utopian or dystopian concepts and applying them to the Global South (*Mind Fuck* loc 1574, 1606, 1880, 1904, 2684). Instead, he draws from the South's pained understanding of itself, and especially from the indigenous Mapuche metaphor of the "imbunche": a kidnapped, tortured, and bewitched child whose orifices are sewn shut and who is set as guardian for a sorcerer's treasure. In this sense Baradit would likely follow fellow novelist Carlos Franz in positing "una identidad imbunchada" at the core of the national self (19). In any case, Baradit updates the metaphor of the "imbunche" by way of a futuristic science fictional perspective into what he calls shamanic cyberpunk, which involves, among other things, spiritually infused AIs (or terrorist bodhisattvas) awakening the Andean earth goddess, Pachamama, who had been hypnotized during the Conquest, to take on her terrible and wonderful challenge of spiritual and political realignment (*Trinidad*; all citations from Baradit's work are translated by Castillo).

The loose trilogy of speculative novels are set roughly in major Latin American cities, including Bogotá, Santiago, and Mexico City, and involve the scientific and political machinations of a series of AIs, astral superbeings, and modified human authorities, some of whom have achieved godlike powers. Their excesses are kept in check by the infighting among themselves, targeted assassinations, interventions by Nepalese shamans, and the Karma Police. In this near-future world, the third child of every family is state property, for whatever purposes the state decides: organ donation, poltergeist creation, military use, or other AI purposes. Among the central characters are the nano-drug-addicted, adolescent girl assassins/police/AIs Angélica, Mariana, and Magdalena, who were created from five-month fetuses extracted from the womb. Access to the command system in their internal web is through cables in their vaginas. Other creative uses of these excess children include:

Crisálidas: twins, one of whom is grown in the other's womb until she is twelve years old, then extracted by caesarean section before first menstruation, when they are linked by hypodermic tubes; and *Poltergeists*: prepubescent children who are inserted in isolation tanks then tortured to death with unimaginable horrors that fix the energy at the moment of their death. There are also oddities like the "traspuesto," who suffers from "una malformación difícil de explicar. Un hombre agónico con su alma desplazada. Su existencia se encuentra traslapada entre su propio cuerpo, un cactus, una roca y una rata" (a malformation that is hard to explain. It is a dying man with a displaced soul. His existence overlaps with that of his own body, a cactus, a rock, and a rat; *Ygdrasil* 9).

In general, Baradit is at great pains to disrupt any possibility of a caring economy, emotional bonds between individuals, or reaching across generations. The mothers of the fetuses are irrelevant; what is important is the monstrous surrogacy, the exchanges between human and animal and machine, that short-circuit any potential for caring relationships. In this sense, the fictions are completely consistent with twenty-first-century postauthoritarian regime societies and a shifting assessment of repression and resistance. They reflect a wholly comprehensible cry of rage from the betrayed children, who blame not only the government for taking their parents away but also their parents for leaving them. This rage has become increasingly visible as the children of the disappeared write their own memoirs and fictions. The heroic aftermath of the immediate postdictatorship period has long since dissipated, and authors are increasingly reflective of more complex emotional strains—examples include some of the authors cited earlier in this chapter, as well as memorialists and filmmakers like Albertina Carri, Laura Alcoba, and Benjamín Ávila.

Baradit's novels focus most insistently on a conflict between various opposing fetus-created forces, manipulated by governments, industries, and astral forces, all of whom have secret double and triple agendas. These fetus derivatives include the *Yámana*: the fetus is installed in a CPU and used as a military AI; *Pensantes*: poltergeist fetuses are transplanted into mare uteruses for three years before being brought into use (the mares have their legs amputated and are hung up in huge warehouses); and *Durmientes*: male fetuses are cultivated within drugged, live anacondas, buried vertically in quartz sand and birthed at age thirty-three, at which point they have sex with a virgin woman, who is killed. They are then awakened and used for psychological, religious, or political purposes, or industrial espionage. In

Trinidad, the character Rogelio is a *Durmiente*. His task is to assassinate Angélica, the AI who blows up the *Yámana* machine by becoming part of it.

Meanwhile, Magdalena, a member of the Karma Police (a force that investigates both current- and past-life crimes), and the living result of a technical error on the part of the government that created her, has been given the thankless and low-priority task of investigating the disappearance of 5,166 orphans, all between the ages of ten to twelve years old, whose mutilated bodies were found in a mass grave in the Atacama desert with their spinal cords removed.[1] This is something that interests authorities only because organ traffickers more typically make more complete use of the bodies they abduct, children who in any case would enter into a vague category of exploitable common property. Angélica, the first soul to fully inhabit cyberspace, collaborates with Magdalena to uncover the nefarious plans of project ENKELI, which uses the human vertebral bone marrow to anchor and fuel wormholes. Angélica, in her capacity as the first such wormhole, is deployed to sabotage the *Yámana* machine, a military construct created with the same goal of opening the astral net as ENKELI. When she is destroyed, the novel reveals that the government has double-crossed Magdalena as part of an internecine struggle and kills her so she can take Angélica's place. Meanwhile, Mariana, the third Chilean assassin—whose body has been dismembered, revived, and her brain modified to house multiple souls—survives to confront the godlike *Perfectos*, *Selknams*, and imbunches that populate *Ygdrasil*.

These women do a lot of killing and likewise suffer tremendous amounts of pain, as they are morcellated and reconstructed, over and over again. For Macarena Areco, one of the few scholars to date to publish on Baradit's work, "La opción de la novela de Baradit es la opuesta a esta estetización: mostrar el dolor del desmembramiento, de la ruptura de la unidad cuerpo/espíritu, de la pérdida del aura y de la conexión, a través de la representación del sujeto abierto como doliente y como disponible para la esclavización" (Baradit's option in his novel is the opposite of aestheticization; he shows the pain of dismemberment, the rupture of the unity of body/spirit, the loss of aura and connection, by way of the representation of a subject open to pain and disposable for enslavement; 846). At the same time, Areco cites an email from Baradit distinguishing his work from splatterpunk precisely along aesthetic lines: "*Splatterpunk* tiene en su origen el 'salpicado,' el chorreo, el estallido de la carne, el goce catártico del *gore* envuelto en la sangre de una víctima agarrada a hachazos. En mi caso el corte y la herida se hacen a sangre fría, con calma, ternura y buscando belleza. Es un asesinato cometido por un cirujano psicótico, pero con profundo respeto estético. Quizá más cerca de Hannibal Lecter . . ." (Splatterpunk finds its origin in the splattering, the gushing, the explosion of flesh, the cathartic pleasure of gore enveloping the blood of a victim chopped up by an axe. In my case the cut and the wound are done in cold blood, with calm, tenderness, and looking for beauty. It is an assassination committed by a psychotic surgeon, but with a profound aesthetic respect. Perhaps more like Hannibal Lecter . . . ; 847). Thus, while Areco sees no possibility of agency in Baradit's apocalyptic work (852), controversially, Baradit would seem to contest this conclusion, pointing precisely to the qualities of something we might tentatively describe as a renewed call for care. This very tentative exploration occurs under a very different set of presuppositions about caring labor—something related to an attenuated and revised understanding of tenderness or beauty—that define his project as responding to an aesthetic and speaking to a particular kind of (psychotic) agency. Furthermore, in some sense, we could reimagine Baradit's extreme aesthetics as a reasoned and methodical, even ethical, rejoinder to the monstrous recent history of his home country, a sur-realist response from the orphans created in the upheavals of late-twentieth-century globalization.

Toward a Science Fictional Bio-Cartography of the South

Science fiction is always to some degree a meditation on the present, and never more so than when we look at *Sleep Dealer*, *Harvest*, *Google Baby*, and Baradit's trilogy together across the biotechnological markets of care in the Global South. In each case, care markets framed in the service of a privileged few mandate that social bonds be fractured in support of capital flows, leaving behind disenfranchised remnant populations whose humanity is increasingly etiolated. In the process, these works highlight the extreme contradictions and hypocrisy of structures rhetorically built on economies of care, while condemning the victims as insufficiently caring. Thus, even more than the orphaned Memo in *Sleep Dealer*, his counterpart, the drone pilot Rudy, stands for the failure of a political system that uses the language of patriotism and care for country to dupe young people into murdering other young people in the service of natural resource control—a theme that Padmanabhan picks up and exploits in a very different direction in *Harvest*, where uprooted families stranded in the poisoned landscapes of hypercapitalist urbanization are forced into a totalized form of clinical labor. Likewise, the reduction of women to annoying appendages to their wombs in *Google Baby* looks forward to the redirections of gestation in Baradit. The abandoned biological children of surrogate mothers, who must suffer the loss of their care in the name of caring for them, are resurrected in the murderous impulses of Baradit's science fictional orphans, as they metamorphose into the protagonists of the horrific gang wars of contemporary Central America.

Yet precisely because the science fiction texts examined in this essay may be read as histories of the unfolding present, they are also susceptible to be bounded by the cartographical imagination. These are stories set in the wastelands of the elsewhere, populated by other bodies, perpetually banished to the south of a future in which we may begin to imagine alternatives to the economies of abandonment. This fractured vision of care, however, "spread[s] out and colonize[s] reality itself" in distinctly Jamesonian terms (371): entwined in the marginalization of same-sex and single intending parents from legal regimes of surrogacy is the simultaneous abnegation of traditionally gendered forms and institutions of care for those who labor to fulfill their aspirations.

It is at the intersection of gender, race, and place, therefore, that we have proposed *bio*-cartography as an embodied approach to the care deficit in the Global South—a South replete with its own internal maps of violent migrations and transmigrations of life yet capable of not just reproducing but also resisting the futures market in life itself. The settings for these insurrections, not surprisingly, are the toxic, polluted, contaminated bodies and borders of Rivera, Baradit, and Padmanabhan's science fiction, in which, as Jaya says, "there is no closeness without risk." This utterance by a science fictional character eloquently conveys the methodological risks taken by our comparative study. By negotiating the site-specific imbrications of displacement, dismemberment, and abandonment in the Indian subcontinent and Latin America while simultaneously framing the science fictional futures of care markets in broader global terms of the South, we attend to the dialectic underlying Kaushik Sunder Rajan's model of "biocapital": "microstructures through which one can discern localized, particular manifestations of global technoscientific phenomena" (97).

In the substantial work on biomarkets beyond borders that has emerged in the last decade, however, the global has tended to subsume the various terrains of the local, regional, national, and subnational engaged in our study across South Asia and Latin America—terrains in which the future as well as the futures markets of reproductive biotechnology grow ever more "sur-real," to quote Baradit. The "sur" here is crucial to this chapter's project of rematerializing gendered, procreative (bio)matter in places that seem to exist only in metaphor. Science fiction lends a peculiar sharpness to what is frequently invoked as the "Global South" but is rarely subjected to deep, place-specific yet comparative analysis across the boundaries of area studies. The literary, mediatic, and cultural texts examined here, set in the "Wild Wests" of re/production in the Global South, be it the Nepali *terai* or the Atacama desert, the slums of Mumbai or factories at the Tijuana borderlands, offer particularly textured topographies of emplaced subjects enmeshed in the migratory circuits of reproductive labor: lost, incarcerated, or annihilated in a global deficit of care.

Note

1. The Atacama desert, famously the driest spot in the world, is the site of numerous mass graves of disappeared people from the Pinochet era (families still regularly take trips to the desert to search for bones). More recently, it is remembered as the location of the 2010 Copiapó mining accident, in which thirty-three miners were buried alive and miraculously rescued two months later.

Works Cited

Areco, Macarena. "Más allá del sujeto fragmentado: Las desventuras de la identidad en *Ygdrasil* de Jorge Baradit." *Revista iberoamericana*, vol. 76, nos. 232–33, 2010, pp. 839–53.

Baradit, Jorge. *Kalfukura: El corazón de la tierra*. Ediciones B, 2009. (Children's fiction.)

———. *Lluscuma*. Ediciones B, 2013.

———. *Mind Fuck Guerrilla! Relatos, fragmentos, canalizaciones y ciberthrash* (*sic*). Amazon Digital Services, 2010.

———. *Policía del karma*. Ediciones B, 2010. (Graphic novel, various websites, videogame, Facebook, blogger, YouTube, sound cloud pages, including mockumentary, fanfic, trailer, etc.)

———. *Synco*. Ediciones B, 2008.

———. *Trinidad*. Ediciones B, 2007.

———. *Ygdrasil*. Ediciones B, 2005.

Bergmann, Sven. "Fertility Tourism." *Signs: Journal of Women in Culture and Society*, vol. 36, no. 2, 2011, pp. 280–88.

Cacho, Lisa Marie. *Social Death: Racialized Rightlessness and the Criminalization of the Unprotected*. New York UP, 2012.

Carvajal, Gustavo. "Una crítica de la (des)memoria: narrativa chilena reciente y la pregunta por el trauma y la justicia a 40 años del golpe." Coloquio Chile actual, 25–28 Sept. 2013, chili-neoliberal.sciencesconf.org/conference/chili-neoliberal/pages/Carvajal_Una_critica_de_la_des_memoria_narrativa_chilena_reciente_y_la_pregunta_por_el_trauma_y_la_justicia_a_40_anos_del_golpe.pdf. Accessed 10 Nov. 2015.

Cooper, Melinda, and Catherine Waldby. *Clinical Labor: Tissue Donors and Research Subjects in the Global Bioeconomy.* Duke UP, 2014.

Courtoisie, Rafael. *La novela del cuerpo.* Casa editorial HUM, 2015.

Ehrenreich, Barbara, and Arlie Hochschild. Introduction. *Global Woman: Nannies, Maids, and Sex Workers in the New Economy,* edited by Barbara Ehrenreich and Arlie Hochschild. Granta, 2003, pp. 1–14.

Fernández Benítez, Hans M. " 'The Moment of Testimonio Is Over': Problemas teóricos y perspectivas de los estudios testimoniales." *Íkala: Revista de literatura y cultura,* vol. 15, no. 24, 2010, aprendeenlinea.udea.edu.co/revistas/index.php/ikala/article/viewFile/5096/4464. Accessed 10 Nov. 2015.

Franz, Carlos. *La muralla enterrada.* Planeta, 2001.

Gilbert, Helen. "Manjula Padmanabhan's *Harvest*: Global Technoscapes and the International Trade in Human Body Organs." *Contemporary Theater Review,* vol. 16, no. 1, 2006, pp. 123–30.

Google Baby. Directed by Zippi Brand Frank. Films Transit International, 2009.

Gurung, Shobha Hamal. "Nepali Female Migrants and Informalization of Domestic Care Work: Service or Servitude?" *Workplace Rights,* vol. 14, no. 3, 2009, pp. 375–96.

Haaretz. 29 Apr. 2015, www.haaretz.com. Accessed 15 May 2015.

Hausner, Sondra, and Jeevan Sharma. "On the Way to India: Nepali Rituals of Border Crossing." *Borderland Lives in Northern South Asia,* edited by David N. Gellner. Duke UP, 2013, pp. 94–116.

Hochschild, Arlie. "The Back Stage of a Global Free Market in Nannies and Surrogates." *Transnationale Vergesellschaftungen,* edited by Hans-Georg Soeffner, Springer, 2012, link.springer.com/chapter/10.1007/978-3-531-18971-0_106, pp. 21–37. Accessed 10 Nov. 2015.

Jameson, Fredric. *Postmodernism, or the Cultural Logic of Late Capitalism.* Verso, 1990.

Kim, Jodi. "Debt, the Precarious Grammar of Life, and Manjula Padmanabhan's *Harvest.*" *Women's Studies Quarterly,* vol. 42, no. 1, 2014, pp. 217–34.

Kumar, Raksha. "Trying to Tame the Wild West of Surrogacy in India." *Al Jazeera,* 14 Jan. 2015, america.aljazeera.com. Accessed 15 May 2015.

Kurlat Ares, S. G. *Para una intelectualidad sin episteme: El devenir de la literatura Argentina, 1974–1989.* Corregidor, 2006.

Landecker, Hannah. *Culturing Life: How Tissues Became Technology.* Harvard UP, 2007.

Maranto, Gina. "They Are Just the Wombs." *Biopolitical Times,* 6 Dec. 2010.

Mathur, Suchitra. "Caught between a Goddess and a Cyborg: Third-World Women and the Politics of Science in Three Works of Indian Science Fiction." *Journal of Commonwealth Literature*, vol. 39, no. 3, 2004, pp. 119–38.

Meruane, Lina. *Fruta podrida.* Fondo de cultura económica, 2010.

Narayanan, Nayantara. "Why the Nepal Earthquake Has Got India and Israel Talking about Cross-Border Surrogacy." *Scroll.in*, 1 May 2015, www.scroll.in.

O'Neill, Tom. "'Our Nepali Work Is Very Good': Nepali Domestic Workers as Transnational Subjects." *Asian and Pacific Migration Journal*, vol. 16, no. 3, 2007, pp. 301–22.

Padmanabhan, Manjula. *Harvest.* Aurora Metro Press, 2003.

Pande, Amrita. "Commercial Surrogacy in India: Manufacturing a Perfect Mother-Worker." *Signs*, vol. 35, no. 4, 2010, pp. 969–92.

———. "Not an 'Angel,' Not a 'Whore': Surrogates as 'Dirty' Workers in India." *Indian Journal of Gender Studies*, vol. 16, no. 2, 2009, pp. 141–73.

Paz Frontera, Agustina, Lara Segade, Valeria Tentoni. "Los años perdidos." *Cuentos raros*, edited by Patricio Zunini. Ediciones Outsider, 2013, www.eloutsider.org/cuentos-raros/.

Pinedo, Rafael. *Subte.* Salto de página, 2012.

Povinelli, Elizabeth A. *Economies of Abandonment: Social Belonging and Endurance in Late Liberalism.* Duke UP, 2011.

Pravinchandra, Shital. "Body Markets: The Technologies of Global Capitalism and Manjula Padmanabhan's *Harvest*." *Science Fiction, Imperialism, and the Third World: Essays on Postcolonial Literature and Film*, edited by Ericka Hoagland and Reema Sarwal. McFarland, 2010, pp. 87–98.

Robertson, John A. "Surrogacy, Israel and the Nepal Earthquake." *Bill of Health: Examining the Intersection of Law and Health Care, Biotech and Bioethics*, Harvard Law Petrie-Flom Center, 4 June 2015, blogs.law.harvard.edu/billofhealth/2015/06/04/surrogacy-israel-and-the-nepal-earthquake/. Accessed 10 Nov. 2015.

Sleep Dealer. Directed by Alex Rivera. Starlight Films, 2009.

Sunder Rajan, Kaushik. *Biocapital: The Constitution of Postgenomic Life*. Duke UP, 2006.

Sussman, Susana. "Khunta." *Revista Axxón*, vol. 154, 2005, axxon.com.ar/rev/154/c-154cuento11.htm. Accessed 10 Nov. 2015.

Vora, Kalindi. "Indian Transnational Surrogacy and the Commodification of Vital Energy." *Subjectivity*, vol. 28, 2009, pp. 266–78.

Contributors

Anindita Banerjee is Associate Professor of Comparative Literature and Chair of Humanities in the Environment and Sustainability Program at Cornell University.

Debra A. Castillo, Emerson Hinchliff Chair of Hispanic Studies, Professor of Comparative Literature, and director of the Latino/a Studies Program at Cornell University, is a past president of the Latin American Studies Association.

Sital Kalantry is Clinical Professor of Law at Cornell Law School, working on comparative feminist legal theory, international human rights, and empirical studies of courts.

Silvia G. Kurlat Ares, an independent scholar working on issues of literature and visual culture in contemporary Argentine and Latin American literature, politics, and cinema, has taught at the Universidad de Buenos Aires, George Mason University, and Johns Hopkins University.

Kavita Panjabi is Professor of Comparative Literature, Jadavpur University, Kolkata, and author of *Unclaimed Harvest: An Oral History of the Tebhaga Women's Movement* (2016).

Karen Smith Rotabi has conducted intercountry adoption and surrogacy research in multiple countries and is Professor of Social Work at California State University, Monterey Bay.

Kumkum Sangari, William F. Vilas Research Professor of English and the Humanities at the University of Wisconsin–Milwaukee, is the author of *Solid:Liquid: A (Trans)national Reproductive Formation.*

Emily C. Vázquez Enríquez is a doctoral candidate in the Department of Romance Studies, Cornell University, and the author of several articles on border environments and reproductive labor.

Sherryl Vint is Professor of Media and Cultural Studies at the University of California, Riverside, where she directs the Speculative Fiction and Cultures of Science Program.

Index

abhuman, 13
adoption, 17–29, 35–36, 54, 100, 106, 141–42
adoption fraud, 9, 17, 21, 23, 27
affect, 2, 3, 5, 12, 53, 56–57, 59–60, 64, 116–17, 121, 123, 126, 129, 131, 133, 137–60, 185; alienation, 138–39, 149–50, 152–53; anxiety, 4, 6, 43, 48, 57, 75, 176; and citizenship, 10; crisis, 116–17, 132; hope, 2, 6, 22, 23, 157, 173, 184, 190; sadness, 138–39, 153
affective labor, 2–3, 80–81, 147, 150, 158
Agamben, Giorgio, 47
agency, 12, 46, 48, 148, 165, 167–68, 175, 179, 185, 208. *See also* autonomy
Agrimbau, Diego, 171
Ahuja, Neel, 77
Aira, César, 169–70
Alazraki, Gary, 127
Alfonso X, 117
American Dream, 189
Anderson, Benedict, 154
anthropocentrism, 61
anthropomorphism, 10, 65
anti-immigration rhetoric, 77
Areco, Macarena, 207–208
"A Requiem for the Earth," 10, 43–44, 46, 48, 64
Argentina, 12, 25, 166, 169, 171, 173–75, 180, 184–85, 201
Argentine novel, 165–86
Assisted Reproductive Technology (Regulation) Bill, 51, 96
autonomy, 12, 35, 67n12, 102, 165, 177–78, 185

Babel, 117, 129–32
Balibar, Etienne, 55, 67n7
Baradit, Jorge, 203–10
Baudrillard, Jean, 176
Baxi, Upendra, 109n5
Bennett, Jane, 5
Bharatiya Janata Party, 50
Bhattacharya, Rituparna, 141, 143–44, 161n2
Bhuwania, Anuj, 94, 102
Bigorre, Diego, 170
bioart, 1
biocapital, 8, 74, 209
bio-cartography, 197, 201, 208–209
bioethics, 173–79
bioinformation, 5, 13
biomarket, 8, 192, 198, 209
biomatter, 5, 6, 192
biopolitics, 8, 62

Bizzio, Sergio, 170
body: altered, 168; artificial, 165–86; as art object, 1–4; as commodity, 12, 80–81, 83–84, 139, 150–51, 158, 177, 198; bioreactor, 1, 3; female, 64, 116, 122, 139, 181; monstrous, 3, 4, 175, 203, 206
border, 6–7, 9–10, 36, 55, 66, 73–79, 84–85, 87–89, 128, 130–31, 140, 142, 189–90, 192–95, 209–10
Braidotti, Rosi, 166, 168, 186
"Breast-Giver," 137, 158, 160
Breece, Julian, 87–88
Briggs, Laura, 26
Brown, J. Andrew, 166
Bunkers, Kelly M., 21, 25, 36

Cacho, Lisa Marie, 202
Cadenas de amargura, 126
Cambodia, 7, 19, 21–26, 36, 51
Cano, Alonso, 117
Cantigas de Santa Maria, 117
Capitalism, 46, 50, 57, 74, 153, 155, 157, 185, 197, 203, 204
care: care market, 8, 87, 189–210; care work, 2–5, 8–9, 11, 56, 66n1, 115, 191, 193–94; child care, 11, 160, 189, 192, 194, 196; eldercare, 5; histories of, 9; semi-care, 1, 4, 6, 8. *See also* affective labor
caregiver, 5–6, 124, 189, 199
Carrillo, Ana, 119, 124
Carson, Rachel, 44
Casa de Ottro, 12, 166, 168, 179–80
Castellanos, Rosario, 116, 121–22
catastrophe, 24–25, 66
Catts, Oron, 1–4
Chaparrós, Martin, 170
Chejfec, Sergio, 170
child laundering, 23, 201–202
Children of Men (2006), 6
The Children of Men (1992), 10, 43, 46, 48
child trafficking, 23
China, 20–21
Chitarroni, Luis, 170
Choudhury, Cyra Akila, 107
clinical labor, 74, 78, 80, 82, 193, 195, 199, 209
clone, 4, 12, 166–69, 174–79
Coelho, Oliviero, 171
Cohen, Lawrence, 85
Cohen, Marcelo, 12, 166–67, 169–71, 179–80, 185
comics, 169, 171
commercial global surrogacy, 9, 17, 29
commodification, 51, 73, 82, 121, 150, 168, 175
Como agua para chocolate, 121
conceptive technology, 62
Constantini, Humberto, 167
Cooper, Melinda, 8, 74, 78, 80, 82–83, 193, 195, 199
Courtoisie, Rafael, 203
cow, 10, 43–44, 56–65, 189
creeping jurisdiction, 100
Cruz, Norma, 25, 27–28
Cuarón, Alfonso, 6, 127
Crossover, 85, 87
crisis, 7, 10, 43, 46, 49, 63, 65, 90n2, 128, 145–46, 168, 170–71, 186n5, 191–92
cruelty, 43, 46, 173, 183
cyborg, 12, 166–69, 179, 181–83, 196

deep ecology, 45
dehumanization, 8, 151
denationalization, 46
Deomampo, Daisy, 31, 103
Devi, Mahasweta, 106, 137, 158–59
Diario de México, 120
Diaz, Porfirio, 122

Dorio, Jorge, 170
Dubinsky, Karen, 25–26
dystopia, 6, 10, 12, 43, 46, 63, 66, 89, 166, 169, 171–72, 180, 205

Eco, Umberto, 178
ecological destruction, 10
Economies of Abandonment, 13, 145, 149, 157, 209
Ehrenreich, Barbara, 8, 194
El corazón de Doli, 12, 166, 168, 173–79
El enemigo, 125
El periquillo Sarniento, 120
enclavization, 10, 43, 56–57, 65
endogamy, 55–56
Esquivel, Laura, 121
Estrada, Luis, 127
ethical medical tourism, 29
ethics, 26, 46, 141, 173, 175, 182, 184
Ethiopia, 19–21
eugenics, 77, 138
exploitation, 9, 22–23, 30–31, 33–36, 74, 79–80, 93, 95, 100, 102, 105–106, 110, 129, 133, 138, 143–44, 146, 149–50, 153, 156, 168, 10
extinction, 10, 43–49, 59, 65–66

Facebook, 59
Federici, Silvia, 57
Feralization, 58, 64
Fernández, Hans, 203
fertility tourism, 52, 140
Fogwill, Rodolfo Enrique, 169–71
Forn, Juan, 170
Foucault, Michel, 62
Frank, Zippi Brand, 196
Fresán, Rodrigo, 170
Friedman, Milton, 204
Fuebel, Daniel, 170
future: imaginary of, 4, 10; promissory, 11, 73–89; reproductive, 55, 66, 83

Garammont, Hubert Carton de, 128
Gardini, Carlos, 165
Gellner, Ernest, 154
gene editing technology, 4
gift, 3, 35, 152, 155, 158
Ghana, 7
Giménez Smith, Carmen, 115
Glantz, Margo, 121
Global North, 2, 3, 5, 10, 80, 198, 202
Global South, 2, 4, 7–8, 10, 46–48, 80, 142, 155, 158, 189, 204–205, 208–10
González Iñárritu, Alejandro, 117, 129
González Rodríguez, Sergio, 128
Goodeve, Thrysa Nichols, 186
Google Baby, 137–38, 196, 200, 208–209
Gothic, 168
Gorjestani, Mohammed, 83
Groza, Victor, 21, 25, 36
Guatemala, 1–3, 7, 9, 17–21, 24–28, 76, 109, 128, 201
Guebel, Daniel, 170
Gutiérrez Mouat, Ricardo, 168

Haraway, Donna, 183, 186
Harvest, 197, 200, 208
Hausner, Sondra, 194
Hayles, N. Katherine, 165
He, Jiankui, 4
health care, 60, 74–75, 77–78, 81
heteronormativity, 51, 67n12
historical fiction, 168
historiography, 120, 167
Hochschild, Arlie, 8, 137, 151–53, 194, 202
Hollow, 79

Huesos en el desierto, 128
humanitarianism, 190
humanization, 60
human rights, 9, 17–18, 21–22, 24, 26–31, 35–36, 129, 132, 177, 204
Human Rights Law Network, 108
human trafficking, 7, 22–23, 36

Ibarlucía, Ricardo, 170
immigration, 22, 75–78, 84
India, 6–7, 9–12, 19, 29–36, 43–45, 48–57, 61, 93–109, 139–42, 144–48, 150–51, 153, 157–60, 190–97, 199, 209
Indian Parliament, 95, 96, 98, 110
Indian Supreme Court, 11, 29, 93, 99
infertility narrative, 45–46, 65
Ink, 75–77
in vitro gametogenesis, 4
Ippóliti, Gabriel, 171

James, P. D., 10, 43, 46, 63, 65
Jameson, Fredric, 50, 75, 185, 209
Jasanoff, Sheila, 75, 89
Jenkins, Barry, 77
Jorar, Karan, 109n3

Kahlo, Frida, 116, 121, 131–32
Kenya, 7, 67n11
Kim, Sang-Hyun, 75
Kráneo, Kwaichang, 171

labor: affective, 2–3, 80–81, 147, 150, 158; clinical, 74, 78, 80, 82, 193, 195, 199, 209; gestational, 193; reproductive, 5, 8, 47, 54, 57, 95, 130, 150, 158, 190–91, 193–95; migration, 47
Laiseca, Alberto, 170
Laos, 36, 51, 67n11
La dictadura perfecta, 127
La fila india, 128
La Guadalupana, 126
La perfecta casada, 118
Las Siete Partidas, 117
legal procedure, 11
León, Fray Luis de, 118
Levitas, Ruth, 173
life: concept of, 3, 165; financialization of, 4, 10; semi-life, 1, 4–6, 8; surplus life, 88; technologies of, 8–9
The Living, 87
Living disappeared, 18
Lizardi, José Joaquín Fernández de, 120
Los bandidos del Rio Frio, 121
Los ricos también lloran, 126
Ludmer, Josefina, 173
Lugones, Leopoldo, 165
Lyotard, Jean-Francois, 139, 149

Mabry, Tina, 85
Maher, JaneMaree, 44
Mairal, Pedro, 171
Malhotra, Anil, 141, 143–44
Manzar, Hasan, 10, 43–45, 65
Maranto, Gina, 194
Marcus, Amit, 176–78
marginalized, 11, 83, 89, 93–94, 101–103, 158, 202
Marimar, 125
market: adoption market, 7, 27; biomarket, 8, 192, 198, 209; care market, 8, 87, 189–210; surrogacy market, 93, 109n6, 191–95
Marre, Diana, 26
Martínez, Tomás Eloy, 167
Maskew, Trish, 18, 21, 26
McBrien, Justin, 45
medicine, 73–79, 85, 89, 186, 193, 200
Meruane, Lisa, 203
Mexico, 6, 7, 11, 51, 67n10, 87, 115–33

migration, 6, 10, 19, 22, 47, 63, 77–78, 129, 191–96, 209
millennium adoption surge, 26
Ministry of Home Affairs, 94, 97, 99–100, 107, 109n3
Modernity, 4, 154, 167
Motherhood, 9–10, 12, 43–44, 48–49, 51–59, 64, 65, 67n17, 116, 126, 138–39, 150, 152–57, 172, 180; adoptive, 18, 21, 23, 28; cow, 10, 43–44, 56–65, 189; genetic, 53; gestational, 53, 55, 148, 191, 196; ontological valence of, 138
Moylan, Tom, 89, 172–73
Mujer, casos de la vida real, 125
Murphy, Michelle, 46
My Nurse and I, 116, 121–22, 124, 132–33

nana, 11, 115–17, 124–31
National Security Act, 58
Nepal, 6, 7, 51, 109n6, 142, 190–94, 197, 205, 210
neoliberalism, 10, 12, 30, 44, 50, 52, 56–57, 59, 62–65, 73–75, 80, 82, 138–39, 143–49, 153–54, 158–59, 165, 171, 203–204
Nielsen, Gustavo, 12, 166, 169–71, 173–74, 176–77, 180, 185
Nigeria, 7
nonentrepreneurial subsistence economy, 62
Nosotros los Nobles, 127

orphan, 18–19, 21–23, 119, 127, 203, 207–209
Ortuño, Antonio, 128
O'Reilly, Justo Sierra, 121
organ trade, 197

Padmanabhan, Manjula, 197, 200, 208–209
Palomo, Beatriz, 120
Pande, Amrita, 140–44, 148, 151–53, 155–56, 158, 194–96
Pauls, Alan, 170
Payno, Manuel, 121
Peace Corps, 17
Pedro Páramo, 121
Pinedo, Rafael, 171, 203
Podalski, Laura, 130–31
posthuman, 12, 165–86
post-vital subjectivity, 89
poverty, 7, 9, 18, 19, 22, 30–36, 64, 84, 119, 126, 128, 187, 194
poverty fatigue, 31
Povinelli, Elizabeth, 13, 145, 149, 157
pregnancy, 3, 30–31, 33, 54, 104, 106–107, 137, 150
public interest litigation, 11, 93–110, 147
public policy, 9, 11, 13
Puig, Manuel, 167

Rajan, Kaushik Sunder, 73–74, 139, 157, 209
Rao, Mohan, 141–43
realism, 167–70, 174, 179
Reati, Fernando, 174, 178, 187n7
Refuge, 83–85, 87
reification, 143, 167, 183
Remigration, 77–79
renationalization, 10, 43, 47, 48
reproduction, 5, 10, 12, 43–44, 46, 49, 52, 55–57, 60, 63
reproductive future, 55, 66, 83
"A Requiem for the Earth," 10, 43–48, 64
resistance, 76–77, 139, 147, 156, 158, 167–68, 172–73, 179, 183, 184, 200, 206
Retrato de familia, 126
Rivera, Alex, 189, 192, 195, 209
Robinson, Lisa, 79

Roby, Jini, 18, 21, 23, 26
Roma, 127
"Ruminations of a Holy Cow," 61
Russia, 7, 19–21, 81

Sagar, Satya, 61
Salomé, 116, 121–24, 131
Samoilovich, Daniel, 170
Sanal, Aslihan, 85
Sangari, Kumkum, 146, 153, 155
Santellán, Matias, 171
Saravanan, Sheela, 103, 148
San Bernardo y La Virgen, 117
Scheper-Hughes, Nancy, 85
science fiction, 4, 12, 23, 73, 79, 165–86, 189–92, 196–97, 199, 203, 205, 208–10
semi-life, 1, 4–6, 8
Semi-Living Worry Dolls, 1–4, 13
Serafín, Pablo, 171
sex work, 2, 26, 30, 50, 103
Sharma, Jeevan, 194
Sharp, Lesley, 85, 90
Silent Spring, 44
Silver Sling, 81–84, 87
Simulacra, 176–77
Sleep Dealer, 189–91, 195, 208
Sloan, Kathryn, 118
social reproduction, 10, 43–44, 46, 49, 52, 56–57, 66n1, 66n3, 66n4, 117, 124, 131
sociotechnical imaginary, 75, 85
Sommer, Doris, 166
speculative fiction, 73–90, 166, 204
speculative technology, 2, 8
Spivak, Gayatri Chakravorty, 159–60
structures of feeling, 159
subsistence, 19, 49, 60, 62–63
surplus life, 88
sur-realista, 203
surrogacy, 2, 6–7, 9–12, 17–36, 43, 49–57, 62, 65, 74, 80–82, 85, 93–110, 137–60, 190–203, 206, 209; altruistic, 11–12, 19, 44, 51–56, 62, 64–65, 98, 139–43, 151, 158, 160; ban on, 7, 11, 43–44, 49–54, 56, 58, 95–96, 99–100, 102, 104–105, 139–44; commercial, 7, 10, 12, 43, 49–53, 55–56, 62, 97–99, 138–58, 190–91, 194; discourses of, 137–60; gestational, 2, 30, 140, 153, 193, 198; public interest litigation on, 11, 93–110, 147; transnational commercial, 7, 49, 153–54
Surrogacy (Regulation) Bill, 51, 96, 98, 139–40, 143–44, 158
Surveillance, 5, 10, 43, 63–64, 66, 75, 84, 119, 146, 194
Sussman, Susana, 203
Suvin, Darko, 75
Swanson, Rosario de, 124
Swaraj, Sushma, 101, 141

Taboada, Carlos Enrique, 127
telenovela, 125–26
Thailand, 7, 36, 51, 67n11
Thapar, Radhika, 102
trade, 13, 55, 62, 138, 142, 144, 173, 186, 190, 193, 197
transplant culture, 85
Tze, Chun, 81

Ukraine, 7, 67n11
Un año en el hospital de San Lázaro, 121
uncanny, 4–5
Under the Same Moon, 117, 129, 132
United Nations Convention on the Rights of the Child, 18
utopia, 73, 75, 166, 171–73, 180, 182–84, 205

Veneno par las hadas, 127
Viñas, David, 167

Vora, Kalindi, 9, 80–82, 85, 150–55, 160, 195
Vourvoulias, Sabrina, 75

Wad, Jayashree, 93, 99, 102, 110n8
Waldby, Catherine, 8, 74, 80, 82, 193, 195
war orphan, 19
Webre, Stephen, 118–19
wet nurse, 11, 115, 119–24, 131, 158–59
WhatsApp, 59

Zurr, Ionat, 1–4

www.ingramcontent.com/pod-product-compliance
Lightning Source LLC
LaVergne TN
LVHW040157080826
844660LV00001B/16

* 9 7 8 1 4 3 8 4 8 1 0 7 4 *